Engagement is going to be the keyword of the next decade. Whether it's employees engaged at work, families engaged in busier and busier homes, or people engaged in an increasingly virtual world, engagement will be crucial. Daniel Montgomery and his coauthors have created a fabulous resource for upping your engagement game. Get a copy and get prepared for one of the crucial issues on the leadership horizon.

—**William Vanderbloemen,** founder and CEO, the
Vanderbloemen Search Group, author of *Culture Wins*
and *Next: Pastoral Succession That Works*

How to Be Present in an Absent World reads like a manifesto for Christian leaders tired of trudging through an world of emptiness. Presence is a powerful—but downplayed—leadership practice that can change the culture of any organization. Daniel Montgomery is a pastor who understands business, and here he shows us how we can experience the fullness of life Jesus promises, even at work.

—**Tom Harper,** CEO, Networld Media Group,
author of *Servant Leader Strong*

Navigating today's leadership and societal challenges as a healthcare professional often feels like treading water in the open ocean. Daniel's coaching and writing brings me safely back to shore. He has an impressive ability to ground me and to foster peace and focus on the journey back to my authentic self.

—**Kim Tharp,** VP, Institute for Nursing and
Workforce Outreach at Norton Healthcare

How to Be Present in an Absent World is unique for being so well-written. It keeps you engaged and turning pages as it drives you to redeem the absence in your life and to become fully present and engaged. People need committed companions present with them in all parts of life: friendships, families, workplaces, and churches. *How to Be Present in an Absent World* is ultimately about those relationships. It journeys with you to find your time, place, and space in the world. It encourages you to collaborate with others in identifying and living out the story God is writing for you according to his purposes.

—**Dave Travis,** retired CEO of Leadership Network, director of
Strategic Counsel to Pastors and Church Boards for Generis

Here's a unique book that meets us at the intersection between marketplace and soul and then guides into self-aware engagement in the hard world of business. If you're feeling dehumanized in your role and responsibilities, this book supplies timely and invigorating gusts of wisdom. Buy it, read it, reflect on it, and then buy it for your team and insist they do the same. You'll be thanked. More importantly, you'll live wiser.

—**Dave Harvey,** president, Great Commission Collective, founder, RevDaveHarvey.com, author of *Rescuing Ambition* and *I Still Do*

The temptation with books on leadership is to rush through to get to the practical how-tos, but this work has made me pause in deep consideration of what it means to truly be present as a leader. It has caused some deeper stirring in my soul. Not easy—but necessary. In a world tempting us to be mindless producers of commerce, I am thankful for Daniel and his team for sharing their wisdom on how to be holistically engaged in the world around us.

—**Dan Hyun,** founding pastor, Village Church Baltimore

Daniel Montgomery, as an experienced churchman and businessman, brings spiritual wisdom into day-to-day life while encouraging us to be more present and practical in our spirituality. Here is soulful direction we all desperately need: a reminder that we are *only* human—and *essentially* human. Professionals of all kinds need to be encouraged and refreshed by what he has to say.

—**Dave Stone,** retired pastor, Southeast Christian Church, Louisville, Kentucky

Daniel Montgomery translates his pastoral experience and wisdom into the business world with surprising agility. A builder of people, he explains with insight and acumen how leaders are not exempt from basic spiritual needs. Far from being preachy, Daniel models a platform of professional leadership, himself led by a heart that follows Christ.

—**Ed Stetzer,** Wheaton College

How to Be

Present
in an
Absent
World

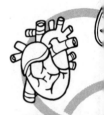

BODY

DISEM-
BODIED

TIME-
FUL-
NESS

ORIENTA-
TION

ETERNAL

SECULAR

DISPLACED

PLACE
FUL-
NESS

PLACED

SACRED

EM-
BODIED

SOUL

BEING-
FUL-
NESS

STORY

ENCHANTED

STORY-
FUL-
NESS

DISEN-
CHANTED

DATA

DISMEM-
BERED

INDIVIDUAL

OTHER-
FUL-
NESS

COLLECTIVE

MEM-
BERED

How to Be
Present
in an
Absent
World

A Leader's Guide to Showing Up, Paying
Attention, and Becoming Fully Human

Daniel Montgomery

With Dr. Eboni Webb and Kenny Silva

ZONDERVAN
REFLECTIVE

ZONDERVAN REFLECTIVE

How to Be Present in an Absent World
Copyright © 2020 by Daniel Montgomery

ISBN 978-0-310-10096-6 (hardcover)
ISBN 978-0-310-10097-3 (ebook)
ISBN 978-0-310-10098-0 (audio)

Requests for information should be addressed to:
Zondervan, *3900 Sparks Dr. SE, Grand Rapids, Michigan 49546*

Cover design: Faceout Studio
Cover image: © Food Travel Stockforlife / Shutterstock
Interior design: Denise Froehlich

Printed in the United States of America

19 20 21 22 23 /LSC/ 10 9 8 7 6 5 4 3 2 1

Contents

How to Read This Book

There's something insulting about a page of instructions for reading. After all, I'm sure this isn't your first literary rodeo. Still, it's helpful for authors and readers to get on the same page (pardon the pun), so I offer the following words of orientation before we begin.

In mapping out this book, Eboni, Kenny, and I struggled to decide whether to write long drawn-out chapters or short concise arguments. In the end, we decided that book-depth, blog-length chapters would enhance your experience, providing manageable pieces of content to work with, principles to apply, and practices to employ. That said, this book wasn't written to be consumed in a single shot. Sure, you could wolf down these pages on the red-eye from LAX to JFK, and I'm sure you'd get a lot out of them. But this book was designed to reward fifteen minutes a day (a chapter at a time) of careful reading followed by personal reflection.

As for the structure of the book, each of the main sections (time, place, body, other, story) contains six chapters and an interlude. The first chapter in each section serves as an introduction. The second makes the case for presence in business. The third through fifth offer further insight and application. The sixth weaves everything together and calls us all to respond to and rest in the truth, goodness, and beauty of God's design for human flourishing. Each interlude, along with scattered insights throughout the chapters, comes straight from Eboni. These sections offer a deep dive into the neurobiology of presence as well as principles and exercises

Eboni employs in her clinical practice. Feel free to skim them first and come back later.

Take your time with this book. Kenny, Eboni, and I didn't set out to write a treatise on presence; we wanted to create an experience. So get somewhere quiet so that you can be present with this book. Set aside your workplace drama, show up, and pay attention to the words on the page. It takes time to become fully human, so give yourself permission, just this once, to slowly roll along. In the end, I trust these pages will reward your patience as you enter fully into the presence for which God made us all.

intro
duc
tion

CHAPTER 1

How Long Can You Keep This Up?

God whispers to us in our pleasures, speaks in our consciences, but shouts in our pains.

—C. S. LEWIS, *THE PROBLEM OF PAIN*

I grew up believing my father was a sandy blond golfer-turned-insurance-broker from Omaha, Nebraska. As a black-haired, olive-skinned kid from Orange County, I never connected with that narrative. Surfing was my bag, not golf, and just the *thought* of golden cornfields was enough to send me running for deep, blue water. That's why a twenty-seven-year-old me didn't flinch to hear my mother eke out these words: "Your biological father isn't who we thought he was. He's a Brazilian hairstylist from Newport Beach, California." My first reaction wasn't anger. Instead, I said to myself, "This explains everything!"

Fast forward. A year later, I'm standing in the lobby of a chic Newport Beach salon staring into the eyes of its owner—my long lost father. I could immediately see myself in him, but all he saw in me was another customer. After the most awkward haircut of my life, I pulled him aside to talk. I don't know what he expected, but I can guarantee it wasn't these words: "I think you're my biological father." I don't know what I expected either, but I can tell you for sure it wasn't that he'd turn away.

I'd spend the next twelve years waiting to find out whether it was true—that this black-haired, olive-skinned man from Newport Beach was really the father I'd been missing my entire life.

The Paradox of Modern Pain

Any effective salesperson will tell you that the key to selling something is to identify a buyer's pain and then offer a cure. In a world where the average consumer sees anywhere from 5,000 to 10,000 brand messages per day, you and I are literally inundated with "remedies" for every little thing that ails us. Struggling under the weight of your hectic schedule? Amazon has over 50,000 time-management resources to help you get things done. Worried you're drifting out of touch with your children? Facebook's Messenger Kids app will help restore that relationship. Think you're losing your mind? There's a mental health app for that—and plenty more if the first doesn't work out.

Absence creates a particular kind of pain. It wasn't until a paternity test confirmed my father's identity that I realized just how much his absence had impacted my life. Personal drive, hunger for relationships, anxiety, insecurity—I began to realize these good and bad features of my persona were rooted in an attempt to deal with the fact that Dad was never in the picture. As I recognized how deeply I'd been shaped by my father's absence, I wondered what *my* presence (or lack thereof) meant for those around me. Was I truly *there* for my wife and kids? Was I engaged or was I going through the motions? Who was I hurting when I failed to show up or truly be present? Did the pain of my father's absence guide me to struggle with and need presence?

This book was motivated by the problem of absence and the pain it causes to us and those around us. Pain is a tricky subject for Christians. Why do bad things happen to good people anyway? That may be a strange question to ask at the head of a book on mindful Christian leadership,[1] but when it comes to God and pain, it's one of the only questions most of us know to ask. Whether the pain comes from poverty, cancer, or terrorism, writers like C. S. Lewis help us to find some comfort in knowing that, underneath it all, God's holy, wise, and good purposes give meaning to the suffering we see out there in the world.

But what about the pain *in us*? What about the everyday grief we suffer as leaders? From the mundane discomfort of one "pointless" meeting after another to the immense heartache of a failed product launch or ministry kick-off, we are surrounded by people and circumstances that seem as though they're designed to inflict maximum psychological torment. It's no wonder 40 million American adults suffer from some form of anxiety disorder right now.[2] Of the 16.2 million who experienced a major depressive episode in 2016,[3] a quick scan of the growing literature on depression among executives confirms that leaders take up more than their fair share.[4]

Psychology aside, what about the *physical* pain tormenting leaders today? Chronic headaches, insufferable back pain, high blood pressure, unexplained weight gain—these are just a few of the embodied afflictions that plague modern leaders. But instead of stopping to consider whether *this* might be the kind of pain God wants to speak through, we pop another aspirin and soldier on. We go to bed late, wake up early, mainline coffee, and skip lunch, all so we can keep up with the never-ending barrage of items on our to-do lists. We beat our bodies into submission, fooling ourselves into thinking that someday we'll be able to cut back, get a good night's sleep, and remember what it feels like to be a human again. But what if that day never comes? What if the perpetual grind slaps us with the absence of forced retirement or early death before we ever realize just how far we've wandered from the path of fully human presence?

The paradox of our moment is this: despite a virtually endless supply of digital and analog therapies, leaders are in more pain than ever—physically, psychologically, socially, and spiritually. We may be surrounded by the most technologically advanced healthcare system in the world, but most of us struggle to get even our most basic medical needs addressed. Psychologically, we're overcome by anxiety and depression. Socially, we're plugged into every social network, yet we feel more disconnected than ever. Spiritually, we wonder if the Bible has any *practical* wisdom to speak into our situation. And in our most honest moments, we can't help but look in the mirror and ask the vexing question: How long can you keep this up?

How long can you keep

- grinding out eighty-hour work weeks before you go down in flames?
- putting your marriage on the backburner before your spouse decides to give up?
- missing your kids' soccer games before they stop looking for you in the stands?
- treating your employees like cogs in a machine before they walk out?
- pushing your life aside before you realize your time is all up?

In this Together

I know the pain of leadership.

Just under twenty years ago, I started Sojourn Community Church in Louisville, Kentucky—a movement that eventually grew into four campuses with over four thousand weekly attenders. To that, we added a church planting network with nearly fifty churches across the country. I found myself leading as the executive of a sprawling organization and a pastor to leaders of all kinds, from worship team leaders to overworked ministry coordinators. I've helped countless others identify their pain and, with God's help, sort through it. And during that work, I encountered my own pain and learned what it meant to let others help me.

In 2017, I left Sojourn to pursue a new avenue of ministry in the marketplace. As a pastor, I'd discipled my fair share of leaders in the corporate world. What I discovered was their desperate need for someone to connect what they heard in the pew with what they lived in the office. They were tired of platitudes about how to be a "Christian witness" at work. They needed more than a talking head. They needed a *leader* like them to wade into the complexity of corporate life and help them learn how to be not just a Christian but a *human being* in the workplace.

With that context in mind, you should know something about the writing team behind this book. While the main voice you'll hear is mine (Daniel), the substance of what follows is a product of collective work: a business consultant, a pastor-theologian, and a licensed psychologist. Why the mix? To speak well about humanity, we need to think carefully about the God who made human beings in his image. That's what Kenny's here for (he hopes). To peer more deeply into the complexities of our design, we need the psychological heft that Eboni brings to the discussion—never mind all the free therapy she gave us in the process.

In what might sound like the setup to a bad joke, Kenny, Eboni, and I walked into a cottage in Louisville and painstakingly labored over this book. My hope is that we made a unique and valuable contribution. This isn't a book on Christian discipleship *per se*, but it'll teach you to be a better disciple at home and in the workplace. It's not a book on theology either, but it offers a biblical and theological take on what it means to be a Christian in leadership. Nor is this a work of management theory or leadership development, but we're convinced it'll take your management game to the next level.

So what *is* this book about? In a nutshell, it's about *showing up to your own life.*

Conclusion: Presence, Absence, and the Journey Ahead

To bring this introductory chapter to a close, Eboni, Kenny, and I want to make a claim in no uncertain terms: the pain we experience as leaders is a function of one thing—*absence*. What does absence look like? We're going to spend the rest of the book fleshing that out. But for now, absent leaders

- spend more time looking at a clock than at their employees,
- build spaces that discourage interaction and wonder why their team can't collaborate,
- burn the wick at both ends until they burn out,
- drive disengagement by neglecting relationships and alienating their team, and
- let their past distract them from engaging the present and charging into the future.

The remedy we're after—the cure we believe will not only rid us of our pain but help us find a new level of fulfillment and success—lies in rediscovering what it means to be fully present as leaders. For now, we'll define that sense of presence as *being* where you are in time and space, fully attuned to your bodily and social presence with a clear sense of where you've been (past), where you're going (future), and how that story impacts the present. Don't worry if that sounds a bit abstract right now. Like absence, our idea of presence is something we intend to fill out more concretely as the book goes on. Before we can do that, we need to get a deeper sense of the *cost* of absence and what presence can do to lift that burden.

Before You Move On

Take a moment to pause with a simple breath prayer. Pray it for as long as you like, feeling yourself relax and become more centered in your awareness of God's presence with you right now.

Breathe in: Abba Father.
Breathe out: I'm home.

CHAPTER 2

The Case for Presence

From 2000 to 2011, Ron Johnson served as senior vice president of retail operations at Apple. From the launch of their first store in 2001 to his departure in 2011, Johnson helped to mastermind the budding tech giant's rise to retail dominance. Challenging the old model of showroom computer sales, Apple's iconic branding and trendy style contributed to more than $2 billion in sales in its first two years. By the time Johnson left, the tech giant had opened four hundred stores worldwide. With more than $4,400 per square foot in revenue, Apple was (and still is as of this writing) the most lucrative retail enterprise in the world.[1]

With that kind of track record, the board of JCPenney made a safe bet tapping Johnson to revitalize its flagging retail operation in late 2011. The stock market agreed, rewarding the company with a bump of more than 10 percent upon the news that Johnson would be stepping in as CEO. What followed, however, was one of the biggest flops in retail history. Under his leadership, revenue dropped 27 percent and the stock fell through the floor.[2] Seventeen months later, the board fired Johnson and invited his predecessor, Mike Ullman, to step back into his old job.

Leader, Know Thyself

Johnson entered JCPenney thinking that what got him to the top in consumer electronics would work just as well in apparel and home retail. Spurred on by his success at Apple, Johnson presented a bold new vision to revamp not just his new company but the entire industry. Johnson was an artist; JCPenney was his canvas. He traded the retailer's old, convoluted pricing scheme for a straightforward everyday-low-price model. He shook up the stagnant feel of department store shopping to create a more bazaar-type environment and opened up mini-boutiques inside each outlet. He even changed the logo—the company's third in as many years.

So what went wrong? Johnson didn't look closely enough at the context. Everyday pricing made sense at Apple (where you could get away with selling everything at sticker price) but not in a department store. JCPenney's everything-on-sale-all-the-time pricing model may have seemed contrived, but the psychological forces behind it were powerful. And what about Johnson's new bazaar configuration? For loyal JCPenney shoppers, the new design was simply *bizarre*. Loyal shoppers felt they'd been snubbed in an attempt to cater to a younger generation. Johnson might've foreseen this if he'd tested his ideas. But when a team member suggested this, his response was as short as it was telling: "We didn't test at Apple."[3]

The Price of Unawareness

It seems Johnson subscribed to what Evgeny Morozov calls "technological solutionism."[4] Morozov, an influential writer in the sociology of technology, has argued at length that Silicon Valley is stocked with leaders who think they can solve the world's problems with a few lines of code. As a product of this culture, Johnson walked into JCPenney with a bulletproof algorithm for success. Instead of opening his eyes to reality, he imposed his vision on an industry that wasn't ready for it. In a word, Johnson was unaware of how his success at Apple had evolved into an earned dogmatism that kept him from thinking clearly about his work.

Tasha Eurich has dedicated her career to studying self-awareness in the workplace. In the book *Insight*, Eurich calls awareness the "meta-skill of the 21st century."[5] She writes: "The qualities most critical for success in today's world—things like emotional intelligence, empathy, influence, persuasion, communication, and collaboration—all stem from self-awareness. To put it another way, if we're not self-aware, it's almost impossible to master the skills that make us stronger team players, superior leaders, and better relationship builders—at work and beyond."[6]

From ten separate investigations including nearly five thousand participants, Eurich discovered one incontrovertible fact: we are oblivious to our obliviousness. Even though 95 percent of people think they're self-aware, only 10 to 15 percent actually are. Kathryn Schulz describes the former demographic well: "A whole lot of us go through life assuming that we are basically right, basically all the time, about basically everything."[7] I can't help but ask: How might JCPenney have fared if Ron Johnson stopped to consider he might actually be *wrong*? Or, to make it more personal, how might your organization do if *you* stopped to consider how your unawareness is holding everyone back?

The Cost of Absence and the Payoff of Presence

The costs of unawareness are unbearably steep at both the personal and organizational levels. The benefits of self-awareness, however, include those qualities that enable success. In that sense, awareness is a necessary step on the journey to full presence. Even so, awareness only takes us so far. The kind of presence we're after is more comprehensive than just knowing ourselves. It spans the breadth of our humanity—thinking, feeling, and doing. So before we ask you to join us on the arduous journey to full humanity, we should zoom out so you can see what's in it for you. What kind of return can you expect to see on your investment in presence?

Absent Leaders, Disengaged Employees

For the past decade or so, employee engagement has been on every business leader's mind. Simply defined, engaged employees actually enjoy working and want to see their companies succeed. Disengaged employees don't. Gallup's most recent *State of the American*

Workplace report (2017) reported that only 33 percent of employees in the United States were engaged at work.[8] The remaining 67 percent were, of course, disengaged. Most of these employees—the *passively* disengaged—still do what they need to do in order to stay on their company's good side and maintain their paycheck. But as many as a quarter of them—the *actively* disengaged—will cut corners, alienate coworkers, and look for ways to hurt the company intentionally.

Gallup estimates that actively disengaged employees cost the United States $483 to $605 billion a year. In addition to productivity losses, these employees jump ship quicker than their engaged counterparts, driving turnover costs through the roof. On a cultural level, their presence continually drains energy and creativity out of the organization. In a striking affirmation of just how damaging these employees can be to a company, Amazon actually pays its disengaged workers $2,000 to $5,000 to quit and never come back. As far as the world's biggest online retailer is concerned, that's a small price to pay for an engaged workforce.

Present Leaders, Engaged Employees

According to Jim Clifton—chairman and CEO of Gallup—widespread disengagement points to the fact that America's abiding leadership philosophy "simply doesn't work anymore," primarily as it relates to workplace culture.[9] We can't write this off as a meaningless nod to the next generation's desire for a kinder, gentler office environment. In 2016, the Society for Human Resource Management (SHRM) showed how "humanizing" workplace culture contributes to real organizational success.[10] Their meta-analysis of 263 studies hammers home the benefits of an engaged workforce:

- 22 percent greater profitability
- 21 percent greater productivity
- 65 percent lower turnover
- 10 percent better customer ratings
- 48 percent fewer safety incidents
- 28 percent less theft

Those numbers alone are enough to force leaders to get serious about how they can better engage their employees. Still, engagement by itself isn't enough. The SHRM report cites a 2012 study from Towers Watson on the difference between *traditional* and *sustainable* engagement. A traditionally engaged employee is one who goes above and beyond on an as-needed basis. A sustainably engaged employee brings their A-game to work each and every day. According to Towers Watson, companies with high traditional engagement scores operated at an operating margin of 14 percent. Sustainably engaged workforces, however, enjoyed a margin of 27 percent—nearly twice as high.

What makes the difference between traditional and sustainable engagement? Towers Watson's answer echoes that of Gallup and SHRM: culture. The companies that enjoy the right kind of engagement are those who intentionally cultivate a human workplace.

We'll talk more about what that looks like in the next chapter. For now, the critical point is that a human culture at work doesn't just happen by accident. Instead, it is *cultivated* by leaders who show up, pay attention, and discipline themselves to be fully present in their work.

Self-Awareness, Leadership Effectiveness, and the Bottom Line

As we saw above, present leaders engage while absent leaders disengage. Not only is that true for workforce performance as a whole but for a leader's personal execution as well. In a study of seventy-two senior executives, the American Management Association found self-awareness to be "the strongest predictor of overall success."[11] Researcher Becky Winkler attributes this to staffing: "Executives who are aware of their weaknesses are often better able to hire subordinates who perform well in areas in which the leader lacks acumen."[12] From a strategic perspective, present leaders are aware of their blind spots and able to build out their teams accordingly. This inevitably leads to higher performance for the leader and his or her organization.

Research on emotional intelligence (EQ) further bears this out. Crudely understood as "people skills," EQ points to the interpersonal dimension of a leader's presence. As Eurich learned in her research, this type of external self-awareness not only strengthens a leader's relationships with employees but actually heightens their perception of his or her effectiveness.[13] A recent study from the University of Pennsylvania further illustrates the positive effects of emotional self-awareness on leadership performance.[14] Participants in the study reported a number of tangible benefits, including:

- significant improvement in effectiveness (100 percent)
- enhanced workplace relationships (79 percent)
- improved ability to identify and manage emotions (86 percent)
- noticeable reduction in stress (81 percent)

All this helps to explain Travis Bradberry and Jean Graves's finding that emotionally intelligent leaders make an average of $29,000 more per year than their "unintelligent" counterparts.[15] Personal effectiveness, of course, can't help but drive the bottom line. British research in the restaurant industry points in this direction, showing that restaurants whose managers scored high in emotional intelligence exceeded average annual profit growth by 7 percent.[16]

Conclusion

Present leaders are emotionally and socially self-aware. They understand themselves and others. They don't just create high-power teams; they engage their employees on a human level in order to draw out their absolute best. More than that, they bring an important sense of humility to every decision. Instead of leaning on past success, they stop and think carefully about their context—within the organization and without. What they're left with is a sustainably engaged workforce ready to execute their vision and outperform their competition in the process. On a personal level, these leaders enjoy less stress, better relationships, more personal satisfaction, and higher pay. Their presence at work gives them the mental space to be truly present with their loved ones at home. This feeds right back into their ability to show up and perform in the office the next day.

In a word, the case for presence is a case for *humanity* in the workplace. Employees crave it. Employers want to know how to create it. We know that's true just by looking at the recent spate of books with titles like *Back to Human, Bring Your Human to Work*, and *Humanity Works*. As a Christian, I can't help but read this trend as a covert longing for the One who came to show us what true humanity looks like. Does that mean I'm out to "Christianize" the workplace? When prospective clients look at my seventeen years in ministry and my work on church leadership, that's often their most pressing question. What I've found, though, is that many expect a "Christian consultant" to be someone who'll slap the proverbial Jesus fish on their organization's bumper. As we'll soon see, there's much more to Christian leadership than painting Bible verses on the walls. We're creatures before we're Christians, *humans* before leaders. In Christ, we get our humanity back, and from him we learn how to lead in a way that embodies our redeemed humanity for the good of our employees and our world.

CHAPTER 3

How Do We Get Our Humanity Back?

*In Louisville, at the corner of Fourth and
Walnut . . . I was suddenly overwhelmed with
the realization that I loved all those people, that
they were mine and I theirs, that we could not be
alien to one another even though we were total
strangers. . . . And if only everybody could realize
this! But it cannot be explained. There is no way
of telling people that they are all walking around
shining like the sun.*

—THOMAS MERTON, *CONJECTURES OF A GUILTY BYSTANDER*

I live in the middle of what I consider the "holy trinity of Kentucky."
Just a few miles from my house lies Churchill Downs—the famous
home of the Kentucky Derby. A few miles further sits Distillery
Row and the (in)famous Kentucky Bourbon Trail. But while more
than a million tourists flock to the Derby or the Trail every year,
my favorite spot is the corner of Fourth and Walnut. Located just a
couple miles from my house, a simple plaque marks the spot where
the famous Trappist monk Thomas Merton rediscovered his humanity. It was 1958, and that spot was just as unassuming then as it is
today. But there, in that ordinary place on that ordinary day, Merton

experienced an extraordinary sense of God's light in and love for human beings. After nearly two decades in seclusion, he realized that humanity wasn't something to be earned in the monastery but a gift to be received from our Creator.

From time to time, I make my own pilgrimage to that corner. As I stand where Merton stood, I can't help but feel what he felt. Drivers race down Walnut, their heads craned over their phones. Nameless, faceless suits rush from one appointment to the next. A sea of strangers float past, each with anxieties, never stopping to look another in the eye. As they do, I'm reminded of all the ways I share in that very same absence. I can't help but think of my own clients—leaders for whom every day is just another smudge in the blur of life as an executive. I want nothing more than to step up to my boardroom pulpit and preach a sermon on what it means to bear the image of God, to shine as brightly as the sun. "If only they could see what Merton saw," I tell myself, "then they could become the leaders they've always wanted to be."

Where Did Our Humanity Go?

In the last chapter, we looked at the upside of presence as it relates to employee engagement, leadership effectiveness, and the bottom line. I also suggested that the case for presence is a case for humanity in the workplace. The two—presence and humanity—go hand in hand. But how? Earlier, I defined presence as being where you are in time and space, fully attuned to your bodily and social presence with a clear sense of where you've been (past), where you're going (future), and how that story impacts the present. As we'll see in this chapter, being present in this way *just is* what it means to live as a human being created in the image of God. The key to presence, then, is learning what it means to be not just *a* human but *this* human— the person God made you to be.

The trouble is, everything we experience seems determined to wage war against our humanity. On a typical weekday, we wake up and choke down a cup of coffee. After a few minutes of small talk with our spouse and/or children, we hop into the car, drive out of the subdivision, and join thousands of familiar strangers as we creep together down the interstate. We park in the garage, walk to the door, and exchange pleasantries with the usual set of actors—the security guard, the person at the front desk, the maintenance worker. We ask how they're doing, but we don't really care. We snooze through the morning huddle, slink into our offices, and prepare to spend the next ten or twelve hours wading through emails.

By the time six o'clock rolls around, we've made 101 connections in the digital world, but we haven't actually *connected* with anyone. We pack up our things and make our trek back up the highway. We drag ourselves through the door, only to sit down to a lukewarm dinner, a disappointed spouse, and a half-hearted greeting from a handful of kids who refuse to put down their cell phones.

This is what life looks like for the average corporate leader, Christian or not. You can call it the rat race, the grind, or just plain "work." Whatever you do, don't call it human.

We Used to Be Human Beings

In 2016, Andrew Sullivan wrote a popular article for *New York Magazine* titled "I Used to Be a Human Being."[1] As someone who spent the better part of a decade in front of a computer, Sullivan laments the dehumanizing effect of "the web." At the height of his success, he enjoyed the prestige of running a profitable media operation with an audience of up to 100,000 people per day. What he didn't enjoy were the four bronchial infections he suffered one year or the way his digital presence made it impossible for him to enjoy life in the real world. Every minute spent online, Sullivan said, isolated him from genuine human encounters. There could be no compromise: "I either lived as a voice online or I lived as a human being in the world that humans had lived in since the beginning of time."[2] In other words, Sullivan's digital presence *demanded* real-world absence. He couldn't have it both ways. In the end, the burned-out writer decided that the only way to reenter reality was to "quit the web," check into a meditation center, and relearn how to experience the world as a genuine human being.

While Sullivan's personal story centers around digital technology, he points to a deeper problem that confronts even the least tech-savvy among us: dehumanization. Our society's addiction to all things digital is only a symptom of a condition that stretches all the way back to the beginning of human history. For too long, people have sacrificed their humanity at the altar of false gods, seeking to find their true identity in sources that ultimately never satisfy. We've often sought our humanity at the expense of others. Slavery, human trafficking, and genocide represent just a few of history's most telling examples. In the corporate world, fluorescent lights, cubicle farms, and TPS reports achieve the same dehumanizing effect. We didn't need Silicon Valley to hand us an Apple in order to rob us of our humanity. The serpent has already taken care of that.

Humanity, Lost and Found

When Sullivan checked out of that meditation center, he was a renewed man—at least for a little while. Before long, the web's call grew too strong, and he was forced to learn how to retain his humanity in the midst of the overwhelming distraction. In the process, Sullivan realized that our struggle with digital dehumanization "is, in some ways, just another tale in the vast book of human frailty."[3] He's right; except the solution does not lie in transcendental meditation or a handful of mindfulness exercises. Rather, it lies in our embrace of the One who came and found us.

Created in God's Image

Sullivan's "book of human frailty" is really a subplot in a much grander story that takes the whole Bible to tell. Its prologue begins with the darkness of nothingness, a formless void, and a work of cosmic ordering. When the dust settles and everything is placed just so, we find a man and woman made in the image of God and charged with the twofold task of management and multiplication (Gen

1:26–28). Image of God (*imago Dei*) is the Bible's way of describing human beings' peculiar dignity and function with respect to all God's other creatures. Parrots can talk, monkeys can think, and even possums come equipped with opposable thumbs. Only *people* are "made in the image of God." Whatever that means, the Bible says it's what makes us human.

So what is it? As theologian Anthony Hoekema points out, the "image of God" can be read as both a noun and a verb.[4] That is, the image is both something we *are* and something we *do*. Humans *are* special; we have a dignity that cannot be taken from us—no matter what. At the same time, the image means we have work to *do* to act out that image, a key first example being to "be fruitful and multiply" (Gen 1:28 ESV). In the ancient Near East, rulers would erect images of themselves throughout the land as a sign of their authoritative presence (Dan 3:1–6). In the same way, human beings represent God in all our being and doing. To summarize, Genesis tells us that we've been made to reflect God's glorious light in all the world or, as Merton put it, to walk around shining like the sun.

Pleased as Man with Men to Dwell

Of course, Genesis 3 happened. The serpent sold, Eve bought, Adam signed, and they all bit the dust as a result. Thus began the tale of human frailty. The key word is "began," for the curse came with a promise:

> I will put enmity between you and the woman,
>> and between your offspring and her offspring;
> he shall bruise your head,
>> and you shall bruise his heel. (Gen 3:15 ESV)

The story wasn't over for God's images.

In the midst of condemnation, God spoke a word of salvation concerning what he would do to redeem and restore fallen humanity. The New Testament presents us with Jesus Christ as Eve's promised offspring—the true image of God who came not only to show us what it looks like to live as God's images but to live and die to renew that image in us (Col 1:15; 3:10). The Messiah, whose ministry was empowered at every step by the Holy Spirit, has poured out that same Spirit so that we can become more and more like him (Mark 1:10; Luke 4:18; Acts 10:38; Rom 8).

If you're not a Christian, it's important you don't misunderstand me here. I'm not saying that everyone outside the Christian faith is somehow non- or subhuman. What I am saying is that from the very beginning God had a plan for humanity, and the reality of human sin and brokenness puts us fundamentally at odds with that good plan. This is the heartbeat of the entire Bible: the Father sending the Son and the Spirit to undo the effects of the fall and restore his broken images. The eternal Son of God emptied himself of his divine prerogatives and became one of us (John 1:14; Rom 8:3; Phil 2:7; Heb 2:14ff.). Jesus walked the earth, died, rose, and ascended to the right hand of the Father—all *as* a human and *for* humans. The Word truly became flesh and will remain so into eternity, all so that we can one day share in his glorified humanity (1 Cor 15:49). There could be no more stunning an affirmation of what it means to be a human being than the fact that God became a man. Thomas Merton recognized as much in his Fourth and Walnut experience: "What more glorious destiny is there for man, since the Word was made flesh and became, too, a member of the Human Race."[5]

By God's grace, *everyone* is rightly considered to be made in his image. You don't need to be a Christian to be human, and you don't need to surrender your life to Jesus to experience some measure of presence in this absent world or to benefit from this book. I've seen too many brilliant models of human presence in non-Christians to ignore that God's common grace is at work in *all* of humanity. Still, as a Christian—and as someone who has both pastored and been pastored—I feel compelled to say that, outside of Christ, that presence will always fall short of God's ultimate purpose for humanity—eternal life in *his* presence. Through his incarnate Son and by his Holy Spirit, our heavenly Father invites us all to embrace David's words:

> You make known to me the path of life;
>> you will fill me with joy in your presence,
>> with eternal pleasures at your right hand. (Ps 16:11)

Our Discomfort with Jesus's Humanity (and Our Own)

Talking about Jesus's full humanity often makes us nervous. In church, we tend to focus on the deity of Christ—and for good reason. We push back against those who would say that Jesus was merely a great moral teacher or an enlightened person. No, we argue, Jesus was (and is!) God. We run straight to passages like Mark 5 where Jesus raises a little girl from the dead, and we say, "See! Only God could do that!" But then our Jewish friends point us to 1 Kings 17 where Elijah raises the widow's son. What about when Jesus fed the five thousand (Matt 14:13–21)? Nope, Elisha had a feeding miracle or two up his sleeve (2 Kings 4:38–44). We could multiply examples, but you get the picture. In our understandable zeal to defend the deity of Christ, we miss the fact that "the predominant reality he experienced day by day, and the predominant means by which he fulfilled his calling, was that of his genuine and full humanity."[6] Yes, Jesus was fully God, but he was also fully man.

Despite our best intentions, the pulpit and Sunday-school classroom often keep us from dealing with the reality of Jesus's humanity and its implications for our own. Much of our thinking about the material stuff of human beings—our bodies in particular—shares more in common with Greek philosophy than biblical theology. If you've ever drawn an overly sharp line between the spiritual and the physical, the sacred and the secular, or the visible and the invisible, then you just might be a Greek philosopher. If you've ever envisioned heaven as you strumming a harp on a cloud, you've taken your cue from Plato more than Paul. If you've ever gone to a funeral and heard something like "heaven gained another angel this week" or sung the words, "This world is not my home. I'm just a passing through," then what you've heard and sung is a presentation of created reality that runs counter to the biblical story.

If the Bible is true—and it is—then eternal glory won't be over yonder; it'll be right here. This world is your home. But it stands in need of serious repair. In the Lord's Prayer, we pray "thy kingdom come," not "may we come to your kingdom." Just as the Son came down, so too heaven will come down to earth (Rev 21). God's plan isn't to nuke his creation but to redeem it and bring about a state of glorious consummation that no eye could ever see, no ear could ever hear, and no heart could ever imagine (1 Cor 2:9). In that redeemed world, we won't be disembodied angels; we'll live for eternity with glorified bodies in real relation to the people around us in God's holy and heavenly place.

Why does all that matter? In downplaying Jesus's humanity, we discount our own. In ignoring the goodness of creation, we remove ourselves from the good world God has made us to inhabit. We overspiritualize the Christian life and draw a thick line between the sacred and the spiritual. And if we hold on to that bifurcated vision, we'll end up living fragmented, subhuman lives. In the name of spirituality, we'll neglect our material bodies. In the name of otherworldliness, we'll ignore our place in this world. In our desire to become "better" Christians, we'll dismiss the wealth of common grace resources (biology, psychology, sociology, etc.) that show us how human creatures work.

Instead, we must push back on all these dualist tendencies, not by running *from* God's truth but entering more deeply *into* it.

Entrepreneurship of Identity and the Plan for this Book

The image of God isn't just something we *are* but something we *do*. According to Hoekema, our being and doing are inherently relational. They involve our relationships with God, other people, and the natural world (i.e., our work).[7] Adam and Eve lived in harmony with God, one another, and the garden they were called to cultivate (Gen 2). After the fall, they (and we) were expelled from God's presence, set at odds against one another, and frustrated in their cultivation (Gen 3; cf. Rom 5). In Christ, we are reconciled to God, one another, and our work (1 Cor 15:17–24; Eph 2:1–22; Col 3:22–4:1). Hoekema adds a fourth dimension: relationship to self.[8] Sin has alienated us from ourselves (Ps 19:12; Jer 17:9; Rom 7:11–12), but Christ has redeemed us from our self-alienation. Christ doesn't just set us free to become some abstract model of a "human" but to pursue our full humanity in the context of our own concrete and gritty individuality. In fact, his example *shows* us how to do this, and his Spirit empowers us to realize the full potential of our human identity.

New Testament scholar Klyne Snodgrass calls us to become "entrepreneurs of identity" as we engage in that project.[9] "All of life," he says, "is lived out of a sense of identity, even if one's sense of identity is confused or unconscious."[10] Grace allows us to look honestly at ourselves and reorient our identities according to the truth of who God says we are. Understood as "the sum of everything that pertains to us and shapes us," identity is that stable sense of self that persists in and through the stories that are our lives.[11] Physical and psychological traits, personal history, relationships, geographical boundaries—these are just a few of the "givens" that influence our stories and, therefore, our identities. We give significant shape to the unfolding of that narrative, but much of it lies outside our control. Redemption is the reality that transcends all these givens and allows us to find ourselves within *God's* all-encompassing story. We actively construct our personal identities in dynamic tension between our actions and the environmental factors that constantly act upon us—all under the grace of God and the empowerment of his Spirit. In this book, we're going to explore the process of identity formation in five dimensions:

1. **Time:** We desperately seek freedom from time, but what we need most is freedom *in* it. From the fixed number of hours in the day to the varied sum of days in our lives, God has given us all the time we need to do what he has called us to do.

2. **Place:** Thanks to buzzing smartphones and lifeless workplaces, we consistently struggle to *be* where we are. Because

God has made a place for us, he calls us to make places in our homes, offices, and cities that cultivate presence for ourselves and others.

3. **Body:** Christians often think of the body as an instrument of the mind or soul. That attitude leads to disembodied living—an absence from the body, which is in desperate need of attention if we're going to think, feel, and act as fully competent human leaders.

4. **Other:** We were made for connection. When we push the idea of rugged individualism to its limit, we isolate ourselves from the social resources God has given us all. We will never reach our potential unless we learn how and when to depend on one another.

5. **Story:** The stories we tell ourselves and others have the power to shape our lives for good or for ill. When we own our story and tell it well, we open up a new vision of reality for ourselves and others that brings life, unity, hope, and a renewed sense of purpose.

Conclusion

As Lauren Tharp, the COO of Leadership Reality, often says, "We're not trying to Christianize the workplace; we're simply trying to humanize work!" As Christians, we should be leading the way in this sphere. Unfortunately, we're not. As we unpack in the following chapters, the walls we've put up between the sacred and secular, spiritual and physical, keep us from thinking well about our humanity in general—much less at work.

Recently, I chatted with an executive managing a very large investment fund about his struggles to humanize the inhumane world of mergers and acquisitions. As the conversation progressed, he lit up. "We're just bringing church to the workplace!" he said. I was turned off right away, all too familiar with pushy evangelism that "fulfills" the Great Commission through managerial imposition. But as I listened, I realized this executive already understood that the church isn't a building; it's a people. Wherever we go, we can't help but bring our churchiness. He was describing an intentional presence informed and empowered by divine presence. And I was all for it.

Gospel witness does demand words at some point. But the most compelling "word" we can speak comes from our transformed and transforming leadership. The workplace redemption we seek will come ultimately through men and women who live and lead in light of the One who put on flesh so that by God's grace we can get our humanity back. In other words, good human development naturally works against the excesses of pushy evangelism.

For Further Reflection

To rediscover our humanity for the good of ourselves, our organizations, and the people we love, we need to adopt a new set of questions:

- What does it mean to be human?
- What is human versus nonhuman work?
- What are practices that dehumanize ourselves and others?
- What are practices that humanize ourselves and others?
- How does God becoming human change our view of human work?

Ask yourself how these look for you in your context. Consider how you might be living a smaller story than the one the Father wrote, Jesus redeemed, and the Holy Spirit is reviving deep within your heart. This is good news for people like us, who so easily forget that we've been made to shine out our humanity—on the corner of Fourth and Walnut and to the ends of the earth.

The Science of Practicing Presence

As I (Daniel) worked on this book, I decided that I wanted the reading itself to be a mindful experience. Beyond making a biblical, theological, and practical case for human leadership, I wanted to include expert insight to help you further understand what goes on in your mind and body as you mindfully approach presence. That's why I've enlisted Dr. Eboni Webb to help explain the neurobiology of presence and, on top of that, give you opportunities to reflect on and practice being mindful. What happens in our brains when we practice presence? How can we integrate this into our lives? That's what she's here to help us understand.

Filtering years of research and clinical experience, Eboni will give you a thirty-thousand-foot view of the brain's response to mindfulness as well as up-close and personal exercises to get you into your time, place, body, social context, and story. You will see her contributions in sidebar sections woven throughout the book: know yourself, check yourself, ground yourself, and imagine yourself. You'll also hear more from Eboni at the end of each section, starting now.

Hey, it's Eboni here. In my counseling practice, the Village of Kairos, we help people build a life worth living through restoring the whole self through therapeutic practices grounded in validation, mindful body awareness, and behavioral change. I hope that Daniel, Kenny, and I can help you move into greater wholeness too.

Have you ever arrived somewhere and wondered, how did I get here? You know you drove from point A to point B, but you don't actually remember the trip. You were lost in your thoughts—or had no thoughts at all, almost as if you were on autopilot.

This trance-like state, known as highway hypnosis, has a benefit: it saves mental energy. But on the flip side, highway hypnosis can be extremely dangerous. When you enter a resting state while driving, your reaction time plummets, which can lead to obvious consequences. Highway hypnosis is to blame for many accidents, and rarely are skid marks found before such a collision.

Like driving, living on autopilot has many unseen dangers—mindlessness and meaninglessness included—and life does not always provide the rumble strips or guard rails that prevent us from disaster. What's needed is to wake up. The goal of mindfulness is awareness, noticing our thoughts, beliefs, and behaviors. Taking a step back and inspecting ourselves from a distance can help keep us on course.

This brings us back to identity. Another helpful metaphor in understanding mindfulness is a tree rooted deep into the soil. Mindfulness, like the trunk and roots of a tree, is the deeply grounded awareness of who you are. Some get mindfulness and meditation confused. By contrast, meditation and other spiritual practices such as contemplative prayer are the leaves of the tree. Mindfulness is a state of being, sometimes called "being present," whereas the spiritual practices are how we support that way of being. Like the fruit, the practices of meditation and prayer demonstrate the health and life of a more rooted self.

Benefits of Mindfulness

In the world of psychology, mindfulness keeps us from taking our neurobiological processes for granted. It's the process whereby you bring your full attention to your experience of the present. Mindfulness is also the state of being aware of all that is around you and inside you. By standing back and inspecting yourself without judgment, you can move from a place of unconscious passivity to a state of being fully present in the moment. The goals of mindfulness include:

- Noticing and respecting feelings, thoughts, beliefs, and behaviors
- Being aware of environmental information and cues
- Decreasing impulsive, passive, and "stuck" behavior
- Decreasing depression and social anxiety
- Increasing emotion regulation and decreasing (ineffective) mood-driven behavior
- Improving connection to experience, enjoyment, and peace
- Achieving higher levels of satisfaction, self-esteem, vitality
- Gaining a greater sense of autonomy[1]

It is human nature to want to understand who we are. We are constantly hunting to find ourselves. You might be tempted to think you simply are your thoughts, feelings, and behaviors. Your thoughts, perhaps, become wisdom that must be obeyed, your feelings are the litmus test for defining your true self, or your actions become the defining characteristic of who you are. Without examination, however, you may be stuck in self-limiting beliefs that proclaim that life will always be this way, in emotions that keep you hidden under the covers, or with inexplicable reactions to stressors that make you doubt what you've always believed about yourself. Mindfulness is a state of being aware of all these parts of you and then choosing to stand as the beloved that you are.

On the other hand, the negative effects of mindless living—much like Sisyphus, who was condemned to push a boulder up a hill for all eternity, only to have it roll back down—is one version of hell. Whether your goal is to be a rooted tree or an attentive driver, whether you want to avoid the perpetual hell of living without awareness or desire to be a more present person, practicing mindfulness is not only supported by Scripture but also proven to be neurobiologically beneficial.

Know Yourself: How Your Brain Works

We all want to experience connection, enjoyment, and peace. Mindfulness affects the centers of the brain involving self-regulation and connection, both intra- and interpersonally.

Here is a short neurobiological lesson: When we are present and mindful, three major areas of our brain are impacted. The *striatum* is located in the prefrontal lobes of the brain, which is fully formed in adults and responsible for attention control. Its job is to help with alerting, orienting, and conflict resolution. The benefits received from mindfulness on the striatum are focus and impulse control. We can then move from being fixated on our emotional state and impulsive thoughts to a more relaxed state that helps us pause and choose what action we are going to take.

Also located in the prefrontal lobes, the *limbic areas* are responsible for emotion regulation. They adjust and monitor your emotional outcomes such as selection, intensity, duration, experience, and expression. Being present brings awareness to these outcomes, which increases cognitive control, decreases hyperactivity, refines cues needed for control, and lessens rumination—that is, worried and spiraling thoughts.

Located between the two hemispheres, the *precuneus*'s job is self-awareness, including: meta-awareness, self-recognition, and self-identity. Mindfulness has the benefits of improving the functions of the precuneus by revealing what's going on inside us and by decreasing our denial. Drug users turn off the precuneus, thereby muting the parts of them with which they do not want to contend.

Does it sound a little complicated? The important thing is that when you are mindful and present, these three centers work together to improve self-regulation and connection both among you and others and within yourself.[2]

Mindfulness and Stress

When you encounter a stressful situation, your body responds immediately. First, your blood flow to the frontal lobe decreases, which, if you remember, is the part of the brain used for problem solving and conflict resolution. The gut also receives less blood, which is why we often experience digestive issues along with stress. Conversely, blood flow increases to the heart and extremities. The sensory system is activated, and all five senses become heightened, leading to hypervigilance.

Additionally, when under stress, your body releases cortisol, often referred to as "the stress hormone," flooding your systems. Excessive cortisol in response to prolonged stress or trauma can have some really adverse effects. First, excess cortisol disturbs the part of the brain responsible for regulating emotions, body temperature, and sleep. It also breaks down communication between hemispheres. Too much cortisol leads to the suppression of the immune system. You know how autoimmune diseases affect 20 percent of Americans? Excess cortisol is to blame.[3]

Mindfulness is a means of reducing our body's stress response. Being mindful can regulate the blood flow to critical parts of your brain and body, prevent adverse effects of excessive cortisol, and increase awareness of automatic responses, all leading to a healthier, more effective way of coping and responding to stress.

How Your Brain Waves Work to Make You Present

Crucial to every aspect of our brain function, brain waves are the patterns of electrical activity affecting our thoughts, feelings, and behaviors.[4] Let's look at one important wave: the gamma wave, which fires the fastest and connects different brain regions, promoting harmony. Looking more closely at the strength of gamma waves, we notice some interesting correlations. High waves are associated with heightened intelligence, deeper compassion, happiness, and memory retention. You can see that high gamma waves parallel many of the goals of mindfulness we looked at near the beginning of the chapter.

In one study of brain waves conducted recently at the University of Wisconsin–Madison, Tibetan Buddhist monks who were long-term practitioners of meditation—remember, meditation is a practice or fruit of mindfulness—were found to have actually altered the structure and functions of their brains. These monks, compared with those new to meditation, demonstrated significantly higher amplitudes of gamma waves, proving their compassion, heightened intelligence, and overall happiness to be not only a subjective experience but a scientifically proven one.

Practicing Presence

As we finish, take some time to reflect: Where do you struggle for self-regulation or self-control? How could mindfulness benefit your daily life? How might mindfulness impact your work environment, home life, and relationships?

The goal is to practice being mindful twice daily, for twenty minutes. The beginning and end of each day has been found to be helpful. Make your practice relevant, interesting, and enjoyable. Mindfulness is essential to effective self-control and is considered a "gateway skill and discipline." Find a comfortable spot to sit. Address any personal or environmental barriers you might have to mindfulness and then ask these questions:

- What is stopping you in your environment from being mindful?
- What obstacles in your body keep you from fully experiencing all the sensations around you?
- Do you criticize yourself, feel shame, or compare yourself to others?
- Do you escape into your thoughts to avoid your body?
- Do you plan events or stay moving to avoid your thoughts or emotions?

The more you begin to acknowledge the answers to these questions, the greater your likelihood for living a deeply fulfilling and present life. Once you are aware of your patterns of mindlessness, you are in a better place to change your behavior.

CHAPTER 4

Where Did All Our Time Go?

How did it get so late so soon?

—THEODOR GEISEL (A.K.A. DR. SEUSS)

I have four kids at home. As best as my wife and I can figure, we've spent 120 nights at field hockey and soccer matches, cross country meets, and basketball games this past year. So, *yes*, we *do* spend a lot of time at sporting events, thank you very much. My eleven-year-old son Levi has always loved basketball, and I've always loved to watch him play. So when my boy nailed a buzzer beater from deep in three-point country to lead his team to victory in one of his games last year, you'd expect me to be the first parent to jump up and cheer. But I wasn't. I was too busy with my phone. When I heard the crowd go wild, I had to ask around just to learn my son had won the game.

I'll never get that shot back. I showed up, but I wasn't present. Whatever text message or email I had to write—I honestly don't remember what it was—couldn't wait for the next morning. At least, that's what I thought. I let my anxiety about time draw me out of that precious moment. The price I paid wasn't just an opportunity to boast in my son but the chance to love, affirm, and build him up in the ways that only a father can. "Never again," I told my wife.

Yeah right. She has to nudge me every time she catches me paying more attention to my phone than her and our kids. There's always someone to talk to, some email to respond to, or some fire to put out. Everybody needs me. Nobody can wait. If only I had more time.

Off the Court and into the Grind

You may not be able to relate to my experience on the court, but I'll bet this scenario sounds familiar. It's 9:00 a.m. For the past hour, you've tried (and failed) to start your to-do list. For some reason, you can't stop stressing about that upcoming meeting with senior leadership. So you distract yourself with a little email. Another hour goes by. It's time to get back in the saddle and make a few phone calls. You reach for the phone but stop as you remember that call you blew yesterday. A little gun-shy, you fire up Facebook instead. You're just going to check in and make sure you didn't miss anything important, of course. Another sixty minutes go by. The phone rings. There's an emergency in production. Two more hours flit away as you scramble to get things back on track. By now, your schedule is a mess, and you haven't touched a single item on your to-do list.

For most leaders, this isn't the picture of an isolated bad day; it's *most* days. And days like these turn into weeks, months, and years. Think of that executive who's missed every one of her daughter's soccer games this season. Think of the leader who forgot to come home for dinner . . . on his anniversary. Think of the entrepreneur who's been holed up in her office for so long that her kids barely remember her face. Think of the sixty-five-year-old widower who spent the past forty years working sixty hours a week, all so he could spend his golden years on a beach with a wife he can no longer hold. Time, it seems, is running away, and there's nothing we can do to stop it.

Out of Time: Time-Anxiety and the Lure of Absence

A 2014 study revealed that one in three Americans slept fewer than seven hours per night. In what the CDC labels a "public health epidemic," far too many Americans put themselves at risk for hypertension, diabetes, depression, obesity, and mental illness (including anxiety).[1] Worse, they endanger others as well. On our roads, sleep deprivation contributes to an estimated six thousand fatal crashes per year.[2] Alongside this devastating human cost, we might consider its economic impact: sleepy workers cost the US economy up to $411 billion a year in lost productivity and increased medical expenses.[3] The numbers seem clear: we have a sleep problem. But why?

Before we answer that question, let's consider another set of statistics. According to a study conducted by Project: Time Off, 52 percent of Americans didn't use all their vacation time in 2017.[4] That means 705 million vacation days went unused, 212 million of them without any option for rollover or redemption. In another study, Glassdoor found that, of the Americans who *do* take a vacation, two-thirds of them ended up working on the road.[5] Why would they do that? For 34 percent, it was for fear of getting behind on their work.[6] Another 13 percent thought they would lose their jobs. And 7 percent said it's because they're afraid of their bosses.

Scarcity and Abundance

Why aren't you sleeping enough? Why is it so hard to break away and take a *real* vacation? As far as statistics go, we might chalk the former up to screaming infants, noisy neighbors, and genuine sleeping disorders. We wouldn't be wrong in that, but when we correlate our sleep deprivation with our reluctance to go on vacation, a different picture begins to emerge. It seems we've forgotten the Psalmist's wise words:

> In vain you rise early
>   and stay up late,
> toiling for food to eat—
>   for he grants sleep to those he loves. (Ps 127:2)

Here's the real problem for most of us: we don't have enough time. At least, we don't *feel* like we do. We're like an anxious high schooler watching the clock run down on her SATs. Time seems *scarce*; if we let it slip away, our entire personal and professional lives will go up in smoke. So we live in a kind of temporal poverty: there's never enough time to get everything done. Consequently, we inflict our time-anxiety on others—at home, in the office, or in line at Starbucks. Scarcity breeds the kind of anxiety that leads us to rob ourselves and others of humanity (just ask that 7 percent of workers who were too afraid of their bosses to take a real break).

Paradoxically, others among us are troubled by the idea that we have *more* time than we need. Have you ever gotten to the end of a busy day in the middle of an even busier season and asked yourself, "How long can I keep this up?" If you have, then your issue wasn't with the scarcity of time but its *abundance*. It's not that you don't have enough time. Rather, you've got too much of it, and you're not convinced today's status quo will be good enough to carry you and your business successfully through to the end.

Whether we feel like we've got too much or too little time, we're letting fear and anxiety define our relationship to time. Our fear of scarcity presses us to anxiety, worry, tension, and overwork. Our anxiety over abundance makes us wonder whether we can keep it all together until the end. On either side, we stop thinking of time as a gift and start treating it as a commodity to be hacked and managed. Instead of receiving time, we manipulate it. And we experience nothing but frustration when we realize time will only answer to one Master.

Where Do We Go with Our Time-Anxiety?

Again, our perception of scarcity creates anxiety over the fact of time spent, while abundance makes us anxious about whether our time will be spent well. In either case, our fixation forces us out of the present. Sometimes, that means we look to the past. Positively, we think back to a golden age when we had all the time in the world to do what we needed to do. Negatively, we fixate on whatever got us into our present time crunch. Other times, we escape into the future. Positively, we look forward to the day when we can sit on a beach and sip little drinks with umbrellas in them. Negatively, we dread the failure we know is lurking around the corner. Wherever we go, we're not here. As the popular yoga teacher and bestselling author Baron Baptiste said, "You are either now here or nowhere."[7]

When we try to cope with our time-anxiety by retreating into the past or the future, we give up our presence and succumb to the lure of absence. Instead of showing up, we check out. We end up dwelling on yesterday's screw-up or psyching ourselves out about tomorrow's big meeting. While we're off in la-la land, the minutes tick away, and the demands of the moment go unfulfilled. The price tag on our absence is immense: procrastination has been estimated to cost businesses up to $10,000 per employee. Corporate America spends billions of dollars every year using the tricks and tools of mindfulness (what some have simply called "present time awareness") trying to increase the productivity of leaders and workers alike.[8]

How Do We Get Our Time Back?

So far, we've talked a lot about scarcity, abundance, absence, and presence. But that all sounds so abstract, doesn't it? What about all those time bandits out there looking to rob us of every precious minute? What about all those interruptions that, estimates say, take up to six hours of a leader's day? What about the fact that 65 percent of us say we're too busy with pointless meetings to actually get important work done?[9] Forget the theory; what *practical* steps can we take to get control of our time?

Ask Tim Ferriss, David Allen, or Michael Hyatt, and they'll each give you a practical method for getting your time under control—at least, for a while. Don't get me wrong; men and women like them are making strides in helping us manage our time. For example, I've found Ryder Carroll's Bullet Journal Method to be a fantastic way to track the past, order the present, and design the future, as his bestselling book claims.[10] He doesn't use the exact word, but

Carroll's method is one of the best practical tools on offer for cultivating *timefulness*.

Yet our problem with time runs much deeper than learning to master our calendar and fend off time bandits. Ultimately, our problem with time does not lie outside of us; it's *in us*. We're running out of time because we're thinking, feeling, and living out of time. In a word, we're *absent*. And the only way to solve our problem is to reenter time and "recover the rhythm and order of man's real nature" as we live within the "appointed times" that God has determined for each of us (see Acts 17:26).[11] This is what I call *timefulness*, and I'll spend the next several chapters unpacking what it entails.[12]

Conclusion

If you've ever looked up at 10:00 p.m. and wondered where the day went, you're not alone. We're all trying to deconstruct the clock and find a way to break free from the constraints of time. What we really need is a better understanding of both time *and* freedom. As Thomas Merton reminds us, the freedom offered to Christians "is not freedom from time but freedom in time."[13] To cultivate that kind of freedom, we need to move beyond our typical mode of pragmatic, bottom-line thinking. There, we'll find all the time we need to

- Work both *in* the business and *on* the business
- Give internal customers (employees) the same respect we give everyone else
- Build businesses where people and places can reach their fullest potential

The word I'm choosing to sum this up is *timefulness*, and we're about to dive deep into how it can help guide leaders into a more fully human (and therefore more productive) way of life.

CHAPTER 5

The Case for Timefulness

I have so much to do that if I didn't spend at least three hours a day in prayer I would never get it all done.

—MARTIN LUTHER[1]

F or Christians, words like Luther's can hurt. We know we need to spend time asking God to search our hearts and show us his will for our work. But when "supersaints" like Luther remind us of that fact, we can't help but feel the weight of our schedules come crashing down upon us. We're thankful the God of the universe has left us an open invitation to sit down and chat, but we've got too much on our plates to take him up on the offer.

Even outside religious circles, leaders feel a similar tension. Empirical data and anecdotal wisdom alike confirm the positive impact of quiet reflection. As we'll see below, as little as fifteen minutes a day of deep thought can provoke a dramatic increase in performance. Still, leaders can't find the time to stop—not even for a quarter of an hour.

My point here isn't to equate prayer and reflection. Nor am I trying to draw a straight line between time with God and the bottom line. Instead, what I want us to see is that we *all*—Christian or not—struggle to let off the gas and hit the brakes, especially in our high-speed, always-on culture. We know we need to pull into pit lane every once in a while but our fear of losing the race keeps us out on the track until we either run out of gas or cut a tire and end up hitting a wall. Either way, we aren't going to finish the race. The question is: How many other people are we willing to take out with us?

Reflection's Return on Investment

In 2014, a group of researchers working in tandem with the Harvard Business School set out to understand the relationship between reflection and performance.[2] To do so, they put together a study using two groups of employees from a corporate call center. In one group, the researchers told employees to go about their work as normal. In the other, they had workers end each shift with fifteen minutes of reflection on what they'd experienced that day. Ten days in, the reflective group outperformed their peers by *more than 23 percent*. Not bad for only fifteen minutes of quiet time per day.

But, you might object, that study focuses on the ground floor. Would it work with executives? Ray Dalio is the founder of Bridgewater Associates—an investment management firm that controls over $150 billion in assets worldwide. In an interview with Business Insider, Dalio shared one of the bedrock principles that helped him go from the humble son of a jazz musician in Queens to a billionaire investor and philanthropist.[3] According to Dalio, "Pain plus reflection equals progress." With every botched decision, Dalio would intentionally slow down to reflect. From each failure, he'd draw a new principle to guide his future action and decision making. Reflecting on and learning from his mistakes—that's the simple truth about how Ray Dalio rose to the top.

Check Yourself: Being Mindful of Your Time

- Reflect on an experience that deeply resonates years after the event originally occurred. What do you remember about it? What made it so special?
- Consider what has been lost in mindless moments that you wish you had savored. Is there a certain moment that you'd like to do over?
- How could you benefit from slowing down? How would this benefit your memory and daily experiences?

A Gift to Be Received

When I make this case with leaders, their eyes usually pop out of their heads. In our high-speed world, the idea that *slowing down* could actually *increase* productivity is laughable. I understand that instinct, but I believe it's rooted in anxiety rather than the reality of time in God's world. Sure, you may not have three hours to pray and reflect like Martin Luther, but you have more time than you think. And if you'll just do it, the practice of slowing down will pay dividends in both your personal and professional life.

If we were to leave things there, you'd probably walk away with the impression that reflection equals results and prayer equals prosperity. That's a heretical game we don't want to play. Worse, it's sinfully reducing fellowship with God to a means rather than humanity's proper and joyful end. Instead, the deeper point I'm after is this: time is a gift from God, and what we do with that gift profoundly impacts what we receive from it. If you live your life at one hundred miles per hour, you'll blow past all but the largest formative experiences that God puts in your path. Worse, when you get to your final destination, you'll look back and wonder where your time went. In a word, you'll realize that you've lived a life of *absence*. The key to getting back our time, then, is to learn how to be fully *present*.

As Saint Augustine noted 1,600 years ago, our experience of time is subjective. If you want to know what that means, just compare ninety minutes watching a good movie with thirty minutes at the DMV. The best work in time management right now takes account of that subjectivity and draws on neuroscience and behavioral economics in order to bend it to our advantage. According to Marc Wittman, "Through mindfulness and emotional control, the tempo of life that we experience can be reduced, and we can regain time for ourselves and others."[4] As I'll argue in the next chapter, all this points in one direction: God has *made* us in such a way that our *presence* in time actually matters to how we experience and make use of it.

Fast or Slow—or Both?

Don't get me wrong: speed can be a good thing. As we'll see in chapter 7, there's a time for fast, and there's a time for slow. What matters most is whether you can tell the difference. In my experience, leaders need to learn the art of *timing*. That's the point Bill Gross made on the TED stage in 2015. As the founder of Idealab—the incubator behind Citysearch, NetZero, and Tickets.com—Gross has launched over a hundred businesses in the past twenty years. In his talk, he drew on that experience to expand on the fundamental difference between startups that win and those that lose. To the audience's surprise, the main differentiator wasn't a company's business model, personnel, funding, or even the product. Instead, it was timing. In a word, the question that determined each startup's success wasn't who, what, how, or why; it was *when*.

Chronobiology—the study of the human body's sense of time—has become something of a hot topic in recent time management work. Daniel Pink's *When* and Michael Breus's *The Power of When* represent two of the more popular works geared toward learning how to hack our daily rhythms for maximum results. As Pink shows, the decisions that affect our lives at every level—marriage, career, daily exercise—are more a matter of "when-to" than "how-to."

Understanding the "when-to," he argues, is the key to strategically aligning our daily activities with our bodies' normal rhythms. Along similar lines, Breus affirms, "There is a perfect time to do just about everything."[5] The path to reclaiming our time demands radical self- and organizational-awareness. In a word, it takes *presence*.

The Value in Numbering Our Days

Timing our days is one thing, but what about *numbering* them? In the Bible, numbering means to take careful stock of how much time you might be able to expect in this life, so that you are better poised to spend it *well*. There is wisdom found in deliberate reflection upon our finite lives. The Psalmist, recognizing the fleeting nature of human life, the depths of human sin, and the reality of God's wrath, invites us to pray:

> Teach us to number our days,
>> that we may gain a heart of wisdom. (Ps 90:12)

David offers up a similar prayer:

> Show me, LORD, my life's end
>> and the number of my days;
>> let me know how fleeting my life is. (Ps 39:4)

As he goes on to say, our days are like a mere breath; they are nothing before God. Even those among us who "seem secure" need to understand this if we're going to make the most of God's good gift of time.

This wisdom is recognized by some of the most insightful leaders of our time too. In 2005, Steve Jobs gave an often-cited address to the graduating class at Stanford. A year after his diagnosis with pancreatic cancer, Jobs praised death as life's greatest invention and invited his audience to live with a keen sense of their inevitable end. In *The Meaning Revolution*, Fred Kofman describes the intense transformation he sees in leaders when they calmly reflect on their inevitable death. At his workshops, Kofman challenges his participants to imagine the ideal version of their funeral. Having lived their fullest life, what would they want their eulogist to say? Then, he does the opposite, asking leaders to imagine their eulogy if they passed away tomorrow. After having them write down their responses, Kofman does a gap analysis, encouraging each leader to account for the distance between the present *real* and the future *ideal*. As I've seen in my own adaptation of Kofman's work, this simple exercise in death awareness can be a game changer.

Conclusion

I get the pain of an overloaded schedule. I understand the intense personal demands of having to show up and be present. But I also know that the cost of absence is far higher than whatever we pay for timefulness. In the last analysis, timefulness demands temporal wisdom. Time is both a gift and a responsibility. If we never slow down enough to be truly *present*, we'll squander that gift in frenzied *absence*. On the flip side, if we misunderstand self-awareness as an invitation to constant navel-gazing, we'll punt on our responsibility to make the most of what God has given. In the end, we need the wisdom that comes from an intimate knowledge of our finitude. Only then will we escape the tyranny of the clock and feel truly free to get our heads back in the game.

CHAPTER 6

The Gift of Time

Time is given us to use in view of eternity.

—HARRY IRONSIDE

If I gave you ten minutes to let your mind wander, where would it go? Would you daydream about the future? Would you drift back to the good old days of your youth? Worse, would the *bad* old days of trauma, neglect, failure, or abuse come to dominate your thoughts? These are the kinds of questions asked by Time Perspective Therapy (TPT).[1] Proponents of TPT, which is an especially effective method for treating combat veterans and executives alike, argue that our perspective on time drastically affects our daily function. If we fixate on past negative experiences, for example, we end up so paralyzed that we refuse to act in the present. Or if we devote all our attention to some anticipated future, we neglect the demands that lie before us right now. To the extent that our imbalance in either direction—past or future—pulls us out of the present, we're *absent* and unable to operate at peak capacity.

If absence is our enemy on the ground, then TPT is our eye-in-the-sky pointing out exactly where we're in danger. To bring it into more familiar territory, TPT comes across as a modern psychological version of ancient biblical wisdom. In Proverbs, we're admonished not to boast about tomorrow at the expense of today (Prov 27:1). In

Isaiah, God tells us not to fixate on the past to the extent that we miss the gloriously new things he's doing in salvation (Isa 43:18). The writer of Hebrews takes up Psalm 95 and urges us to listen to the Spirit's voice *today* (Heb 3:8). Indeed, now is the time; today is the day of salvation (2 Cor 6:2). The point is clear: God cares about our *presence* in time. He wants us to be timeful.

Ground Yourself: Mindful Eating

Timefulness can seem abstract. Use this simple exercise to practice savoring the present moment—literally. As you do, note how this simple act of noticing helps you attune more mindfully to your wider world.

- Choose a favorite treat or snack that you can sit and eat for a minimum of 3–5 minutes. Turn off any distractions (e.g., TV, social media, etc.)

- Begin by taking in the sight of your treat. Notice it's texture and form.

- Observe its smell and its weight in your hand or on the edge of your utensil. Become aware of any memories or images that emerge as you take in your treat visually and aromatically.

- Notice how your mouth prepares to receive your first bite.

- Don't swallow quickly but notice how you experience the taste. Notice the savory, sweet, sour, bitter, or salty flavor on your tongue.

- Notice how your throat prepares to swallow and your belly receives this bite.

- Pause after swallowing and notice any sensations. Allow your senses to broaden to the environment around you. Try to "stitch" this savored moment in time. Where are you? Who are you with?

God's Gift of Time

For leaders, our ability to manage everyday complexity demands *presence* in time. We need to let the wisdom of past experience and the prudence of long-range thinking inform, not eclipse, our decisive action in the present. To do that, we need to understand something about time—past, present, future—and what it means to live and lead as human beings in God's world. More specifically, we need to understand that time is a *gift*.

A theologian named Francis Turretin once described God's eternity as "the interminable possession of life—complete, perfect and at once."[2] The key word there is *life*. In the mystery of God's creative goodness, he decided to share his perfect eternal life with time-bound creatures like us. For that reason, time is not the contradiction of eternity. Instead, it is the arena or "space" in which God has chosen to live alongside human beings. It isn't an enemy to be vanquished or a commodity to be hacked but a gift to be received and extended as you live, move, and have your being with others. God has given and will give us all the time we need to do what he has called us to do—no more, no less.

Sometimes, timeful presence demands momentary absences from our busy schedules. In both my church and consulting experience, I've found retreat to be one of the most practical and helpful ways to take an intentional time-out for the sake of our time-in as leaders. During the early days of Sojourn, I made it a point to get away for at least two days at a time—sometimes, even a week. Extended retreats can be challenging in the business world, but the soul therapy is worth every minute spent. My challenge to leaders is to begin with a half day per quarter and two consecutive days per year. I bill these times as "time experiments," and I've yet to meet a leader who hasn't come away from one of our retreats with a greater sense of timefulness and presence.

A Time for Everything and Everything in Its Time

I've met plenty of young leaders who think they're going to be the first to strike the perfect balance between life and work. On the outside, I nod along graciously. On the inside, I laugh. Early on in our marriage, my wife and I realized quickly that balance was nothing more than an illusion. Life isn't about keeping everything in perfect stasis. Instead, it's about moving and grooving with the natural rhythm of life's seasons. Sometimes, you need to accelerate and grow. Other times, you need to take a moment (or a month) to slow down and recover. A year into our marriage, fresh out of seminary and already starting a new church, we found ourselves in an intense season of challenge and growth. Nearly twenty years later when it came time to transition from the church to the marketplace, we found ourselves in a similar time of acceleration and sacrifice—only, this time with four kids and a mortgage added into the mix.

No great leader has ever managed the overwhelming complexity of home, work, and health by chasing the great white whale known as balance. Instead, they've learned how to adapt to the seasonal nature of time in our world. They've discovered that life is a series of decisions, each season provokes a leader to ask which area or domain of life needs the most attention *right now*: health, relationships, finances, marriage, children. Where the search for balance enslaves us to the impossible task of focusing on *everything* all at once (a contradiction in terms), comfort with the rhythmic nature of life sets us free to allocate our resources dynamically as each particular season demands.

One of the reasons we seek balance rather than rhythm is our faulty perceptions of how time is supposed to work. Reacting to pagan ideas of eternal return (think of the movie *Cloud Atlas*), many

Christians have preferred to think of time as strictly linear. On that understanding, time moves the same way we do when we drive to work—from point A to point B as efficiently as possible. There is no ebb and flow, no give and take. Our job is to simply hop on the timeline and try to make the most of every moment. This leaves us feeling frustrated, exhausted, and dehumanized when the ordinary circumstances of life—family, illness, traffic—keep us from squeezing every last ounce of productivity out of each available moment. What we find in Scripture, however, is a strong affirmation of the cyclical—or better yet, *seasonal*—nature of life.[3] Our journey through time should be less like the morning commute and more like a scenic drive—sometimes fast, other times slow, always ready to slow down and savor the moment, but never unwilling to step on the gas when necessary. This gives us the freedom to ramp up when we need to and throttle down when life throws obstacles in our way, all without feeling like we've failed in our quest for maximum productivity.

To start living more like human beings and less like productivity machines, we need to reorder our lives to the ordinary flow of God's creation. In the beginning, God ordained the twenty-four-hour cycle of day and night as the basic unit of time (Gen 1:5, 8, 13, 19, 23, 31). The pattern of God's creative work (six days on, one day off) and the fourth commandment give rise to the significance of ordinary work weeks (Gen 2:1–3; Exod 20:8–11). The timing of feasts and festivals to follow cycles of sowing, growing, and harvest also served to order the lives of God's people in the Old Testament (Lev 23). Even the human lifespan was used as a fundamental measure of time (Gen 15:16; 50:23; Ps 90:10; etc.). In sum, time wasn't measured by the clock but by the everyday rhythm of natural life.

But can life in the natural world really tell us everything we need to know about time? The "Teacher" seemed to think so. In Ecclesiastes, we find a profound reflection on time "under the sun," as it might be perceived by a nonreligious person. In Ecclesiastes 1:4–11, we start with its apparent meaninglessness (Eccl 1:11). In chapter 3, however, we get a glimpse of its goodness. Time is God's gift, the Teacher tells us (Eccl 3:10–11). God has given us a sense of eternity, yet he also gives us temporal limits as an invitation to praise (Eccl 3:12, 14). Even if it *is* all meaningless, the Teacher says, the momentary fruit of our labor is a blessing from God (Eccl 3:12–13).

Time: Redeemed and Redeeming

Ecclesiastes is wisdom literature; it defies a straightforward reading.[4] The opening and closing verses form a frame around the book, inviting us to read everything in between similarly to how we'd read the sayings of Job's foolish friends. Much of what they say sounds good but falls apart in light of the rest of Scripture. According to Old Testament scholars Tremper Longman and Raymond Dillard, it is "not that everything that is said is wrong, but nearly so."[5] Thanks to its frame, the book itself invites us to transcend his limited perspective, to climb above the sun, and to see the real nature of time.

In the New Testament, Paul helps us do just that. He tells us about God's eternal plan to right everything that's gone wrong in the world, a plan that revolves around Jesus, whom God sent forth in "the fullness of time" (Eph 1:9–10 ESV; cf. Gal 4:4). Jesus's life, death, resurrection, and ascension is the act of God that, according to N. T. Wright, brought heaven and earth together.[6] In Christ, it's as if the time, space, and matter of heaven have entangled with that of earth. In his work on the Psalms, Wright describes this current entanglement: "God's time and ours overlap and intersect, God's space and ours overlap and interlock, and even (this is the really startling one, of course) the sheer material world of God's creation is infused, suffused, and flooded with God's own life and love and glory."[7] God's life in eternity is marked by the light and love shared by the Father, Son, and Holy Spirit.[8] He has extended that eternal fellowship to *us* by sending his Son in the fullness of time to be and bestow that life, light, and love to all God's people for now and forevermore (John 1:4; 5:24; etc.).

Redeeming the Time

We've been created and redeemed for life with God in his world. At the bare minimum, that should tell us that time is inherently meaningful—even when long lines at the post office, insufferable quarterly meetings, and delayed flights scream otherwise. More than that, it should tell us that God is profoundly invested in our engagement with time. He literally gave his Son so that we could spend a lot of time—at least ten thousand years and then forevermore—with him.

Here are four differences that you should make in how you approach time:

Perspectival: As the Lord of time, God gives it to us as a gift to be enjoyed and used for his glory and our good. Do you spend more time reminiscing about the good ol' days than you do trying to make *these* days better? While Scripture calls us to remember God's goodness in the past (Exod 13:3–16), it also tells us to get off our duff and act (Prov 6:4–14). Are you paralyzed by the fear of what may come? Again, we're told to leave the future up to God and to live faithfully in the present (Jas 4:13–17).

Relational: If the life God shares with us is relational, then our time should reflect that social reality. As Alan Burdick says, "Time is a social phenomenon. This property is not incidental to time; it is its essence. . . . Life is one great adaptation to the when of others."[9] The people we engage with are worth more than the time it takes to engage with them. We can trust God with the gift of time, even as we extend that gift to others.

Prudential: Time isn't a static reality to be manipulated at our whim. Time management skills are important, but presence in time is more about practical wisdom than dialed-in scheduling. The men of Issachar weren't noteworthy because of their efficiency or productivity but because they "understood the times and knew what Israel should do" (1 Chron 12:32). We'll unpack this at length in the next chapter.

Moral: Time is both a gift and a responsibility. Proverbs has plenty of examples of those who make foolish use of their time (Prov 6:4–14). Moreover, Paul tells us to redeem the time as we live in the midst of a twisted and crooked generation (Eph 5:16; Phil 2:15). We are accountable for our time; we'll one day have to answer for the use we've made of it.

Conclusion

We have seen the value of timeful presence, and now we've taken a deeper look at what time *is*—the space in which God shares his infinite, eternal life with finite, created images. That space takes shape in the created rhythms of days, nights, weeks, seasons, and our ordinary human lifespan. All this is a gift from God. These are the working conditions in which we can join him in cultivating the world as we look forward to the day when he brings history to its culmination. It is the privilege and responsibility of leaders not only to live and lead in time as God has made it but to create spaces and structures for others to do the same.

The Gift of Time

Principle: Time isn't a resource to be manipulated but a gift to be received. Because God has numbered our days, we can live in the freedom of knowing that he has given us all the time we need to do what he's calling us to do.

Practice: Set aside fifteen minutes each morning to pray over your schedule. Ask God to free you from anxiety over all there is to accomplish and for the faith to trust that he has already gone before you into your day.

CHAPTER 7

Leadership at the Speed of When

I used to believe that timing is everything. Now I believe that everything is timing.

—DANIEL PINK

Netflix, Uber, Airbnb—these are just a few of the companies that have risen to dominance in recent years. Interestingly enough, each was a miracle of *timing*. Without the fall of Blockbuster and the rise of widely available broadband internet, Netflix would be just one of a thousand now-defunct internet entertainment outlets. Without radical shifts in the economy that left millions searching for additional employment, Uber never would've amassed the drivers it needed to succeed. And without the recent recession and Americans' desperate need for additional cash, Airbnb never would've convinced homeowners to rent out space in their homes to complete strangers.

For business leaders, timing isn't *just* about launch strategy and market penetration. It's more granular than that. Every day, we're faced with a raft of decisions, big and small. As Daniel Pink points out, these decisions often depend much more on timing than they do technical know-how.[1] Anyone who's expanded too soon or waited too long to correct or replace a failing subordinate can tell you that the timing of a decision is at least as important as its execution. John Maxwell calls this the "Law of Timing," and he summarizes its importance in four bullet points:

1. The wrong action at the wrong time leads to disaster.
2. The right action at the wrong time brings resistance.
3. The wrong action at the right time is a mistake.
4. The right action at the right time results in success.[2]

A perennial challenge for leaders is to take the right action at the right time. The trouble is, the pace of modern business demands that we unhesitatingly treat *now* as the right time. The Teacher of Ecclesiastes tells us that for everything there is a season (Eccl 3:1), but the teachers at Wharton, Booth, and Sloan remind us of how short that season truly is. So before we can say something about *when*, we need to say something about *speed*. More specifically, we need to understand the forces that lean on us to move quicker than we, our organizations, or the market truly demands.

Burning Desires and Emotional Dumpster Fires

Every day, it seems, we're forced to make a choice: Will we be the tortoise or the hare? An idealistic young bootstrapper might opt for the former. Slow and steady wins the race, right? Sure, until an investor comes along to remind her that the hare didn't lose because he was fast; he lost because he was foolish. Today's marketplace isn't interested in slow, deliberate action. Leadership at the speed of modern life demands *urgency*. The early bird gets the worm, and the first to market—whether in smartphones or submarines—wins the prize. As Malcolm Gladwell has said, "The most successful entrepreneurs not only have courage and imagination; they also have a sense of urgency. They're not willing to wait. They have a burning desire to get something done."[3]

But what happens when we mistake a "burning desire" for an emotional dumpster fire? As John Kotter argues, leaders often confuse urgency with high-functioning anxiety. They try to fight back complacency by injecting a frenzy of activity into their organizations. Driven more by fear than by intentionality, leaders ramp up the pace, thinking the best way to maximize output is to crank the corporate machine up to eleven. As a result, "[The leader's] employees scramble: sprinting, meeting, task-forcing, emailing—all of which create a howling wind of activity. But that's all it is, a howling wind or, worse yet, a tornado that destroys much and builds nothing."[4]

One of the best ways I've found to protect myself from fear-driven frenzy is the simple discipline of journaling. There is no right or wrong way to journal. Some find it helpful to review today; others find it more helpful to preview tomorrow. I try to adopt both approaches in my practice, often recording a Psalm in my journal and adapting it into a prayer of reflection, anticipation, correction, and supplication. That simple act of writing and praying slows me down enough to flip off the autopilot and reengage my heart *in the moment*. When my time-anxiety tries to take over, a simple pen and paper are usually all I need to pause, reflect, and immerse myself in the present without stirring up an unnecessary whirlwind of unproductive busyness.

Slow It All Down Then?

Not so fast. Not all urgency is false urgency. Speed driven by mission and conviction is good, especially if it's marked by competence. In their book *Speed*, John Zenger and Joseph Folkman make the case for fast, competent leadership.[5] Based on their research, Zenger and Folkman found that leaders who execute competently only have a 3 percent probability of becoming "extraordinary."[6] But if they're both right and fast, that probability jumps to 96 percent. Here's where this really matters: the top 25 percent of leaders—in terms of speed—are twice as effective as their counterparts. Moreover, they increase the percentage of highly committed employees by 50 percent. A literal change of pace, as long as it's driven by urgency instead of anxiety and punctuated by competent execution, might just be the thing leaders need to engage a stagnant workforce.

Still, while it may be true that employees want genuinely fast leaders, that's not all they want. When *Harvard Business Review* surveyed nearly 20,000 workers, they learned that people perform at their highest level when four basic needs are met: physical, emotional, mental, and spiritual.[7] In other words, engagement and retention require more than fast leadership; they need fast *human* leadership. As I've witnessed firsthand, though, leaders tend to put the emphasis on speed over human need. Carl Honoré brings out the dehumanizing tendencies of fast life and leadership over against the humanizing benefits of going slow:

> Fast is busy, controlling, aggressive, hurried, analytical, stressed, superficial, impatient, active, quantity-over-quality. Slow is the opposite: calm, careful, receptive, still, intuitive, unhurried, patient, reflective, quality-over-quantity. It is about making real and meaningful connections—with people, culture, work, food, everything.[8]

We might expect Honoré to advocate that we all slow down, but he doesn't. Instead, he urges balance: "Be fast when it makes sense to be fast, and be slow when slowness is called for. Seek to live at what musicians call the *tempo giusto*—the right speed."[9]

Getting Our Speed Right

So which is better? Fast or slow? The final answer is a big, fat "it depends." A wide range of factors affects your pace as a leader: personal health, institutional harmony, life cycle, and market factors, among others.[10] Your *tempo giusto* ultimately depends on how you "understand the times" and react to the reality in and around you and your organization. In sum, your pace will be determined by your *presence*. To respond to the moment, you need to be *in* the moment. If you only know how to operate at one speed, it's likely because you've flown too far from reality to realize just what the present demands of you.

I've had to learn that lesson. You could say I'm blessed with what leadership experts like to call "a constellation of mentors." Godly advisors, coaches, mentors, and counselors have pushed, challenged, and stretched me to do more than I ever thought was possible. When Lyle Wells at the Flippen Group called me out on a blind spot in my leadership, I listened. Lyle was responding to what he'd observed in my leadership and on a 360 assessment. Top-flight leaders generally share a common bent toward high urgency and intensity. Their leadership engines run hotter than most, and mine was no exception. As we saw above, this is typically an asset for leaders, but as it is with most things, our greatest strengths can also be our greatest weaknesses. I had allowed my intensity to run over the more laid-back members on my team. Paradoxically, I needed to let off the gas if I wanted the team as a whole to pick up speed.

Suprachiasmatic Nucleus Expialidocious

To lead well, we need to regain our sense of mastery of time and timing. Pace matters, but knowing that doesn't answer our more concrete question: *When* is the right time to act? In recent years, chronobiology—the study of time *in our bodies*—has become increasingly relevant to work on time management. The basic idea goes something like this: Our brains are chronologically tuned to the normal patterns of daylight and darkness. The biological equipment (the suprachiasmatic nucleus) that governs our bodies' sense of time (circadian rhythm) evolved over a long period of time, most of which came *before* Thomas Edison and his light bulb. Now that we're in the age of artificial light and late-night Netflix binges, everybody's circadian rhythm is all out of whack. The consequences include insomnia, fatigue, poor health, and mood disorder—all of which practitioners of chronobiology claim to be able to alleviate.

Some Christians would take issue with the evolutionary cast of human beings' chronobiological development. The concern is fair, and it raises the question as to whether the God who created night and day could not similarly furnish his created images with the biological equipment they need to live in sync with his good creation. Holding those types of objections in reserve, chronobiology still opens up a new realm of awareness that we'd be foolish to ignore. As we saw in the last chapter, human beings are time-bound creatures. In principle, there's no reason why we couldn't explore our chronobiology in the same way a cardiologist might study the human heart. Still, we would need to maintain a robust commitment to our human responsibility to act in time. When it comes to our inaction or laziness, "my suprachiasmatic nucleus made me do it" will never be an acceptable answer.

Check Yourself: What Chronotype Are You?

A *chronotype* is the behavioral manifestation of underlying circadian rhythms. Your chronotype shows your propensity to sleep at a particular time during a twenty-four-hour period.

Take a chronotype test and find out your chronotype. This one happens to be our favorite: https://cet.org/assessment/confidential-self-assessments/.

Bringing Together Who and When

Michael Breus is one of the foremost popularizers of chronobiology. In *The Power of When*, Breus makes the bold claim that there is a perfect time to do just about everything.[11] Breaking human beings up into four basic chronotypes—dolphins, lions, bears, and wolves—Breus helps readers understand their bodily rhythms and time their activity accordingly. The payoff of this new awareness of our bodily rhythms is the ability to time "everything": when to wake, when to sleep, when to eat lunch, when to take your medicine, when to make love, and so on.

Daniel Pink offers a similar perspective in his book *When*, which is tailored to a business-oriented audience. For 75 percent of people, he says, each day is split into three sections: peak, trough, and recovery.[12] Our chronotype determines how and when we live through that pattern. In general, we are most alert, confident, and enthusiastic in our peak time. That all takes a nosedive after lunch, followed by recovery in the afternoon. If we make the mistake of trying to perform a critical task while we're in the trough, we'll perform at about the same level as if we had a few glasses of wine.

To combat the ill effects of mistiming, Pink encourages two kinds of breaks: vigilance and restorative. A vigilance break is that ten-minute breather you take to collect yourself before walking into a critical meeting. A restorative break is that five minutes you're supposed to take every hour or so. I say "supposed to" because few of us rarely take restorative breaks as often as we should. That's a mistake, says Pink. Citing a report from the productivity software company DeskTime, Pink reports that high performers "work for fifty-two minutes and then break for seventeen minutes."[13] Long story short, the people who get the most done are the ones who recognize their need to drop what they're doing and go out for a stroll.

Conclusion

As Breus and Pink show us, the trick to making the best use of our time is to understand our natural rhythm. Timing your leadership activity requires *presence* in your own body—knowing not only who you are but *when* you are. Do you do your best work late at night? Are you an insufferable monster just after lunch? Is an early afternoon nap your saving grace? It's time we start paying attention to questions like these and allowing their answers to positively shape the way we structure our days. This may seem minor, but these are the low-level adjustments that will inevitably pay off in the long run. By dialing in our daily rhythm—that is, our embodied timefulness—and expanding that sense of awareness out to the organizational level, we'll train ourselves to become the kind of leaders who instinctively take the right action at the right time.

Leadership at the Speed of When

Principle: The best leaders don't let the urgency of leadership short-circuit their own embodied sense of timing. Always in tune with the present, they know when to jog and when to sprint as they lead people toward the finish line.

Practice: Fit restorative breaks into your schedule this week. Every hour on the hour, get up and take a five minute walk around the halls. Remember, you're not slacking; you're ramping up your impact for the next hour.

CHAPTER 8

You're Going to Die

From quixotic quests for the "Fountain of Youth," to pseudoscientific practices like bathing in blood or having sex with virgins, humans have a long, odd history of trying to put off death. In recent decades, some have turned to a host of fanciful options, from cryogenic freezing to parabiosis, which is a theoretical treatment that transfers plasma from young donors to older recipients. These radical attempts to overcome death are being pursued by tech moguls like Peter Thiel, Max Levchin, Ray Kurzweil, and others.[1]

Yet, as Jeff Bercovici reports, a trend in the opposite direction has emerged in Silicon Valley. While some leaders continue to spend billions attempting to eliminate death, others have learned to embrace their inevitable date with the Reaper as a catalyst for better living in the present. Picking up on an ancient philosophy called Stoicism, these leaders have adopted a new mantra: "The man who fears death will never do anything worthy of a man who is alive."[2] As Steve Jobs so effectively communicated to that graduating class of Stanford students (see chapter 5), the impending reality of our death invites us to heed the words of the Stoic Marcus Aurelius: "Execute every act of life as though it were your last."[3]

Christians and the Art of Dying

For lovers of lifehacking with a desire to maximize every possible moment (think Tim Ferris's *4-Hour Workweek*), death is a powerful motivator. There's nothing like a stiff deadline to get us going! But do *Christian* leaders share this positive take on life's finitude? According to Rob Moll, the answer is likely no. In fact, Christians have gotten so pro-life that we've forgotten what to do with death.[4] Moll shares a study from the *Journal of the American Medical Association* in which religious people, 95 percent of whom were Christians, ended up three times more likely to opt for aggressive medical treatment at the end of life, even in the face of incredibly long odds. And when it came to end-of-life planning, Christian patients were often the least prepared and most confused. All told, Moll's take is as accurate as it is condemning: "Our churches are not teaching us to die well."[5]

Christians are right to perceive death as an enemy, but what does Christ's victory on the cross tell us about how we should overcome that foe? Jesus confronted his impending death with a sense of purpose that shaped all he said and did on his life-long road to Calvary. Jesus's righteous life and sacrificial death represent the embodiment of that wisdom to be found in learning to number our days (Pss 39:4; 90:12). Paradoxically, when we refuse to seek that wisdom by denying death's presence, we plunge ourselves into a type of temporal absence. As theologian Jürgen Moltmann has said, "To push away every thought of death, and to live as if we had an infinite amount of time ahead of us, makes us superficial and indifferent. . . . To live as if there were no death is to live an illusion."[6] In suppressing our thoughts of death, we idolize life and foolishly indoctrinate ourselves into the cult of speed. This idolatry "leads to fast living: to fast food, to fast cars, to fast relationships, to fast meetings."[7]

Does all this mean we need a healthy dose of Stoicism in our Christian lives? Not exactly. Stoicism is ultimately a form of fatalism that denies biblical teaching about God and the true nature of created reality—including life and death. Yes, the Bible teaches us to number our days, but it doesn't teach us to live as though death were our natural end. Death is the wage of sin (Rom 6:23), a decidedly unnatural consequence of humanity's refusal to accept God's gracious invitation to life. Even so, death *will* be defeated in the end

(1 Cor 15:26). We're called to live as partakers of the eternal life we have hidden in Christ as we wait for its full revelation in the future (John 5:24; Col 3:3–4). If you ask Peter, the prime motivator for godly living in the present isn't the day of our death but that day when the Lord will come like a thief to right all that has gone wrong and usher in the new heavens and new earth (2 Pet 3:1–10).

Terror or Training?

In the Pulitzer-prize-winning *The Denial of Death*, Ernest Becker argued that every human being is driven by his or her desire to thwart death. From skyscrapers to social networks, everything we do is an attempt to transcend our finite existence and find some scrap of meaning that will last beyond the grave. The thirty plus years of research behind terror management theory (TMT) has sought to both confirm Becker's argument and expand on it. In the book *The Worm at the Core*, psychologists Sheldon Solomon, Jeff Greenberg, and Tom Pyszczynski use TMT to double down on Becker's thesis: "The terror of death has guided the development of art, religion, language, economics and science. It raised the pyramids in Egypt and razed the Twin Towers in New York."[8]

If read as a sociological attempt to reduce the origins of our faith to a mere revolt against mortality, Christians will rightly find TMT problematic. What it does reliably show us, however, is how people behave in light of what *they believe* about the finitude of human life. The more conscious we are of death, the closer we cleave to those values, systems, and behaviors that give us a sense of transcendence. All it takes is a gnarly patch of turbulence or a near miss on the highway to scare us to death. In those moments, we're reminded of the distance between the life we *want* to live and the one we're actually living. As we saw in chapter 5, advisors like Fred Kofman are tapping into that tension in order to help leaders reckon with their mortality and use their awareness of the end to influence their leadership in the here and now.[9]

Steve Jobs, Jonathan Edwards, and You

Training for death isn't exactly a new development in the history of thought. The medieval world feared "sudden death," not because it cut their time short but because it deprived them of the opportunity to prepare for the next life.[10] According to Peter Kreeft, "They feared not thinking about death more than death itself."[11] This death awareness informed the two medieval maxims of *memento mori* (remember death) and *respice finem* (look to the end). Instead of viewing their day of death as a tragic and meaningless end, medieval Christians understood it to be a day of new birth (*dies natalis*) in which they passed from this shade of reality into true, heavenly Being.[12] Today, says Kreeft, we've got that precisely backward: "People *hope* for 'a sudden and unprovided death' so that they might *not* have time to think about it. They fear thinking about death more than death itself!"[13] Why else would Steve Jobs need to stand before an audience and remind them to stop living as though their time on earth was unlimited?

With all due respect, I disagree with Jobs when he says, "Death is life's greatest invention."[14] As we saw above, death is life's greatest foe—an unnatural consequence of sin and an enemy to ultimately be defeated. That doesn't mean, however, that death can't continue to motivate the way we choose to live in the present. We have a rich history of Christians who've used death as a powerful catalyst for reflection (*memento mori*). Jonathan Edwards (1703–58) represents just one example of many. In the 1720s, Edwards wrote up a list of seventy resolutions—personal commitments spelling out how he intended to live as a devoted follower of Christ. Here are a few of them (with my own emphasis in italics):

1. Resolved, that I will do whatsoever I think to be most to God's glory, and my own good, profit and pleasure, in the whole of my duration, *without any consideration of the time.* . . .

5. Resolved, *never to lose one moment of time*; but improve it the most profitable way I possibly can.

6. Resolved, to live with all my might, *while I do live*.

7. Resolved, never to do anything, which I should be afraid to do, *if it were the last hour of my life.* . . .

9. Resolved, *to think much on all occasions of my own dying, and of the common circumstances which attend death*.[15]

Edwards died an "early" death at the age of fifty-five, just weeks after assuming office as the president of the College of New Jersey (which later became Princeton University). In that "short" life, he managed to play a key role in the First Great Awakening, write at least seventy-three volumes worth of material, and become America's greatest theologian. I wonder if Edwards could have done all that without a vivid sense of his mortality driving his resolve to use every moment of time in the most profitable way he possibly could.

Conclusion

Reckoning with our mortality brings a new sense of clarity to everything we do. It compels us to stop living with our regrets and to start actively building a legacy. It reminds us that we have a responsibility to those we leave behind. It's time we stop ignoring the inevitable. Unless Jesus comes back first, neither you nor I can escape the fact that our time is going to come. But, unlike Becker and his followers, we know that death can never have the final word. You're going to die. But if you're in Christ, you've already begun to live. It is God's gift of life—not humanity's fear of death—that gives all our earthly moments their significance. So live your life in light of the end. Don't ignore it. At the same time, don't forget that the Lord of time is as present and sovereign in the end as he is the beginning, as well as every moment in between.

You're Going to Die

Principle: Death is the common lot of humanity in this fallen world. Knowing our days are numbered, present leaders resolve to live each moment for the glory of God and the good of others.

Practice: Put thirty minutes on your calendar to reflect on your own inevitable end. Who do you want by your side in your final moments? Who will be there when they lay you in the ground? What will they put on your tombstone? How will you be remembered?

CHAPTER 9

The Blessing of Timefulness

At various points in this book, we've painted pictures of leaders who live *out of time*. Racked by anxiety, they try with all their might to milk as much as they can out of every last minute of the day. They lock themselves into mortal combat with the clock and sacrifice relationships with coworkers and loved ones at the altar of productivity. Squeezed by the unrelenting pace of modern life, they mistake busyness for business, inflicting their organizations with a false sense of urgency that does more to destroy than to upbuild. When an inevitable brush with mortality comes—either through the death of a loved one or bad news from the doctor—these leaders double down on their efforts to beat the clock, only to find themselves on the losing end.

Clocks and Seasons: A Tale of Two Times

The ancient Greco-Roman world of our New Testament had two ways of looking at time: *chronos* and *kairos*. *Chronos* referred to static, linear time—the kind of time you'd measure with a watch (i.e., a chronometer). *Kairos*, on the other hand, dealt less with quantity than quality. To speak of time in a kairotic sense is to point to its fitting-ness: "The Lord GOD hath given me the tongue of the learned, that I should know how to speak a word in season (*kairos*) to him that is weary."[1] So 2:30 p.m. may be a great time (*chronos*) to jump on a call as far as your calendar is concerned, but if 2:30 p.m. is the groggiest part of your day, then it's ultimately the wrong time (*kairos*).

According to Douglas Rushkoff, the always-on world of smartphones and 24-7 email has led to a near-total eclipse of *chronos* over *kairos*.[2] In the ancient world of sundials and lunar calendars, the natural rhythms of time left plenty of room for life to happen. The turn from analog to digital timekeeping, however, left us with a conception of time as a static number—an abstract symbol with no sympathy for the fuzziness of life in the concrete world. Those unforgiving digital numbers on our smartphone and laptop screens condition us to focus less on rhythm and more on ruthless efficiency. Our hours and minutes become like dollars and cents to be hoarded rather than the generous space in which God has called us to live with him and others.

We used to measure time by the position of the sun. Now we measure it by the cesium-133 atom and its 9,192,631,770 oscillations per second. When literally every *nanosecond* counts, *chronos* has no time for *kairos*: "Either show me the bottom-line impact of an hour spent building relationships, or talk to me about something else." We try to squeeze production out of every minute, yet we forget how many of those minutes God has intended us to use for "nonproductive" activities like rest, reflection, and relationship.

Precision, of course, isn't the only factor in this equation. Data plans, Wi-Fi, and the smartphone have all conspired to take every kairotic moment captive. With each ding, we're forced into the realm of *chronos*. We used to live with a sense of imagination about what the future might bring. Now we live in compulsive anticipation—always waiting for the next buzz from our smartphones.

Redeeming Time

Time—both *chronos* and *kairos*—is God's gift to us (chapter 6). To realize the blessing of timefulness, we need the wisdom to disentangle the two—to distinguish between the *chronos* of fiscal calendars and the *kairos* of cultural formation. According to Thomas Merton, we can see the wisdom of that distinction in the emptying of Jesus's eternal "equality with God" for the sake of his service in time.[3] In the fullness of time (*chronos*), God sent his Son for our redemption (Gal 4:4–5). Consequently, now is the favorable time (*kairos*)—today is the day of salvation (2 Cor 6:2). Worship is where we go to celebrate the fact that the eternal Son has come for time's redemption. As Eastern Orthodox churches proclaim at the head of the Divine Liturgy: "[Now] is the *kairos* for the Lord to act."

At this point, the typical move for a Christian take on time management would be to shame you into better stewardship: "Today is the day, so you better get to work, you ungrateful sinner." No doubt, that's a message many of us need to hear. But in my work, I've found that leaders need more redemption than condemnation. They need to know that the God who marks out the "appointed times" of our lives did not allow David to go into the grave until he "had served God's purpose in his own generation" (Acts 13:36). The God who teaches us to number our days is the Sovereign Creator who numbers those days before we're even born (Pss 90:12; 139:16).

You have enough time to do what God has called you to do. Stop living in fear of time's scarcity and start walking in the freedom won for you by the Lord of time.

Ground Yourself: Observing a Minute

- **Round 1:** Take out the stopwatch on your cell phone and push start. Turn over your phone and sit until you think a minute has elapsed. Check the phone. How close did you get?

- **Round 2:** Set your timer for one minute and count your breaths until the timer goes off. Note the number of breaths.

- **Round 3:** Return to the stopwatch and push start. Turn over your phone and count your breaths to the number you achieved in round 2. Compare the time variations from round 1. Were you closer to a minute by being present with your breathing versus with your thoughts?

Sabbath: Your Freedom to Rest in Time

Paul calls us to redeem our time in the midst of an evil world (Eph 5:16). The language he uses comes from the realm of commerce. In a sense, we're called to buy back our time from a world that wants us to squander it, which in this case means living out of step with the freedom established by the gospel (Eph 5:1–2). In Christ, we've been set free from the modern world's fixation on scarcity. As Thomas Merton put it, everyone in contemporary society "is obsessed with lack of time, lack of space, with saving time, conquering space, projecting into time and space the anguish produced within them by the technological furies of size, volume, quantity, speed, number, price, power, and acceleration."[4] But if time is an abundant space that God has set out for us to enjoy life and partnership with him, then the word *scarcity* no longer applies.

Christ has come from "above the sun" to free us from our fixation with *chronos* and our schedule addiction. He has not conquered time so much as liberated it. The freedom of Christians who think well about these things "is not freedom from time but freedom in time."[5] The key to redeeming our time isn't to join the world's obsession with *chronos* at the expense of *kairos*. Rather, we need to rediscover a sense of time that's not measured by the clock—to "recover the rhythm and order of man's real nature."[6] Chronobiology sets its sights on that prize but falls short unless it turns to God to learn what "real nature" actually is.[7] We need to recover the rhythm and order of God's *created* nature—that is, the rhythmic world in which days, nights, seasons, and lifetimes mean as much to us as seconds and minutes.

In the beginning, that natural rhythm included the principle of sabbath: six days on and one day off (Exod 20:8–11). When God liberated Israel in the Exodus, he set them free from their 24-7 bondage to the Egyptian labor market and commanded them to pattern their lives after his created rhythm for work and rest (Deut 5:12–15). Later, when the religious leaders distorted that good principle into just another form of bondage, Jesus came as the Lord of the sabbath to set his people free once more (Mark 2:23–28).

Not only can we apply the sabbath principle to the way we order our weekly schedules, but we can also apply it to the way we live freely in time. To help you do that, this chapter will close with a simple exercise: stop, trust, and enjoy. You can expect to see it repeated near the end of each major part of the book. The purpose of this exercise is to still our hearts before God (stop), turn to him for help (trust), and receive the good gifts he has given and will give (enjoy).

- **Stop:** Embrace sabbath as an opportunity to unplug from the constant pressures of the modern world. Embrace the freedom to retreat, knowing that God has given you all the time you need to both work and rest.
- **Trust:** We often ignore rest because we feel as though time is passing too quickly. Fight against that misconception by scheduling times of solitude. In those moments, meditate on the goodness of God's gift of time.
- **Enjoy:** Quit trying to get more time from God. Start celebrating the time he's given you. Intentionally grasp opportunities to play, all the while praising God for giving time as something to be enjoyed and not simply used.

Time and the Brain

We've all heard the phrase "seize the day." *Carpe diem.* Where does this idea of seizing time come from? The wing-footed Greek god of time, Kairos, was said to have had a long lock of hair hanging from the front of his head, suggesting that you could only grab Time from the front as he was coming toward you. Once he passed you by, there was nothing you could do.

Chronologically speaking, time doesn't change for anyone. Yet time flies by when you're having fun or stretches on when *War and Peace* is required reading. During catastrophes, time warps into slow motion and is often described as if it stopped entirely. Thus our experience of time is subjective, psychological, experienced, and episodic.[1]

Time Happens in a Context

The brain organizes both space and time in the temporal lobes. Your ability to relive moments from your life is called episodic memory. When you recall a memory, you see it replaying in your mind's eye, or the hippocampus. That image bank is anchored in time (the when), place or space (the where), and content (the what).[2]

Memories are stored in the hippocampus, which sits directly next to the amygdala (the part of the brain that regulates emotions). Our experience of time becomes more meaningful and whole when our brain layers all five senses on top of these episodic memories.

The key to slowing down time is to be mindful of all the layers available to us in the present moment. Your senses stitch into the memory, securing it in time and place. In other words, savor the moment, or yes, seize the day.

Savoring Bends Time to Your Will

I teach clients and other therapists to S-A-V-O-R the moment. Savoring is not easy. It takes work. But it can help as you journey toward being present in all aspects of your life. Here are the five steps to S-A-V-O-R:

S—*Study your senses.* Become aware of your five senses. What do you see? What do you smell? What do you hear in the foreground and the background? What does the seat feel like under you? Is it cold or hot? What flavor does your tongue notice? Is it bitter or sweet? Are your palms sweaty?

A—*Attune to your inner thoughts and feelings.* Now take your gaze inward. What thoughts come up? Do you feel excited or nervous or content? Are you experiencing fear or self-criticism? Are you happy or sad?

V—*Validate without judgment.* Savoring a moment requires the ability to integrate all the information our brains are receiving and then name it. Naming, as Laura Vanderkemp says, is taming.[3] Naming a feeling or experience validates our memory of it. We cannot change what we cannot name. Placing words on the emotions, senses, thoughts—the what and the when—solidifies another layer of experience.

O—*Occupy the entire experience.* Immerse and extend yourself fully into the corners of the experience. Take it all in. Take command of yourself in the moment. Inhabit it. Submerge yourself in the ocean of the moment.

R—*Remove distractions.* Multitasking is an illusion. We cannot fully immerse ourselves when there are multiple things competing for our attention. When we remove distractions, we become more efficient as all of our resources are focused on that moment.

As an example, I decided to savor Christmas day using the gift my husband had given me that morning. I turned off the TV, set my new Amazon Echo to play jazz, and began to notice all my senses. The pine scent of the Christmas tree, the twinkling lights in my living room and those coming through the window, the lull of the soft trumpet, the warm cup of tea in my hand that I lovingly took the time to steep the full recommended five minutes. All of this led me to a holiday memory that felt rich and somehow seemed to last a long time.

When we decide to "veg out," we make a conscious choice to block out any sensory input. At the end of a weekend in which we binged on Netflix and ate too much processed food, we wonder *where did my weekend go?* Just like highway hypnosis, vegging out is a retreat from the outside input that nourishes and sharpens our experience.

The beautiful thing about our brains is that they let us hold on to the awareness of all our senses at the same time. We can further deepen our savoring by recalling past memories and contemplating future desires. When we are able to S-A-V-O-R, time is no longer our master but our servant. We can bend time to serve us.

PLACE FUL- NESS

SECULAR

DISPLACED

PLACED

SACRED

CHAPTER 10

Where Are You?

Sunrise is still a few hours off. It is way too early. You're driving down the highway, but you don't quite remember how you got there (highway hypnosis). That 4:00 a.m. wake-up call came too soon, especially since you spent half the night answering emails while your partner snoozed peacefully beside you. Before you know it, you're at the office sleepwalking past a sea of dimly lit cubicles. The faint hum of fluorescent lighting only perpetuates your half-hypnotic trance. You walk into your office, plop down in your chair, and swivel toward the window. A faint glimmer of moonlight on the tree in the parking lot reminds you of the time you and your kids went for a hike last year. Then you remember that you haven't spent more than five minutes outside in the last month. In fact, the only contact you've had with nature is the stock desktop wallpaper on your laptop.

Wherever You Go, There You Aren't

Most leaders today are captive to the portrait of absence I painted above. In 1994, Jon Kabat-Zinn released his popular *Wherever You Go, There You Are* as a response to this very issue. Using mindfulness as a sort of "technology" of presence, Kabat-Zinn argued for meditation as a "human activity which at bottom is about not trying to improve yourself or get anywhere else, but simply to realize where you already are."[1] Twenty-five years and nearly a million sales later, it seems he touched a nerve. But *why?* Why do we need some guy with a typewriter (or a laptop) to tell us where we are? Don't we know already?

Yes and no. Thanks to our GPS-enabled phones, we (and Google) know exactly where we are at all times. Even so, the same technology that plots us on a map can drag us away mentally and emotionally as we read the latest headline or covet our neighbor's trip to Acapulco. Technology isn't the only contributor to our sense of absence, of course, but it has amplified our ongoing struggles with presence. No matter where we let our attention go and no matter why it happens, our absence as leaders is contagious. If we don't do something about it, we'll become like a queen bee presiding over a swarm of dehumanized, disengaged, and marginally productive drones.

We've Lost Our Sense of Place

In our digitized world, where we can work just as well in a Starbucks as we can in an office, we've all grown disconnected from the importance of the physical places we inhabit. When so much of our interaction happens over Skype, Slack, and Gmail, who cares *where* you are as long as the Wi-Fi works? But as we'll see in the following chapters, your sense of place is about more than the chair you just happen to be sitting in. Until we understand what place is and why it matters, we'll be stuck in the limbo of *displacement*.

Displacement is a broad term that describes the lived tension between physical presence and spiritual, emotional, and psychological absence. Displacement is

- missing your kid's buzzer-beater (see chapter 5)
- loving your home but hating your neighborhood
- feeling like you're doing the work God has called you to do, but being surrounded by people and places that won't cooperate
- looking up from your phone to find you've missed everything your spouse just said

- "waking up" behind the wheel of your car to realize you've been zonked out for the past six miles
- realizing you just spent $180 on a meal without having a meaningful conversation
- having one of your kids grab you by the face just to get you to notice them

Displacement is the ongoing struggle to *be* where we are. When we use our smartphones to turn the house into another satellite office, we're displaced from the wonderful gift of rest and refuge the home provides. When our office space is divided by lonely corridors and isolated meeting rooms, we're displaced from all that jargon in our mission statement about collaboration, creativity, inspiration, and synergy. When our only interaction with nature is Fluffy's morning tinkle in the backyard, we're displaced from the natural world that God has invited us to cultivate. If we're going to survive, we need to recover our sense of place.

From Displacement to Placement

If displacement is our absence from physical space, then what can bring us back? In the next few chapters, I'm going to argue for *placefulness* as the antidote to absence. Placefulness is both a disposition and a practice. It's the commitment to be where you are and the discipline to create spaces—at home or the office, in your neighborhood or city—that facilitate presence for yourself and others. Both aspects of placefulness feed on one another as the places we make can draw us into a deeper sense of presence.

A word of warning: God made his images for presence. To be fully human is to live before God and reflect his presence in the world around us. If placefulness is about stepping more fully into that vision of humanity, then we can expect all the antihuman forces of darkness to rise up against us. We see that every time we set up a workshop, and the executives who *paid* us to coach them end up frittering away our time and their cash on their cell phones. We hear it every time a leader complains about the amount of time his employees spend on Facebook or Netflix instead of contributing to the organization. We feel it every time we lug a laptop with us on a family vacation for fear that completely disconnecting would somehow cause a disaster.

But those are only the *external* pressures that displace us. What about the *internal* motivators that constantly draw us out of the moment? Those executives I just mentioned aren't playing Candy Crush; they're doing important work. Why? Because they're afraid that presence *here* entails an absence *there*, and that the only solution is to "be" in two places at once. Instead of trusting their team and experiencing the freedom of delegation, their lukewarm presence becomes a functional absence. In trying to be in both places at once, they end up in neither. Remember what Baron Baptiste said: "You're either now here or you're nowhere."

Whether it's the fear of missing out or dropping the ball, something *in us* wants to drag us away. The recent explosion in new media technology not only cultivates that internal penchant toward absence but *facilitates* it. As we learned in chapter 3, our connection to the digital world comes at an expense to our embodied engagement with the world. No matter how close we feel on Facebook, or how efficient we are with Skype, the ones and zeros of online interaction will never replace the eyeball-to-eyeball connection of two human beings in one place.

Yet our technology continually seeks to enslave us. Americans spend over eleven hours per day interacting with media like movies, television, radio, internet, and video games.[2] Even when we're not consuming media, our media consumes us. Email, instant messaging, breaking news, a friend's latest social media post—these are just a few of the distractions that pull us out of the moment. Wherever we go, they follow.

Conclusion: Get Real

Look, I'm no Luddite. I've got six tabs open in my browser right now. Notifications keep pinging at the top of my screen, inviting me to answer a text from my wife, respond to a client, and watch the latest episode. My phone is face down on the table, but I can still feel it buzz. And in the back of my mind, there's a constant tug of that long-overdue vacation my family's been hounding me for.

The trick to overcoming displacement isn't pretending those things don't exist or retreating into a monastery. Instead, it's recovering a robust sense of place. In the modern classic *Celebration of Discipline*, Richard Foster talks about solitude, not as a retreat from life but as the discipline of quieting yourself *in place*.[3] In the following chapters, we're going to see what that looks like in the spheres of home, neighborhood, work, city, and nature.

CHAPTER 11

The Case for Placefulness

In January of 2019, thrift stores across the nation enjoyed a tremendous spike in donations. According to one spokesperson for Goodwill, the Washington DC area saw a 66 percent rise in giving, with one store posting a 367 percent increase over the previous year.[1] What was behind this meteoric rise in generosity? Two words: Marie Kondo. In 2014, Kondo's *The Life-Changing Magic of Tidying Up* inspired millions to weed through their belongings and get rid of everything that didn't "spark joy." As a direct result, *Time* magazine named her one of the top one hundred most influential people of 2015. And when her Netflix series *Tidying Up with Marie Kondo* dropped, a whole new horde of devotees loaded their minivans and headed to the nearest Goodwill.

Why did Kondo strike such a nerve? To be sure, the cultural phenomenon she started wasn't just about tips and tactics for clearing out your bedroom closet. After all, any schmo could spend a few minutes on YouTube learning how to fold clothes. And it doesn't take a Netflix special to sell the benefits of spring cleaning. No, what Kondo did was teach people to reimagine their *place*—to rethink their stuff through the lens of lifestyle, joy, and fulfillment. Where hoarding threatened to transform the home into a museum, Kondo stepped in to remind her viewers that "the joy and excitement we feel here and now are more important" than that old softball jersey your wife keeps begging you to throw out.[2] At bottom, tidying up isn't about decluttering your space as much as it is about reclaiming your life: "The space in which we live should be for the person we are becoming now, not for the person we were in the past."[3]

Losing Our Place at Home

People flock to Marie Kondo for her promise of a new and better life—a restorative experience played out in the mundane spaces of our everyday lives. But can an ordinary place like the home exercise such immense power on our well-being? We don't have to take Kondo's word for it. There's a bevy of research out there to show that cleaning your house can lower stress, boost productivity, spark creativity, and keep your teenagers from ripping each other (or you!) to shreds.

It doesn't take but a moment's reflection to realize why all that is true. Our home is our place of rest and refuge. When we let it fall to pieces, we deprive ourselves of one of the last safe places we have in this world. We rob ourselves of one of the simplest, yet most profound sources of energy we know. But apart from letting the laundry pile up, there's another subtler way you and I can transform our place of refuge into just another stress-inducing pile of brick and mortar. I'll give you a hint: we carry it around in our pocket.

If everyone's house is their castle, then the realities of 24-7 connectivity have swum the moat, scaled the walls, and stormed the keep. In one emblematic study, 40 percent of respondents believed it was ok to return urgent work emails during family dinner.[4] For those of us who wouldn't go quite that far, our smartphones still manage to find a spot on the table somewhere to the left of the salad fork. Even if we resist the urge to answer every buzz, research shows that just having the phone on the table is enough to ruin the experience for everyone else.[5]

If we can draw on Genesis 1–2 for a moment, our home is supposed to be our garden. The dinner table is meant to be the shade tree where we go to find life. But when we let digital messengers creep in from east of Eden, we turn our home into just another workspace. We make ourselves absent from the people and places that make us. And then we're surprised when stress, fatigue, and burn-out come knocking at the door.

The Impact of Place on Corporate Culture

Placefulness isn't just about making our own place but making it for others too—especially those we lead.[6] Leaders tend to discount the impact of space on their employees. According to David Kelley, founder of the international design firm IDEO, "Space matters. We read our physical environment like we read a human face."[7] What do employees "read" when they walk in to see enclosed desks shot off long, lonely hallways? What do conference rooms with massive tables that keep people as far apart as possible say about your attitude toward collaboration? Most offices, Kelley says, "were designed according to an industrial labor model, from a time when our work was tethered to big machines and our status was rooted in the size of our office space."[8] That's why, when Kelley started IDEO—a decidedly *non*industrial enterprise—he and his cofounders knew they would have to design a space to cultivate their cultural values of innovation, collaboration, and creation rather than one-size-fits-all office work.

In chapter 2, we looked at the current stats on engagement and the impact of culture in winning back our employees. Can your sense of place make *that* kind of cultural impact? According to Rex Miller, Mabel Casey, and Mark Konchar, the answer is a resounding yes:

> Changing the design of the workplace gets to the heart of all the issues that make work complicated, distracting, and energy draining. . . . Changing space brings managers and leaders back in touch with how the work really gets done and back in

touch with the people and the hidden culture that embodies the real drivers behind behavior and performance.[9]

To back up their contention, Miller, Casey, Konchar, and their collaborators traveled the country looking at the most engaging workspaces and their impact on the workforce. Exploring organizations like Google, the Bill and Melinda Gates Foundation, and Cummins, they saw just how place and culture feed into one another: "The spaces—the actual designed places for work conferencing, exercise regimens, eating, walking, and the like—reflected the values of the company, and also shaped the patterns of behavior and interaction."[10] They discovered that the greatest companies felt like foreign countries and their employees like passionate, engaged citizens. Productivity, creativity, and pretty much every other *-ivity* you can imagine improved as a result of those companies' efforts to craft places to match their values.

Is Your Space Killing You?

According to Simon Sinek—bestselling author and TED Talks phenomenon—our jobs are literally killing us.[11] More than 10 percent of the workforce is on antidepressants,[12] and 60–80 percent of doctor visits (primary care) include a significant stress component.[13] In fact, 83 percent of employees are stressed at work, contributing to $300 billion in lost productivity due to stress-related issues.[14] According to a 2013 Harvard Medical School study, 96 percent of senior leaders feel burned out.[15] The corporate wellness movement—of which mindfulness is a significant part—has recognized statistics like these as a clarion call to make meaningful changes to both culture and space. Companies like Google are actively redesigning workspaces to encourage physical activity. Not only does this encourage employees to improve their health, but the knock-on effects of exercise translate directly to increased energy, productivity, and collaboration. Just going for a walk is enough to boost creative output by 60 percent.[16]

Along with this turn to corporate wellness, organizational experts are learning that placefulness requires a renewed awareness of our need for nature. In *The Nature Fix*, Florence Williams gathers a dizzying array of scientific evidence to show that our growing disconnect from nature is ruining us physically, psychologically, and spiritually. "Over recent decades," Williams says, "we have come from dwelling in another world in which the living works of nature either predominated or were near at hand, to dwelling in an environment dominated by a technology which is wondrously powerful and yet nonetheless dead."[17] While more research is still needed, a litany of studies have shown that time in nature can boost mental energy, relieve stress, improve concentration, spark creativity, and even fight cancer. That said, Williams's prescription is simple, yet vital: "Go outside, often, sometimes in wild places. Bring friends or not. Breathe."[18]

Conclusion

If timefulness was a matter of finding our *when*, then placefulness is about finding our *where*. According to George Michelson Foy, "'Where' is the primal question."[19] Foy's book *Finding North* offers a fascinating look at the art of navigation, its effects on the brain, and the spatial dimensions of human existence. What Foy shows with data and analysis, we might find in the book of Acts. The appointed times and geographic boundaries that God has marked out for us play a far greater role in shaping our individual identities than we will ever truly grasp (Acts 17:26). As Marie Kondo discovered, millions of people are eager to remake their place precisely because of the power their places have to make them. On the shadow side of that reality, Simon Sinek reminds us that our places hold the power to unmake us as well. The next few chapters will challenge us all to embrace a vision of placefulness that allows us to shine a light in the shadows and to begin cultivating places of presence for our good, others' joy, and God's glory.

Check Yourself: What's in Your Space

We inhabit the places of our life, and in many ways they reflect our inner experiences. Have you ever been in a room and felt disconnected? You might even silently remark, "This isn't anything like me. Something is off. I don't like this at all." This is an inner marker that we are visiting a space rather than inhabiting one. The more we resonate with a space, the more at home and grounded we can be within it. Choose a space (like your office or bedroom), and in the corresponding box list your priorities, demands, wants, and shoulds. Does your space reflect your needs? If not, perhaps mindfully consider changes to make the space more of what you require.

Priorities	Demands
Wants	**Shoulds**

CHAPTER 12

There's a Place for Us

In October 2018, more than a million viewers tuned in to HGTV . . . on every single day.[1] In fact, I can't tell you the last time I sat in a waiting room and *didn't* have to endure fifteen minutes of *Property Brothers*. Markets don't lie, and if our nation's obsession with better homes and gardens tells us anything, it's this: the places we live *matter*. In this section, we've got our sights set on placefulness—the attitude and practice of presence in space. In this chapter specifically, we're going to unpack what that looks like in our homes and neighborhoods. To begin examining that, we first need to understand our placefulness within the cosmic perspective of *God's* place-making.

A People and Their Place

In the beginning, God created a people and made them a place— Eden (Gen 2:15–25). But the people rebelled and got themselves cast out (Gen 3:17–19). Still, God loved his creatures, so he made a nation out of a nomad, Abraham, and promised that wanderer's offspring a *new* place (Gen 12:17). Yet the people rebelled again, and God spit them out of the promised land (Lev 18:28). Still, God loved his creatures, so he promised to bring them back (Jer 29:14). When the time was right, he sent the light of the world to call his people out of the darkness and into his kingdom of marvelous light (John 1:4–5; Col 1:13; 1 Pet 2:9). But that heavenly kingdom came with an earthly address—not just a small strip of land in Palestine but a transformed world (Rev 21:1). Until that day, when heaven comes to earth, Jesus has gone ahead to prepare a place for God's people, even as they prepare a place for him (John 14:2–3; Eph 2:22).

That's the pattern. God creates a people and he makes them a place. Sometimes, that place is spiritual: the kingdom is "in your midst" (Luke 17:21). Sometimes, it's physical: a garden, a city, a nation, a world. The beauty of biblical religion is that we don't have to separate the two. As we saw in chapter 6, God has brought together eternity, space, and time in Christ. The Father sent the Son into a Podunk Jewish town to usher in the redemption of the entire world. And if *that* place mattered, then so does yours.[2]

Unwrecking Your Home

Our homes are gifts from God. They are—or at least they should be—places of rest and refuge. Isaiah looked forward to a day of salvation when the people of Judah would live in "peaceful dwelling places" (Isa 32:18). They'd enjoy "secure homes" in an insecure wilderness and "undisturbed places of rest" in a restless world. We'd do the prophet wrong if we read his words as an automatic guarantee of a happy home life in Christ. Still, what we find here is a glimpse of what a reconciled home looks like: an outpost of gospel sanity in a world that's gone certifiably insane.

This is the place God has made for us, even as he calls us to make it for ourselves. Proverbs 24:27 says:

> Put your outdoor work in order
> and get your fields ready;
> after that, build your house.

Don't overspiritualize this. The call to build your house has just as much to do with swinging hammers and scrubbing walls as it does with having a heart-to-heart with your teenager. And this concerns both women and men. Husband or wife, sister or brother, unlaunched millennial or unwelcome couch surfer—God calls each one of us to step into the challenge and blessing of placefulness at home.

But what does that look like? This isn't HGTV and I'm not Chip Gaines. I don't have "design hacks" to peddle. What I do have, though, is a framework to help you think intentionally about how you can turn your home into a place of joy, peace, rest, and refuge for you and the ones you love.

- **Sight:** Design impacts our well-being. The colors we paint, the furniture we buy, the kitsch we put on the walls—there's no getting around the profound effect aesthetics can have. You don't have to be a designer, but time spent intentionally designing your place will pay psychological dividends in no time.
- **Sound:** Whether it's the pitter patter of little feet or the Arcade Fire blaring out the other side of your teenager's earbuds, ambient noise can make or break an environment. Take charge of your soundscape by springing for a Bluetooth speaker and making music a regular feature of life in your home.
- **Smell:** Before people got wise to this trick, real estate agents would pop a tray of cookies in the oven before every open house. Why? Because nothing says "home" better than the smell of fresh-baked cookies. In case you're not sold, take a whiff of your coffee tomorrow morning and see what happens. Scents have a powerful effect on mood and performance. Don't neglect the way your home smells.
- **Space:** How do you use your space? Do you have an inner sanctum—a place where you can escape? An office with a door that locks, a comfortable chair, a reading nook—these are the inner spaces that each person in your home needs in order to retreat, recharge, and reengage life at their highest level.
- **Sanity:** As we saw in the last chapter, 24-7 connection means you can expect the entire world to try and rob you of presence at home. What will you do to protect yourself from the pull of digitization, distraction, and diffusion?

Neighborhood: Loving the Place You Live

The average American will move more than eleven times in his or her lifetime.[3] One out of every four Americans moves every five years.[4] With those kinds of mobility numbers, it's not difficult to imagine why making a home might seem foreign to us. When your next move—whether for work, school, or retirement—is always on the near horizon, investing yourself in a new home and neighborhood can seem like a waste of time. The alternative, however, is a perpetually displaced existence that threatens to rip us apart from the inside. Worse, it creates the kind of breakdown in community life that leaves us all more susceptible to various shades of extremism.

Melody Warnick is a journalist with an interest in exploring the connection between people and their place. In *This Is Where You Belong*, Warnick tells the story of how she made Blacksburg, VA, *her* new place.[5] There was nothing special about Blacksburg. Warnick had just moved six times and decided she was tired of living a displaced life. The story she tells isn't just the quirky adventure of a young mom making her way in a new city; it's a deep dive into the psychology of place attachment coupled with a call to renew our lives by reconnecting with our communities.

At Sojourn, Warnick provided a paradigm for how we would fight back displacement in our church and engage the city of Louisville. At a broad level, her categories and strategy (see below) enabled us to engage Louisville and make our place in the city in a new way. As a church, we sought to bless the city. And as individual church members, we each learned to indwell our neighborhoods with more intentionality and a deeper sense of place. Thanks to that newfound placefulness, we were able to tap into a wellspring of opportunities to engage our neighbors with the gospel and invite them to come find their place with us.

Most significantly for leaders outside the church world, Warnick learned in the process of making Blacksburg her home and doing her psychological research that the things that keep people rooted and engaged don't center on promotions or opportunities but on geography and attachment. If we love where we live, we engage our work. If we don't, we won't. As we'll see more clearly in the next chapter, placefulness in our homes and neighborhoods pays dividends at the office. But before we do, though, we need to look at how Warnick made Blacksburg her new place: cartography and choreography.

Cartography: Mapping Your Place

In behavioral geography, a "mental map" describes our first-person perspective of an environment. Thanks to GPS, most of us have outsourced our mental mapping to Google. As a result, handheld navigation isn't just changing the way we interact with the world. It's rewiring our brains.[6] The London cab service is one of the best in the world. Before they can get their license, cabbies are required to memorize the city's twenty-five-thousand streets, as well as every landmark within a six-mile radius of Charing Cross. Preparation for the exam takes about three or four years. On account of this intense exercise in mental mapping, researchers have found that the London Cab driver has a *larger* hippocampus than the average person.[7] As a result, these drivers exhibit an incredible capacity for spatial thinking—a crucial element in critical thinking and decision making.[8]

Mental mapping doesn't just exercise your leader-brain. It enriches you as a human being, as well. The ability to think spatially about our neighborhoods provides a framework for narrating our lives. Think back to the most vivid moments in your life: that first kiss with your spouse, the birth of your first child, your high school graduation. Odds are, you remember exactly where you were in that moment. The same dynamic happens when you wave hello to a neighbor or enjoy a nice chat with the owner of the corner store. With each of these experiences, Warnick says, you put a pin in your mental map. Together, these maps and pins enhance your sense of place in the community.

Choreography: Making a Place

In chapter 9, we learned about the difference between *chronos* and *kairos*. Well, it turns out the ancient Greeks made a similar distinction with respect to place. Aristotle thought of place as *topos*, or "a mere location, a measurable, quantifiable point, neutral and indifferent."[9] This is where we get our word "topography," and we can think of it as a point on a map. In addition to *topos*, Plato talked about *chora* as place in "[it's capacity] to resonate to the immediacies of human experience."[10] More simply, we can think of *chora* as *topos* with a story. For Moses, the difference between a random bush (*topos*) and holy ground (*chora*) was the presence of the Lord, the God of his fathers (Exod 3:5–6). For me, the difference between a random intersection and holy ground is the presence of a marker with Thomas Merton's name on it (see chapter 3).

In ancient Greece, the amphitheater was created to be a space where *topos* and *chora* meet—particularly on the circular platform where the *chorus* danced, sang, and narrated the unfolding drama.[11] This is where we get our word choreography, and it points out one of the many ways in which human beings long to imbue spaces with meaning. We see this in the Bible, of course, when Old Testament patriarchs like Abraham and Jacob erect monuments to mark significant meetings with God (Gen 12:7; Gen 22:18). The presence of God turned the *topos* of Bethel into a *chora* of promise and provision.

What does all that have to do with placefulness in a neighborhood? Without *chora*, you're simply living in a *topos*. In her book, Warnick tells the story of Jay Leeson, a student at Asbury Theological Seminary, and his efforts to rally a community behind Leonard Fitch and his local grocery store.[12] The store had been in the family for fifty years and served as an institution in Wilmore, Kentucky. Hit hard by the economic downturn, Fitch couldn't keep his doors open. When Leeson heard, he *choreographed* a group of volunteers from the community to repaint and refresh the store. They called themselves "Fitch's neighbors," and in repainting that store, they revitalized Fitch: "New paint has given me new life!" Leeson decided to *make* his place, and in doing so, he transformed his *topos* into a *chora*. More accurately, he reinvigorated the *chora* that already existed by inviting his neighbors to restore an institution they all knew and loved.

Where are those institutions in your neighborhood? How can you *choreograph* your neighbors in order to make your community a better place for both you and others? One way my wife and I have been able to do that is through our yearly Christmas party. Living on the border of rapid gentrification, our neighbors include an eclectic mix of everything from lower-class eccentrics to upper-crust executives. A couple blocks in one direction, you've got one of the most dangerous neighborhoods in the country. A couple blocks in the other, you've got million-dollar historic homes. Every year, we open up our doors and invite that hodgepodge in to celebrate the season. My wife makes the invitations and the kids deliver them door to door. Everyone's invited to mix it up in our home: conservative and liberal, rich and poor, young and old, black and white, Christian and atheist, Baptist and Unitarian. It may not seem like much, but parties like this choreograph the neighborhood. They turn our *topos* into a *chora*.

Conclusion

As I put the finishing touches on this chapter, I can see a gaggle of middle-school girls posing for group shots at the local coffee shop. This is nothing new; they're here daily. What are they doing? Say what you want about kids these days and their Instagram accounts—these girls are *making* this little coffee shop *their* place. Like Zack and Kelly at the Max or Norm and Cliff at Cheers, they're drawing on their own brand of social interaction to make this *topos* a *chora*. What will you do in your home this week to make it your place? How will you relearn and reconnect with your community this year? In a word, how will you cultivate placefulness in the place you live? This is the ground floor and foundation of rediscovering presence in your personal and professional life.

There's a Place for Us

Principle: Without a place, leaders flame out. We need to *make* and *protect* our homes and neighborhoods so they can become spaces of love, joy, peace, rest, and presence.

Practice: Plan a one-day, in-home retreat. Shut off every connection to the outside world and commit your family to a day of full presence. Read books, play games, cook a meal together, and *talk* to one another. If you don't have a family to do this with, invite a good friend or significant other to join you.

Check Yourself: Choreography in the Neighborhood

HOW TO MAKE YOUR *TOPOS* A *CHORA*

- **Walk more.** When was the last time you went for a walk in your neighborhood? Go home and look up walkable cities and find out your city's walk score.

- **Buy local.** Where do you go to buy local products? Find one item and buy it from a locally owned business.

- **Get to know your neighbors.** How many neighbors have you shared a meal with? Join your neighborhood association and throw a block party.

- **Do fun stuff.** What is the best way to have a good time in your neighborhood? Prioritize showing up when you are invited to a party. Connect the things you love and your hobbies with what is available in your neighborhood or city.

- **Explore nature.** What makes you feel close to nature

where you live? Invite friends for a hike or a ride through the countryside.

- **Volunteer.** Where do you regularly see brokenness in your city? Find a place to volunteer.

- **Eat local.** What local food do you love or haven't tried? Find a place in your town to become a regular.

- **Become more political.** Who are your city officials? Read a local news source or attend a city council meeting.

- **Create something new.** What is something you have made or started in the past that you can continue to cultivate? Be a creative initiator and organize a place-making project in your town.

- **Stay loyal through hard times.** What hardships has your neighborhood or city been through? What negative persona does it have? Read about your town's history and treat people with kindness.

CHAPTER 13

Out of the Shadows

MAKING YOUR PLACE AT WORK AND IN THE CITY

Recently, I spoke with an executive who'd just kicked off a massive turnaround at her office. She whispered to me, "There are ghosts in this place." No, she wasn't talking about Slimer or Jacob Marley. Instead, she spoke with hushed tones about the unseen influence of her company's decades of placelessness—the "ghosts" of disengagement, lost morale, apathy, and resignation. She was coming to realize that the ghosts haunting her organization weren't simply a matter of psychological *culture* but the actual physical *space* in which her organization worked.

In *Places of the Heart*, neuroscientist Colin Ellard describes this phenomenon, teasing out the ways in which our setting influences our thinking and doing. We understand this intuitively, of course. Why else would we be drawn to the magnificence of Notre Dame or the kitschy banality of a Six Flags? As Ellard observes, "But even though we all feel and respond to the design of a building at an emotional level, and even though those feelings influence what we do when we are there, we most often don't have the time or inclination to dissect our daily responses to place or make sense of them."[1] As Ellard points out, we *feel* the effects of our place, yet we rarely slow down long enough to actually acknowledge them. In a word, we've grown placeless.

Learning to Live in the Nonplace

According to the anthropologist Marc Augé, we are living in "super-modernity," an age marked by the overabundance of time, space, and individualism.[2] In the past, we all had our places. From the bar where everybody knew your name to the deli where Frank knew just how to cut your pastrami, places were deeply invested with meaning and story. Today, we're surrounded by nonplaces: super-markets, airports, hotels, and so on. To take a mundane example, consider America's favorite "local" restaurant: Applebee's. The irony of your local Applebee's is that it's designed to look like it belongs everywhere, yet consequently, it belongs nowhere. Sorry, Ricky Bobby, but the fact that any given Applebee's reflects nothing of its actual local neighborhood constitutes a stunning example of a nonplace. You could extend this phenomena to any of the soulless, placeless chain stores and restaurants that bespeckle the landscape of suburbia.

These nonplaces are designed for two things only: transience and consumption. Nobody drops into Walmart to connect with their cashier, and I sincerely doubt my next-door neighbor at the Marriott would be interested in joining me for a run. These nonplaces also provide the tempting yet deadly allure of anonymity. Like the serpent in the garden, they hold out the false promise of freedom from every social obligation and constraint. As far too many business travelers have learned, you can be whoever you want in a hotel bar: single or married. But just as a pair of scissors liberates the kite from its string, the so-called freedom of the nonplace will only end in one result: disaster.

The Shadowy Side of Displacement

For leaders, nonplaces are just another symptom of our displacement. But this isn't just about us; it's about our employees and volunteers, as well. Displaced leaders breed placeless followers. When our place of employment becomes just another nonplace in the supermodern world, disengagement is never far behind. For leaders in general, then, pure self-interest demands we get serious about our presence and that of our employees. For Christians, in particular, placefulness is not only a gift we've received in Christ but a blessing we're called to share with others—especially at work.

The journey from *topos* to *chora* (see chapter 12) involves a give-and-take between the places we make and the places that make us. As Churchill said, "We shape our buildings, and afterwards our buildings shape us."[3] In chapter 11, we briefly joined Rex Miller, Mabel Casey, and Mark Konchar as they traveled the country looking for engaging workplaces. The best companies, they told us, felt like foreign countries—thick with a deep sense of pride, meaning, and purpose. Space, they learned, was a proxy for culture. The places designed by these companies "reflected the values of the company, and also shaped the patterns of behavior and interaction."[4] In sum, these companies built their place, and their place built them.

Alongside the good, Miller, Casey, and Konchar saw plenty of the ugly. One of their more interesting discoveries was the distinction between *official* and *shadow* culture.[5] A company's official culture, they say, is that jargon scribbled down on a piece of paper or a website somewhere. It usually mentions boiler-plate virtues like integrity, service, teamwork, and diversity. The shadow culture, on the other hand, is that set of virtues written on the walls. Those values often run counter to the official culture: the "ghosts" of hierarchy, control, command, fear. These companies are the most resistant to change because spatial redesign usually brings those deeply held shadow values into the light of day. Once again, these companies built their place, and their place built them. Only this time the product was nothing like what its leaders envisioned it to be.

Making Your Place at Work: Nine Objectives

The question here isn't which values a business should have but whether your place communicates *your* values. As Miller, Casey, and Konchar point out, our workplace structures are often relics of the way things were done in the past rather than how they're done today. I can tell you from personal experience that companies run into serious displacement issues when they trumpet a platform of innovation and collaboration, yet their day-to-day life takes place in chopped-up spaces that haven't been updated since 1982. That tension between place and values can't help but hamper a company's execution: "If your office reflects past attitudes about work, no matter how often your company hosts town hall meetings, provides improved team dynamic training, or offers employee engagement workshops, you can't overcome the habits of how you live."[6]

How do you turn your *topos* into a *chora*? In their eminently practical guide, Juriaan van Meel, Yuri Martens, and Hermen Jan van Ree lay out the nine most important objectives in designing physical workspaces. But place is about more than just physical space; it involves culture as well.[7]

1. **Reduce costs.** Disengagement is the price you pay for dehumanized workspaces. Your baseline objective should be to create a place where employees can be fully human.

2. **Increase flexibility.** Give employees with the physical, mental, and temporal space to do the work the way it *needs* to be done—not the way it's *always* been done.

3. **Improve productivity.** Output is no longer measured by the hour or the square foot. Develop spaces around maximizing *people* first, and productivity will follow.

4. **Encourage collaboration.** Compartmentalized workspaces can breed toxic forms of competition, while more flexible spaces invite healthy collaboration.

5. **Stimulate creativity.** A strategic blend between open space for collaboration and private space for reflection is crucial to enabling your employees to tap into their best creative energy (see chapter 8).

6. **Express the brand.** Branding is storytelling, and the place you make at work is just one more opportunity to embody your corporate story.

7. **Attract and retain.** Office environment is a key factor in attracting and retaining the best workers. Cultivate an environment that equips employees with the resources they need to do their best and most fulfilling work.

8. **Support cultural change.** Place-making is about living out your values in space. The place you make at work *will* make the people who indwell it. Use place to effect positive change.

9. **Steward environmental impact.** Generally, consider energy conservation and waste management (i.e., good environmental citizenship). Doing so opens a broader vista into the connection between your company and its geographical context (i.e., corporate citizenship).

Understanding Your Place in the City

Every company is a citizen. Whether it's a neighborhood startup or a global juggernaut like Facebook, each company has a responsibility to inhabit its local context well. Speed plays a crucial role in that dynamic. Every city has its speed. Louisville is slow, and I like it that way. Like a twenty-mile-per-hour stretch of the road, Louisville takes its time. A city like Nashville, however, runs much faster. At fifty miles-per-hour, Music City is growing exponentially, making it a hot-spot for new startups and corporate expansion alike. Even so, Nashville might as well be a go-kart track compared to the super-speedway that is Los Angeles.

As a church planter in a slow city like Louisville, I had to learn that the pace drilled into me by my Orange County upbringing wouldn't cut it in Kentucky. To serve my city and church well, I had to match pace with my environment. Twenty years later, I'm consistently tasked with helping business leaders realize the same thing. Our cities have speeds, and if we don't match pace, we'll either outstrip or lag behind our environment. This is just another form of placelessness. If we allow it to go unchecked, not only will we alienate our neighbors, but we'll prevent our employees from finding *their* place in the community.

Corporate Citizenship

Matching pace is only one part of rediscovering a company's place in its city. A truly placeful company is one that inhabits its context as a productive citizen. Part of that, of course, means learning the lay of the land. During our first major capital campaign at Sojourn, I felt that God wanted me to help our church get a sense for its place in Louisville, past and present. So I used twenty slides to walk us through 150 years of the city's spiritual history. I highlighted the many tributaries of faith that had welled up into the evangelistic current in which we found ourselves swimming. I wanted our "hip, cool" church to see how the Catholics had been the first to break holy ground in Louisville, followed by the Baptists and other conservatives who were fighting against the spiritual dead end of Protestant liberalism. I knew that if we were going to be theologically deep and evangelistically wide, we needed to know that we stood on the shoulders of others. Especially for our largest donors, the impact was palpable. The placeful practice of tracing Louisville's spiritual history helped them see how the small part we played figured into the much bigger story God was writing in our city and, through it, the nations.

Just as placefulness had helped us to serve our community better as individuals (see chapter 12), it enabled our *organization* to become a much more productive citizen in Louisville. Thanks to social media, that kind of citizenship is no longer just a value-add. It's *essential* to every organization's survival—church, business, or otherwise. Corporate Social Responsibility (CSR) has become an imperative in the contemporary marketplace. Americans want to work with and buy from companies that prioritize responsibility, care, issue advocacy, environmental protection, and generosity.[8] According to one study, 78 percent of consumers believe that social and environmental impact is just as, if not more, important as making a profit.[9] Another study found that 64 percent agree that business leaders should spearhead change instead of waiting for the government to do it.[10] In fact, a 2015 study showed that 66 percent of them are willing to spend *more* on a product if it comes from a socially responsible company.[11] The emerging picture is this: the road to profitability cuts directly through social responsibility. Pursue the former with everything you've got, but if you fail to do so as a responsible corporate citizen, you'll end up harming the bottom line.

From an engagement perspective, turnover rates have been shown to drop as much as 57 percent among employees who give and volunteer through company outreach.[12] *Harvard Business Review* found that 89 percent of senior executives say that collective purpose drives workers' job satisfaction.[13] We've seen this done well with one of our clients in Louisville. This company recently committed itself to serving local schools. Specializing in logistics, they decided the best thing they could do was enlist their employees to gather and donate the classroom supplies teachers were lacking. This simple and meaningful gesture served a real need in the community. Moreover, it reinforced the company's core values and motivated its employees to *own* the mission in a new and vivid way.

Conclusion

People make places and places make people. That's as true of an office, church, or nonprofit as it is of your broader geographical context. To slip into placelessness is to allow the "ghosts" of disengagement to haunt the shadows and turn your organization into a nonplace of disengaged, dehumanized mediocrity. Don't let that become your reality. Instead, create a place where *topos* can become *chora*. Cultivate an environment in which the values you've written on paper can find their natural expression in the everyday flow of engaged people doing engaging work. As a redeemed human, receive the gift of placefulness by creating a redemptive place in which others can do their best work. If you want to "Christianize" the workplace, start here. In this place shaped by gospel freedom, the words you "write on the walls" will give powerful support to the words you *speak* about Jesus.

Out of the Shadows

Principle: Displacement lurks in the space between *official* and *shadow* cultures. Placefulness at work and in the community bridges that gap. It enables us and others to live, lead, and work at our highest levels.

Practice:[14] Gather your senior leadership. Put up a whiteboard and brainstorm your ideal work environment. Prompt your team with positive descriptors: high-energy, collaboration, productivity, and so on. Dream up a space that embodies those characteristics. Plot out what it'll take to move from your current space to that ideal environment and commit to incremental action.

Do you lead a distributed workforce? If so, encourage each employee to envision his or her own space. How can they cultivate placefulness where they are?

Ground Yourself: Sitting Mindfulness

We are learning that in all areas mindfulness means we have to slow down. Here is an exercise you can do anywhere.

Quietly sit for three minutes and simply notice what is going on in your environment:

- **Internally:** Look on as an outside observer. Let your thoughts, emotions, and urges pass by without examining them.

- **Externally:** What is happening around you? What information is coming through your five senses: What are you tasting, smelling, feeling, seeing, and hearing?

CHAPTER 14

Rediscovering Your Place in Nature

*I'd stopped to give him a telescope view of a
long-billed curlew, a species whose magnificence
is to my mind self-evident and revelatory. He
looked through the scope for two seconds before
turning away with patent boredom. "Yeah," he
said with his particular tone of hollow politeness,
"it's pretty."*[1]

—JONATHAN FRANZEN, "DAVID FOSTER WALLACE"

David Foster Wallace isn't exactly a household name, but his unconventional writing style earned him an avid readership, a Pulitzer Prize nomination, and a place on *Time* magazine's Top 100 list of novels. For all his literary genius, Wallace was a deeply troubled man. He struggled with depression, alcoholism, and drug addiction until he took his own life in 2008.[2] In the words quoted above, Wallace's close friend and literary rival Jonathan Franzen reflects on just one element of Wallace's turbulent existence: he simply couldn't relate to or enjoy nature. Says Franzen, "I understood the difference between his unmanageable misery and my manageable discontents to be that I could escape myself in the joy of birds and he could not."[3]

Could learning to escape into the joy of birds have saved David Foster Wallace? Maybe. We'll never know. But what we *do* know is this: most of us are suffering from what Richard Louv has called "nature deficit" disorder.[4] Less a diagnosis and more a set of empirical and psychological observations, Louv laments our growing alienation from nature and its negative impact—particularly on kids. Thanks to urbanization, new media technology, and a host of other factors, Americans today spend a meager 7 percent of their time outdoors.[5] As a result, we're more anxious and less self-aware than we used to be. Our circadian rhythms are out of whack, and our sunlight-deprived brains lack what they need to preserve mental health. We may not suffer as acutely as Wallace did, but the price we pay in terms of physical, cognitive, and spiritual health grows clearer every day. Learning to escape into the joy of the birds may just be what we all need most.

Renaturing the Office

In the workplace, we can see the cost of our nature deficit. According to research out of the University of Oregon, a 10 percent uptick in sick time used could be chalked up to a lack of sunlight and greenery in or near the office.[6] Think about the cost of absenteeism and what a 10 percent recapture of employee productivity—not to mention recovered healthcare costs—could do for you. To back up that thought, another study reported that increased exposure to nature increased employees' sense of well-being by 15 percent.[7] Based on numbers like these, one estimate says a few simple nature-minded adjustments like added sunlight and increased access to green space could save employers as much as $2,000 per employee per year.[8]

This dovetails with the research we briefly introduced in chapter 11. Study after study has shown that time spent outdoors can improve short-term memory,[9] restore mental energy,[10] relieve stress,[11] improve concentration,[12] spark creativity,[13] and much more. An entire industry—experience-based design—has grown up and thrived on the simple proposition that spaces designed to maximize exposure to nature actually net positive gains for the companies that inhabit them.[14] The joy of the birds, it seems, does more than make us better people; it makes our *places* better as well.

This is My Father's World

Before we go any further, I want to stop and address an elephant in the room. In our technologically advanced age, strong claims about the health and productivity benefits of nature tend to strike us as granola-fueled pseudoscience. Especially for us nonmillennials who didn't grow up with a Whole Foods on every corner, all this "back to nature" stuff strikes us as a new-age spin on old-school paganism. But should Christians be quite so skeptical? When God spoke the world into being, he dropped humans into a garden temple, not a concrete jungle (Gen 2:15). In that original green space, God's good creation existed in harmony with the people who were made to work and keep it. A tree stood in the middle of that garden; its fruit was the stuff of everlasting life (Gen 3:22). We no longer live in *that* place, but that doesn't mean God has fully revoked his good gift of nature. After all, we still get to look forward to a day when the leaves of that garden tree will provide for "the healing of the nations" (Rev 22:2). Until then, God will keep on making his sun to rise and rain to fall as he provides for his creatures (Matt 5:45; Gen 8:22; Jer 5:24).

This is our *Father's* world, and we must never worship and serve the creature rather than the Creator (Rom 1:25). But we also have to remember that this is our Father's *world*. Why shouldn't we benefit from a closer connection with nature? Martin Luther once said, "God is entirely and personally present in the wilderness, in the garden, in the field."[15] Still, we're losing touch with the green spaces where God would speak. If Jesus showed up today and talked to us about the lilies (Matt 6:28), I wonder how many of us would know what they looked like without having to Google it first. We shouldn't be surprised; our alienation from nature is nothing new. When Adam and Eve sinned, they were kicked out of the lush garden and into a place where nature was no longer their friend (Gen

3:17–19). Their worst descendants—Cain and his offspring—turned into those wicked city-builders who misappropriated the good gifts of nature for their own self-exalting ends (Gen 4:17; 11:5–9).

Don't get me wrong; the city isn't the enemy. In Babel, the problem wasn't the people's attempt to build an ancient skyscraper, but their pride in thinking they could "make a name for themselves" by climbing up into heaven. In the new creation, every scrap of human boasting is set aside as garden and city come together in beautiful harmony. Think of it like a glorified Central Park. Infinitely better than a momentary refuge from the chaos, that beautiful garden will *constitute* our life in God's eternal city.

Imagine Yourself: A Rocha USA

A Rocha USA's mission is to restore both people and places through collaborative, community-based conservation. They resource Christians to care for creation where they live by building a network of hands-on conservation projects in communities across the nation. Through partnerships with individuals, churches, and community groups, they provide content, curriculum, and a network of support for improving local habitats and increasing biodiversity. Find your local chapter's calendar and add some of their projects to your calendar: https://www.arocha.org/en/a-rocha-usa/.

Taking a Bath in Nature

The flip side of alienation is infatuation. Again, the Bible doesn't mince words about putting creation before the Creator. With that crucial precaution in place, the concrete-jungle dwellers among us might consider other parts of the world where the nature deficit isn't quite as acute. In Japan, for example, the practice of shinrin-yoku ("forest bathing") reflects a deep sense of connection with nature as a source of well-being. The bath isn't literal. Instead, it's an exercise in mindful immersion as participants disconnect from urban life and plunge themselves deep into the woods. According to one study, the practice reduces cortisol—the hormone that affects stress.[16] Another study showed that forest bathing helps control blood pressure and blood sugar levels.[17]

Indeed, in Finland, forest-bathing (*metsänpeitto*) is nearly a way of life. The country itself is about 74 percent covered with trees. In fact, one third of Helsinki, the nation's capital, is covered in trees and green spaces. Compare that to a paltry 8.5 percent in Chicago. In Finland, regular time outdoors is a part of the fabric of life. In one vivid example, school days are structured so that kids spend 45 minutes in the classroom and 15 minutes outside—hot or cold, rain or shine. As long as the temperature is above 20 degrees, those kids head outside! At the risk of reductionism, it seems Finland's on to something we often miss with respect to nature. While we're busy trying to bring home the bacon, the Finns are outside picking berries. That may not seem like the most productive use of their time. But if the World Happiness Report is right, and Finland really is the happiest country in the world, I don't think they care.[18]

Take a Hike

In her book *Nature Fix*, Florence Williams provides her own perspective on our nature deficit, complete with plenty of research to back up her own call to the wild. Interestingly, Williams devotes an entire chapter to walking.[19] That's right—walking. In it, Williams reminds us of the ancient practice of *solvitur ambulando* ("in walking it will be solved"). Aristotle, Augustine, Wordsworth, Dickens, Kierkegaard—these giants of Western thought and literature all spent a great deal of time walking around. In fact, Aristotle's disciples came to be known as the *peripatetics* (wanderers) because they spent so much time on their feet. Why all the walking? Because, deep down, people have always known by common experience what we modern types have had to rediscover through science: walking helps you think.

For several years, business leaders have capitalized on the value of walking. Beyond the obvious health benefits of getting out of your chair and going for a stroll, research has shown that walking increases blood flow to the brain, improves learning and memory, and enhances creative thinking.[20] More than that, walking creates a better environment for honest, open exchange between employees. And since we can never forget engagement, the *Harvard Business Review* discovered that employees who participated in walking meetings were 8.5 percent more likely to be highly engaged.[21] Steve Jobs, Mark Zuckerberg, Richard Branson—this is just a handful of leaders who've sworn by the walking meeting.

Step Out and Breathe In

I've already shared these words from Florence Williams, but they bear repeating: "Go outside, often, sometimes in wild places. Bring friends or not. Breathe."[22] As we've seen in this chapter, nature is *good* for us. And why shouldn't it be? God made us for this world, and he made this world for us. As I shared earlier, I've got nothing against cities and high-rises, but it's time we reconnect with the good creation all around us. What does that look like?

1. **Rethink your space.** If a full redesign won't fly, there are practical steps you can take to increase your exposure to natural light and greenery. Even nature photography has been shown to mimic the effect of time spent outdoors.
2. **Get outside.** Nothing beats the real experience. Start by getting outside for at least fifteen minutes a day. Eat your lunch at a park bench, linger in the front yard after you get home from work. Do *something* to put yourself outside every day.
3. **Go for a walk.** Kill two birds with one stone by taking at least one meeting per day out on the walking path or sidewalk. Both your bottom line and your waistline will thank you for putting in the extra steps.

Conclusion

My youngest child, Georgia, is an explorer by nature. Since she's my baby, I'm acutely aware of how brief our time together truly is. Eager to savor these precious moments before her childhood evaporates, Georgia and I have started taking what we call "explorer walks." With no destination in mind, she and I will stroll down city sidewalks and brick alleys into deserted buildings, collecting artifacts as we go. Each time, we come home with an impressive haul of glass shards, train spikes, pictures, plants, tree bark, strange pieces of metal, and so on. In her young eyes, every bit of it is fodder for the imagination and a treasure to be enjoyed.

Georgia's unmitigated sense of wonder never ceases to energize me. One day when we were walking, she asked, "Daddy, do you ever wonder what it was like when there were just trees and no buildings?" She may not have had the language to describe it, but Georgia was envisioning Eden in our neighborhood. As she wondered aloud about what this world once was, my precious little girl was stirring in me a deep longing for what this world will be—not just Eden restored but creation perfected in the new heavens and new earth. This must be what Jesus was getting at when he said, "Truly I tell you, unless you change and become like little children, you will never enter the kingdom of heaven" (Matt 18:3). God has made us for this place and one day he will finally remake this place for us. In that day, we will escape once for all, not into the joy of the birds but into the joy of the Lord for whom, from whom, and through whom all things were made.

Rediscovering Your Place in Nature

Principle: God made us for this world, and he made this world for us. To be all he made us to be, and to perform in the way he designed us to perform, we need to get back into nature.

Practice: Go for a stroll in the woods. Stop to appreciate *everything*: the bubbling brook, the tall tree, the bright sky. When you do, praise God for that specific beauty. Ask him to cultivate in you a deep sense of wonder over all he has made.

CHAPTER 15

The Blessing of Placefulness

Several years ago, I was invited to spend seven days rafting down a 187-mile stretch of the Colorado River with a group of biblical scholars. Why me? Let's just say, it's not what you know but who you know, and I just so happened to know a scholar who thought I'd like to meet the crew's very special guest: John Piper. In case the name isn't familiar to you, John Piper is an author, theologian, and pastor who's had a powerful influence on Christians across the world for the past several decades. To say I had a man-crush on Piper would be an understatement. For a long stretch of time, I was so influenced by Piper's Christian hedonism—the idea that "God is most glorified in us when we are most satisfied in him"[1]—that whenever someone would ask me to clarify my faith convictions, I'd simply say, "I'm a Piperian."

In *The Pleasures of God*, Piper said, "Without a spiritual wakefulness to divine purposes and connections in all things, we will not know things for what they truly are."[2] A spiritual wakefulness is exactly what I was feeling as he and I rafted down the Colorado River together, taking in the indescribable grandeur of God's good creation. Like a good little fanboy, I took every opportunity to sit by, raft alongside, hike with, and talk to Piper during the trip. One night as we sat in the depths of the Grand Canyon and took in the beauty all around us I said, "John, you should write about the pleasures of God in the Grand Canyon." His response was classic Piper, "Before the foundation of the world God ordained that we would be sitting here having this conversation soaking in the glory of his creation." He sure did. Praise God.

From Displacement to Placement

Piper took my advice and wrote about that trip in a book called *A Peculiar Glory*. In it, he tells the story of another day on the river when a rainstorm washed out our lunch and left us wondering whether we might prefer a hotel room in Vegas to a raft in the Grand Canyon. We chose, however, to *be* where we were. What came next?

> We boarded our two large, blue, motor-driven rafts and set out down river. The rain stopped and the sky started to clear, when suddenly, almost simultaneously, dozens of waterfalls burst out into the river in front of and behind us from the walls of the canyon. Some of these were gigantic, falling a thousand feet. . . . The guide explained what had happened. He said that during a hard rain the water in the gorges comes down from the steep sides and builds and builds until it is a rushing river—a rain-made temporary river in a place where it almost never rains. . . . It was stunning. Then he said, we might not see the likes of this in the canyon for another hundred years.[3]

Whether it's the discomfort of a sudden rainstorm, the draw of a buzzing phone, or the deadening influence of a lifeless workplace, we all deal with the constant allure of placelessness. When we fail to *be* where we are, we miss out on the waterfalls of grace God places right before our eyes. Where are *you* right now? Are you sitting in your easy chair, riding on a bus, waiting to board a flight? Does it make any difference? I hope you're convinced that a deep sense of your place in the world matters not just for you but for your family, friends, neighbors, colleagues, and employees. In chapter 11, I defined placefulness as both a disposition and a practice—something we *are* and something we *do*. As we close out this chapter, I want to invite you to envision the transformative effect presence can have on your life and leadership if you take the call to placefulness seriously in your home, neighborhood, work, city, and world.

Home: A Place to Call Your Own

Laura Ingalls Wilder was right: "Home is the nicest word there is." Our homes are God's gifts to us. They are (or, at least, they *can* be) outposts of Gospel sanity and places of rest for our weary souls. But for all the peace and presence our homes offer, they become places of strife and absence when we allow the outside world to come barging in through the Wi-Fi. What would change if we learned not simply to make our homes places of presence but to jealously guard them against the enemies of digitization, distraction, and diffusion? How would the presence we come to enjoy there enrich our lives? What would your life look like if every day began with a good night's sleep and a meaningful breakfast conversation with your spouse and kids? How would your psychological and emotional health improve if each day ended with a similar time around the dinner table and an hour or two of time with your family? What's going to serve you better in the long run: a place you can call home or a place you can finally reach inbox zero?

Work: A Place to Make and Be Made

John Stewart is a friend, developer, and contagiously joyful Christian leader. John's design firm, Encompass, specializes in sensory informed design (SID), an approach that marries neuroscience and architecture to create luxury spaces for boutique hotels, resorts, and casinos. The feel of a door as it swings, the impression it makes on first sight, the sound a latch makes when it engages—SID optimizes as many of these sensory inputs as possible to create immersive spaces that transform the people who inhabit them. When I mentioned this to Eboni, it immediately resonated in terms of her own clinical practice. Whether it's the beauty of a hotel lobby or the calibrated safety of a therapeutic environment, sensory input shapes us in profound ways.

Our senses tell us more about an environment than words ever could. Like fish out of water, we will never succeed in spaces that inhibit our humanity. If everything about our work environment screams absence and isolation, no amount of positive culture work can create a present, engaged workforce. There's no getting around it: we make our place and our place makes us. Placefulness calls us to live in that dynamic—not simply to show up at work but to create a place where everyone else can show up as well. How would things change if your employees no longer had to work around the constraints of their physical space? What if they consistently found themselves enabled—even encouraged—by their work environment? How do you think your organization would grow if you got your fish back into the water?

Nature: A Place to Find Healing

When was the last time you went for a walk? I don't mean that dash from your parking spot to the door. I mean a *walk*—thirty minutes to nowhere on the shoe-leather express. We tend to look for health and happiness in the latest dieting fad, workout program, or self-improvement book. There may very well be a place for those things, but sometimes the simple beauty of an afternoon by the lake can be all we need to quiet the noise of modern life, reconnect with the Maker, and receive the deep soul healing he intends for each of his wayward creatures. As the book of Job reminds us,

> But ask the animals, and they will teach you,
>> or the birds in the sky, and they will tell you;
> or speak to the earth, and it will teach you,
>> or let the fish in the sea inform you.
> Which of all these does not know
>> that the hand of the LORD has done this?
> In his hand is the life of every creature
>> and the breath of all mankind. (Job 12:7–10)

Sabbath: Your Place of Rest

At the end of chapter 9, I invited you to view timefulness as an invitation to rest in God's good gift of time. Now, I want to do the same with respect to placefulness:

Stop: Turn your home into a place of sabbath by unplugging from the outside world—especially work. Consider your home to be a retreat from the enemies of digitization, distraction, and diffusion.

Trust: Whether you are in your home, at the office, or out in the woods, rest knowing that God has you exactly where he wants you. Quiet your FOMO by engaging in solitude and meditation as you spend time with God in prayer.

Enjoy: Celebrate the fact that God has made a place—this place—for you. He has called you to partner with him as he turns the whole earth into a venue for his glory. Play in your Father's world, and praise him for his creative goodness.

Increasing Your Mindfulness of Place

How can you increase your mindfulness of place?

- Imagine organizing the spaces you inhabit to promote wellness and a balanced stimulation of your senses. Do you have an office that offers natural light versus fluorescents? Have you brought nature into your space?

- Imagine redefining your sacred spaces. What resources might be needed for you to enjoy the fruits of your labor?

A Place for Everything

Pastor John Faison Sr. of Watson Grove Missionary Baptist Church once reminded me of the intimate connection between past, present, and place. He said something like, "When we have to overcome our past in order to show up and be present; our sense of arrival is imbued with meaning. Our sense of place is derived from what we have left behind." To be mindful of our present place, we must acknowledge our past.

Where have you lived, worked, and had important experiences? What events happened in that location (*topos*) that gave the place— and you—meaning (*chora*)? These important places shape your sense of and need for place; the places you have pass through *and* the places you inhabit matter.

What Should Be in Your Place?

Mindfulness of place is the ability to identify what should be in your place, reflecting your personal mission, vision, and values and filled with your sense of purpose.

Mission in your place: What's your life calling? What change are you working for? How do you want to be a conduit of change? If your mission is to help orphans, your place should have space for children.

Vision in your place: Where do you see yourself in five years? Can you grow to your fullest where you currently reside? If not, maybe you should move. In every new place, ask yourself what you want there. How do you envision yourself interacting with your city? What kind of outdoor lifestyle do you see yourself living? Is there a nearby ocean, river, or mountain? If your vision for life includes being in nature, you should be intentional about the places you choose to live.

Values in your place: If you value discussing personal issues like I do, you should make sure your space is safe for talking and listening. If you value knowledge and effective leadership like Daniel, you should make space for learning and leading. If creativity is your core value, you should have a space where you can create. What do I need from my place? What do others need from me in this place?

Protecting Your Place

As busy Americans wired for productivity and success, we often neglect our need for places that are set apart. Executives and business leaders find themselves at a breaking point because they have not protected their places. The demands of work are often a priority. Work is where we commit most of our time. Yet as we reflect on our lives, many of us would say that work is not what we value most. Consequently, as we focus on the other places of our lives—home, family, community, spiritual life—we are filled with greater purpose and connection.

Protecting our places from the intrusions of others' demands is vital. Leaving to go to work helps define the difference between family time and work time. Leaving work for home gives us an equally pleasurable experience. I "get to go home." I "clock out" for the day.

Just as we mindfully monitor what we keep out of our places, screening what we invite in is as equally crucial. Screening what we allow into our places should become part of our routine. Overscreening keeps us from making connections—we exclude good things, maybe everything, from our place. Underscreening forces us to make too many connections—we allow too many things to occupy our minds. This is why we don't go grocery shopping when we are hungry! Too much input!

Mindlessness about your place keeps you from experiencing place as a gift. Being mindful about your place gives you pleasure, rest, and the freedom to enjoy things in their proper place. From designing beautiful and inspiring places to enjoying, maintaining, and protecting them, we are neurobiologically wired to care for our places.

BODY

EM-
BODIED
SOUL

BEING-
FUL-
NESS

DISEM-
BODIED

CHAPTER 16

Leadership, an Out-of-Body Experience?

A fifty-five-year old man named Bill walks into his psychologist's office. His bones creak as he settles down into a soft leather chair. He shifts ever so slightly, looking for just the right position to quiet the aching in his back. His head is pounding; it's been that way ever since his anxiety attack last year. Six months later, he's still on medical leave trying to figure out what comes next. The day before it happened, Bill was at the top of his game, leading a company of five hundred employees through a period of unprecedented growth. The day after, this high-powered CEO found himself laid up in a hospital bed, struggling just to get a cup of Jell-O. And now he's sitting in a chair, talking to a psychologist about why he just can't get up off the mat and back into his corner office.

Eboni sees patients like Bill all the time in her counseling practice. They come to her with the mind of a thirty-year-old: sharp, determined, unrelenting. But though the youthful spirit is willing, the middle-aged body is weak. Hard-chargers like Bill try to ignore their limitations by skipping sleep, guzzling coffee, popping pills, and eating like college sophomores, but they end up paying the price for it *in their bodies*. Anxiety disorders, autoimmune disease, stroke—these are just a few ways the body has of telling us, "Enough!" Still, what sends patients like Bill into Eboni's office isn't exactly a desire to hear what their bodies are trying to say. No, Bill wants to know how to *ignore* his body so that he can get back to work. "Mind over matter" is his motto. If only Eboni can give him the right combination of psychological tips and tactics, then he can get back on the saddle and charge headlong into his life of trains, planes, and seventy-hour workweeks—that is, until he dies of a heart attack in five years.

Splitting Ourselves in Two

Like most men in his culture and age demographic, Bill has learned to identify himself by his work. If he's not a Fortune 1000 CEO, he's nothing. Therefore, he will continue to offer up his body as a living sacrifice until he finds himself entirely consumed. As Christians, of course, we'd want to say some things to Bill about what happens when we put the idols of self and career before God, but to mention the spiritual in this scenario seems like a category mistake. Bill's *body* is the problem, not his *spirit*. Unless I've got a prayer pill for anxiety, Bill isn't interested in what I've got to say about sabbath rest, quiet meditation, and long, lonely walks in the woods.

Bill's idea of the split between spirit (mind) and body seems to be the default in our modern age, even among Christians. This idea (what philosophers call mind-body dualism) stretches back as far as Plato and hits its high-water mark in the seventeenth-century philosopher René Descartes.[1] According to Descartes, human beings are made up of "two substantially distinct entities (mind, or soul, and body). . . . Moreover, it is the immaterial soul, not the corporeal body, that constitutes the person."[2] That is, "I" can somehow exist without my body.[3] The "real me" is what's on the inside; all this bodily stuff is unreal and destined to pass away.

For antireligious types who'd like nothing to do with souls and spirits, this kind of dualism is a fiction: human beings are physical things all the way down, and the mind is just brain chemistry in action. For Christians, though, the Bible says we're more than mere cells and synapses. Without necessarily affirming the dualism of Plato and Descartes, the Bible teaches that human beings are embodied souls (or ensouled bodies). Words like *flesh, spirit, body,* and *soul* are used to describe human beings from different angles. Paul speaks of flesh vs. spirit, body vs. soul, and outer- vs. inner-self (e.g., 2 Cor 4:16). Scripture uses this language not to split human beings in two but to describe one person from two perspectives. Ultimately, Scripture presents human beings as a duality of mind/spirit and body. But the question is: Have we pressed that duality too far?

Never the Twain Shall Meet

To counteract antireligious efforts to write spirituality off as mere psychology, modern Christians often feel obligated to draw a sharp line between the body and the mind, soul, and/or spirit. This split lives in harmony with a host of other dualisms many of us live with—faith and reason, religion and science, sacred and secular, Chick-fil-A and KFC. To be sure, unless we want to collapse the mind into the body, we need *some* form of dualism. But as we will see in chapter 17, the Bible does not draw the same bright lines that we do. We don't have to delve any deeper into philosophy to see what happens when we tear asunder what God has joined together.

Instrumentalization: For Bill, his body is little more than an instrument for executing the vision he carried in his mind and spirit. The trouble is, our bodies contribute a lot more to our mental and spiritual states than we typically realize. And Bill's bodily neglect landed him in serious mental, physical, and emotional trouble.

Compartmentalization: When we divorce the body from the mind, we lose sight of the link between "mental" states like depression and "bodily" states like fatigue and malnourishment. Then we get irritated when we end up paying a psychologist to tell us to eat better, sleep more, and exercise.

Dehumanization: If the unity of body and soul is an essential feature of being human, then a hard split between body and soul ultimately robs us of that humanity. Worse, it encourages us to dehumanize others. As we'll see in the next chapter, terrible things happen when we treat ourselves and others like machines.

Ground Yourself: A Contemplative Prayer

Pray this prayer by Thomas Keating.

Welcome, welcome, welcome.
I welcome everything that comes to me today because I know it's for my healing.
I welcome all thoughts, feelings, emotions, persons, situations, and conditions.
I let go of my desire for power and control.
I let go of my desire for affection, esteem, approval and pleasure.
I let go of my desire for survival and security.
I let go of my desire to change any situation, condition, person or myself.
I open to the love and presence of God and God's action within.
Amen.

Which line is the most difficult for you to pray? What does that reveal about you and your emotions?

From Disembodiment to Embodiment

The fundamental problem for Bill *and* the rest of us is this: we are absent from our bodies. We behave as though our "real" selves don't include our skin and bones. As a result, we are hopelessly bewildered when our bodies stand between us and who we think we should be. Even worse, we ignore how our *bodies* affect everything we do, including "mental" activities like strategic planning and decision making. We go through the motions, oblivious to how everyday rituals *form* us—kneeling in prayer, hugging our children, shaking hands with coworkers, slouching in the conference room.

What we need is a richer conception of the body and its holistic effect on the entire range of our lives as leaders. We need to move from disembodiment to embodiment.

In keeping with the running theme, this section provides a vision of *beingfulness*. Bodies are an essential feature of being human. If we are going to be present to ourselves and with others, then we need to make peace with our bodies. Beingfulness means reestablishing the holistic connection between body and soul and learning to live in the strength of that unity. Embodiment entails *action*, doing things in the world by means of our bodies. That might sound abstract right now, but beingfulness is a *practical* reality. And it's through embodied practice that we enter more deeply into the presence for which God made us.

Conclusion

What have you done with your body this week? What has your body done with you? I'll admit, those are weird questions to ask. But in their strangeness, we catch a glimpse of how far we have to go to understand the impact of our bodily existence on our lives. Where would Bill be if he'd taken his embodiment seriously? Would he be on medical leave, staring down the barrel of a forced retirement and an identity crisis? We may not see ourselves in Bill—but I'll bet that twenty years ago he wouldn't have seen himself in Bill either. Far too many of us are in a downward spiral; we just haven't realized it yet. It's time we wake up and pay attention to what our bodies are saying before it's too late.

CHAPTER 17

The Case for
Beingfulness

In the last chapter, I described beingfulness as the practical rec-
ognition of our embodied reality. But what does that mean for
leaders? It isn't too hard to connect the dots between bodies and
productivity: eat right, exercise, and get some sleep so you can perform at your highest level. That's true enough, but I want to take you
in a slightly different direction for two reasons. First, I wouldn't be
telling you anything you haven't already heard from your general
practitioner or the umpteen articles in the magazines in her waiting
room. Second, to zero in on health as a productivity hack would lead
us into the same instrumentalist trap we saw with Bill in the previous chapter. As we'll see, our bodies are more than just machines
for getting things done.

I want to head down a road that leads to a deeper conception of
our humanity. On that journey, we'll learn how embodiment affects
the way we carry ourselves, think through important decisions, and
influence others. In the coming chapters, we'll look at each of these
embodied realities, what they mean, and how to train your sense of
bodily *presence* for the good of your leadership at home, the office,
and church. Before we do that, let's look at a few examples of beingfulness in action.

Body Language: Monologue or Dialogue?

In the 1971 book *Silent Messages*, Albert Mehrabian famously reported that 93 percent of what we say comes not by words but through tone and body language. This rule has been misinterpreted and misapplied by communications experts the world over, but its basic insight is spot on: we communicate more with our bodies than words could ever say. Dirty looks, folded arms, exasperated eye rolls—nonverbal cues like these signal anger, disappointment, and contempt. Every time a parent or teacher scolded us to stand up straight and look them in the eyes, they were teaching us this subtle lesson: don't let the nonverbal contradict the verbal. You can't say, "I love you," with a scowl on your face, and you can't connect with people if your eyes keep darting all over the room.

We know what our bodies can say to others, but have we considered what our body language might say to *us*? Amy Cuddy, a social scientist out of Harvard, took up that idea when she stepped onto the TED stage in 2012.[1] In a talk that has now been viewed over 51 million times, Cuddy illustrated the connection between body language and brain chemistry. Most vividly, she focused on a study that examined posture. The participants in the study were split into two groups. Cuddy had the first group stand in a power pose for two minutes—arms held high, chest puffed out. She asked the second group to sit in a weaker position—shoulders slouched, head hung low. Before and after, Cuddy measured testosterone and cortisol levels. For quick reference, highly effective leaders tend to be high in the former and low in the latter. Among those who stood in the power pose, Cuddy found a 20 percent increase in testosterone and a 25 percent decrease in cortisol. In the weak group, she found a 10 percent decrease in the former and a 15 percent increase in the latter. In another study, Cuddy had subjects do their pose and then sit with an interviewer. When observers watched the interviews on video, they all described the power posers as the sharpest participants by far.

What's the payoff, here? Cuddy certainly doesn't want us to

walk into our next interview or board meeting and puff out our chests as if we were trying to scare off a black bear. The power pose isn't about fake power as much as it's about embodied presence. By taking a few minutes to strike a pose (in private!), you can stimulate the processes in your body that enable you to rise to the occasion and be *who you are* in the moment rather than a shrunken, timid version of yourself. For Cuddy, it's not about faking it till you're making it; it's about faking it until you *become* it. And what you'll become is a fully present, wholly engaged leader who earns the respect of his or her followers.

Check Yourself: Five Core Movements

Noticing our physical sensations and how they relate to our experiences of ourselves is a key factor in growth. Our bodies move in what can be categorized into five core movements: surrender, push, reach, grasp, and bringing home. Tracking the five main ways your body moves and how you feel about the movements can allow your body and your conscious mind to work in balance and allow for the release of unresolved energy.

Sit with both feet firmly planted on the ground so that you have full access to your body. Be aware of how your body responds to these five core movements:

- **Surrender:** Allow your body to be supported entirely by the couch or chair that you are seated upon.
- **Push:** Press down with your hands or feet. Notice how it feels in your body.
- **Reach:** Imagine reaching out for something. Extend your hand in front of your body.
- **Grasp:** Imagine grasping something in your out-

> stretched hand.
> - **Bringing home:** Return your extended hand back to your body. Notice the sensation in your body.
>
> Now ask yourself:
>
> - Which movement felt the best?
> - Which didn't? Why?
>
> By determining which movements felt most or least comfortable, you can see where your body is lacking in integration. Since the body will always find a way to homeostasis (i.e., balance), you can either participate in healthy choices that move you toward integration (i.e., practicing boundaries with relationships) or wait for your body to force it (i.e., collapsing from fatigue and being forced to ask for help).

Make Up Your Mind (and Body)

Dave Ramsey, a nationally syndicated radio host and bestselling author on personal finance, won't hire a new employee without taking him or her out to dinner. The catch is, Dave's wife gets to go and so does that employee's spouse. If Mr. and Mrs. Ramsey leave that dinner with anything less than a peaceful feeling, you better believe that the applicant's chances are toast. Now, the Ramseys don't do this with every applicant. The dinner typically comes on the heels of a months-long process chock full of applications, interviews, and evaluations. Ramsey starts with deep analytics and intentional process, but at the end of the day, his (and his wife's) "gut" makes the call.

Today, the sprawling field of decision science offers professional deciders a host of methods, frameworks, and techniques to help them think scientifically about every option on the table. The literature tends to revolve around cognitive processes—how we *think* about the decisions we make. But as many in the field now recognize, there's more to deciding than thinking. After all, what kind of statistical analysis did you run before you proposed to your spouse? How much logical deduction entered into your last car purchase? As any good salesman will tell you, most of life's decisions are made emotionally. Logic comes second.

As we'll see in chapter 19, our thoughts and emotions are bodily realities. Experts in embodied cognition have long observed the connection between our bodies and thoughts.[2] In terms of decision making, "people are embodied creatures who rely on movement to drive and navigate their own priorities as decision makers."[3] Our bodies connect us to our environment and drive our thoughts, actions, and emotions. Analytics are important, but our "gut" plays a legitimate role in decision making.

How can this help rather than hinder us? How do you train your gut to reliably produce thoughts and emotions that correspond to reality and make wise decisions?

The Bodily Price of Dehumanized Work

In July 2013, a thirty-one-year-old Japanese journalist named Miwa Sado died of heart failure.[4] Why did her young heart stop beating? According to a ruling from Japanese labor regulators, Sado was the victim of *karoshi*: death by overwork. In the month prior to her demise, the young journalist had logged a blistering 159 hours of overtime with only two days off. I wish I could say her death was an anomaly, but *karoshi* has become something of an epidemic in Japan. In 2016, nearly 1,500 instances of *karoshi* were reported, although the actual number is certainly higher.[5] Japanese officials have sought to fight back *karoshi* through a strict regime of sanctions discouraging employers from overworking their employees. Some have had to pay as much as 130 million yen (more than $1 million US dollars) in damages to victims' families.[6]

In Japan, the root cause of *karoshi* runs much deeper than greed or workaholism. It's cultural. Japanese business is ruled by hierarchy; in general, the lower you are on the totem pole, the more likely you are to be treated like a nameless, faceless machine to be used and abused until you flame out. Sound familiar? We may not have the same cultural expectations that would drive people to work themselves *literally* to death, but how many times have we encouraged our junior employees to "pay their dues" by working the same eighty-hour workweeks we did when we got out of college? Whatever one might say about the "snowflake" generation, millennials are taking over the workforce in droves, and plenty of research shows that work-life balance ranks high on this generation's occupational wish list. Like it or not, the realities of high employment and a shallow labor pool are going to demand that leaders quit treating their employees like machines if they want to compete for the next generation's best and brightest.

Conclusion

Beingfulness is a practical reality. Our bodies change the world for both ourselves and others. Ignoring that embodied reality doesn't erase it; disembodied living is less a matter of living outside the body (as if that were possible) and more of habitually neglecting the body. In a word, disembodied leadership is *absent* leadership. Worst of all, disembodied leaders don't just misuse their bodies; they abuse their followers. As we saw with *karoshi*, there's a way to abuse our employees without laying our hands on them. Reclaiming embodied presence is about more than diversity and inclusion, harassment and #MeToo—though it certainly isn't less than those things either. Beingfulness will empower you to respect the bodies of those you lead and in the process make you a more effective leader. Doing so will *rehumanize* you and your workplace, engaging both yourself and others at the level of everyone's deepest longing—to know and be known as human beings created in the image of God.

CHAPTER 18

Embodied Stress

AN UNEXPECTED FRIEND

When it comes to the battleground of life with a teenager, our daughter Stella was our second tour of duty. Our son Elijah was our first, and when his testosterone spiked, I knew how to handle his boyish attempts to assert himself. Stella was different. She felt feelings, and she wasn't afraid to express them.

Shortly after my daughter first decided to follow Christ, we sat down to unpack what that meant. She was high on Christ, but it wasn't long before Stella off-loaded a raft of anxieties. "Dad," she wept, "I have doubts and I'm afraid. I can't stop them. I try and I pray but they don't go away." To her newly converted mind, piety and anxiety occupied two distinct spheres. If you wanted to be a good Christian, you had to master your emotions, right?

This was a defining moment for Stella. When I think about it, I'm reminded of something Eboni told me: "We must learn to *befriend* our emotions." In that moment, I had to get real with my daughter. She wasn't alone. I'd felt everything she felt and continue to feel it today.

The question for her, me, and you is this: What do we do with our emotions? The gospel doesn't liberate us from emotions. It sets us free to befriend them, to observe what's going on in our hearts and ask deep questions about ourselves in the presence of the Lord.

We can't *think* our feelings into submission any more than we can *convince* ourselves to fall in love. Rather, we allow our emotions to usher us into a deeper dialogue with ourselves in God. Like Stella, we learn that God can handle our emotions. If that was true for my teenage daughter and her anxiety, then it's equally true for whatever leaders might be struggling with right now.

Anxious Sinners in the Hands of an Angry God?

Do you struggle with anxiety? Jesus and Paul have three words for you: don't be anxious (Matt 6:25–34; Phil 4:6). Problem solved, right?

If only it were that easy. Many well-meaning Christians have pointed their anxious brothers and sisters to verses like these, counseling prayer and repentance without giving a single thought to the *embodied* elements of anxiety (chronic pain, drug side effects, hormonal imbalance, etc.). On the flip side, dualists ship their friends off to a psychologist without ever thinking to pray and call their pastor. Which is right? Are stress and anxiety spiritual ailments in need of prayers or medical issues in need of pills? Are our stressed-out brothers and sisters rotten sinners or victims of biology?

Good news, things aren't that simple. For one thing, not all anxiety is sin. Paul describes *himself* as anxious for the churches (2 Cor 11:28 ESV). On top of that, the apostle approves Timothy's genuine "anxiety" for the welfare of the church in Philippi (Phil 2:20). In each case, the Greek word is *merimnao*, and it refers to a deep sense of concern that can either be positive or negative. The difference lies in the response to anxiety's circumstances. For example, genuine concern for our children is valid, but it becomes sinful when we functionally deny God's existence by fretting about their every move.

With all that in mind, we might look again at all those biblical words that seem to condemn anxiety. Is Jesus dismissing our anxiety or inviting us to submit it to his love and care? Is Paul chiding us for being ungrateful or challenging us to shift our perspective in prayer? Does Peter rip into us for our anxiety, or is he calling us to place it in the only hands that can hold it (1 Pet 5:7)? Rather than condemning every instance of stress and anxiety, the Bible calls us to *do something* with what we're experiencing in our hearts, minds, and bodies. Especially in the Psalms, the moments of our deepest distresses are precisely when God meets us (Pss 94:19; 102:2, 5, etc.).

Embodied Stress and the Power of Negative Thinking

What do stress and anxiety have to do with the body? According to psychologists, stress is a situational response while anxiety is a settled disposition. Stress primes our bodies to respond to trying circumstances (think of how your body reacts when you think you're about to get into a car accident). As a settled disposition, anxiety corresponds less to the facts on the ground and more to what's going on inside our hearts, minds, and bodies. OCD, PTSD, social anxiety—each of these labels describe different ways our *bodies* respond to perceived (real or not) circumstances.

The fact that the Bible calls us to *do something* with our stress and anxiety seems to assume that "nonphysical" activities like thinking and praying can have real effects on the physical states that cause our distress. That shouldn't surprise us; if God can reach down and bring a dead person to life, then why couldn't he answer our anxious prayers with a quick hit of serotonin *ex nihilo*? But is a direct intervention from the outside the *only* way God interacts with the bodies he designed? Is it possible God has created our bodies to "use" stress in a certain way? If so, then how?

In *The Upside of Stress*, Stanford University psychologist Kelly McGonigal describes a radical shift that took place in her own thinking about stress. For years, McGonigal towed the traditional line on stress: it's bad for you. Thanks to a study on the relationship between stress and mortality, however, McGonigal changed her mind. In that study, the mortality rate between low-stress and high-stress individuals was found to be nearly identical. What gives? If stress is bad, shouldn't the latter have died at a higher rate? Here's the catch: for the high-stressed individuals who didn't hold a negative view of stress, the mortality rate was indeed similar. But for those who *believed* stress was harmful, the risk of dying rose 43 percent.[1] Call this the power of negative thinking. It isn't stress that kills; it's our stress about stress.

Tending and Befriending Your Bodily Responses

According to McGonigal, "Many of the negative outcomes we associate with stress may actually be the consequence of trying to avoid it."[2] On standard evolutionary accounts of human development, stress evolved as a real-time response to immediate danger (e.g., a lunging lion or an attacking tribe). Since most of us have long since left the world of fight-or-flight behind, our bodies have learned to respond to the "immediate danger" of an important test or a grumpy deacon by initiating what McGonigal calls the "challenge" and "tend and befriend" responses. The former is what our bodies do to prepare for a nonlethal threat like an approaching manuscript deadline. The latter is similar, except that the specific chemical released is oxytocin, which prompts you to suppress your flight instinct, reach out to others for support, and face down your stress. If we think of stress as purely negative, then we tamp down these bodily responses and prevent them from positively impacting our performance.

One doesn't need to share McGonigal's precise evolutionary viewpoint to affirm her insight into the body's response to stress. Her emphasis on positive thinking has the potential to revolutionize how we perform in tense circumstances. If she's right, we should stop viewing stress as an enemy and more as a resource. "In many ways," McGonigal says, "the stress response is your best ally during difficult moments—a resource to rely on rather than an enemy to vanquish."[3] In sum, training yourself "to view anxiety as excitement, energy or motivation can help you perform to your full potential."[4] Befriend your body, and your body will tell you what you need to do to reach your highest level.

Conclusion

In chapter 17, we considered the connection between bodily posture and brain chemistry. As Amy Cuddy showed us, the power pose is an effective way to prepare for activities like job interviews, sales presentations, and public speaking engagements. The pose anticipates those stressful environments and uses bodily posture to prime our brains and prepare us to move forward with confidence and a deepened sense of presence. If McGonigal is right, then "befriending" our stress might just be the mental component of the power pose, challenging us to bow up and face whatever lies before us.

As Christian leaders, it's important we keep this all in perspective. Considered by itself, stress is neither a friend nor a foe but an opportunity to seek the Lord in our bodily distress. It's only when we trade faith for fear that we cross the barrier from valid concern to sinful anxiety. In those moments, we're called to lift our hands, not just in a power pose, but *in prayer*. The Psalmist cried out in distress to the Lord (Ps 118:5–6). On the eve of battle, the Israelites were told to remember that God was with them (Josh 1:9). When the people were stressed about their material provision, Jesus pointed them to the birds and flowers as evidence of their Father's abiding care (Matt 6:25–34). When the church was scattered in exile, Peter reminded Christians to cast their anxieties on Jesus (1 Pet 5:7). This doesn't mean tossing our anxieties overboard (i.e., denying them) so much as laying them on the back of the One who is powerful enough to carry them and us to safety.

Embodied Stress: An Unexpected Friend

Principle: When we write stress and anxiety off as sin, we ignore what our bodies are trying to tell us. We need to acknowledge and befriend these responses, even as we take them to God to hear what *he* would say through them.

Practice: Next time you feel your heart rate quickening and your blood pressure rising, stop and notice your circumstances. What triggered this stress? Was it a person? A deadline? A daunting task? Take a deep breath and offer up that trigger to God in prayer.

Check Yourself: ACE Inventory

ACE stands for Adverse Childhood Experiences. According to an ACE study, the rougher your childhood, the higher your score is likely to be and the higher your risk for later health problems.

Find your score here: https://www.npr.org/sections/health -shots/2015/03/02/387007941/take-the-ace-quiz-and-learn -what-it-does-and-doesnt-mean.

CHAPTER 19

Learning to Think with Your Heart

M eet my friend Larry. Larry has had a couple crazy years. Three months after we partnered to devise a leadership development track for his company, he began to develop heart issues—a dilated aortic root, to be precise. Before his diagnosis, Larry was a wildly successful business developer and an Ironman triathlete. For decades, he used extreme physical activity as a kind of therapy. Out on the road or in the water, Larry found a place to amp up his adrenaline and tamp down the pain of leadership. When the doctor's orders took away his physical outlet, Larry spent even more time in his business, searching for the same high he used to find biking in the mountains of Idaho. In his mind, that was the only way to sustain his intense lifestyle. A year after his diagnosis, Larry hit a wall that no amount of bicycle-induced and business-inspired adrenaline could help him climb. For thirty-six years, Larry's wife, Janet, had been his emotional rock. She'd stuck by him through years of intense struggle. So when Janet's face went numb, and a neurologist told her she would need immediate brain surgery, everything in Larry's world stopped—at least for a little while.

Confronted by his and his wife's mortality, Larry tried to drop everything so that he could focus on Janet in recovery, but the business wouldn't let him. He'd spun an intricate web of partners and deals from which he just couldn't break free. Physically, he was leveled; he literally could not stomach the risk involved in his work anymore. Larry's mind wasn't ready to admit it, but his body was telling him it had hit a wall. Much like Bill (chapter 16), Larry learned to keep his body in its place with a steady dose of adrenaline. With that hormonal muzzle gone, Larry's body was finally able to speak for itself. He had no choice but to listen and do what his heart was telling him.

The Body Knows

We'll pick up Larry's story later in the book. For now, I want to invite you into a quick exercise. Imagine there's a keyboard in your lap, and type the word "fingers." Go ahead and set this book down for a minute. What happened? It was probably a bit awkward, but I'm willing to bet your fingers went where they were supposed to go. How did they do that? Did you think about it, or did you let your fingers do what they've been trained to do by constant practice? Typing at a keyboard, tying your shoes, using a fork—these are just a few examples of the embodied knowledge that you and I carry around with us every day. In far too many ways to count, we simply know what to do without having to think about it. This is how our bodies are supposed to work.[1]

We were made to live *through* our bodies. It's only when something goes wrong that we began to focus our attention *on* them instead. When's the last time you thought of your elbow? Unless you've been hitting the tennis court lately, it's probably been a while. Yet without your elbow, you wouldn't be able to hold a book—like this one. In this bodily sense, every action we take in the world is a "lived truth."[2] My body *knows* the chair I'm sitting in is stable enough to hold me, even though I didn't inspect the legs before I sat down.

We can extend this bodily sense of knowledge to relationships (I *know* I'm safe around my wife), places (my body *knows* I'm in my living room), and even moral decisions (that pit in my stomach is my body's way of *knowing* when I've done something wrong). I don't know these things through a process of logical deduction: people who give hugs are safe; my wife gave me a hug this morning; therefore, my wife is a safe person. Only Spock would think like that. Rather, I just *know* my wife because of our twenty-plus years of experience together. Examples like these are why epistemologist (i.e., philosopher of knowledge) Esther Lightcap Meek isn't afraid to describe our knowledge as *incarnate*: "Plato just turned over in his grave. But it's the kind of view of knowing that I think a bodily resurrected Jesus would confirm. Not to mention a world-making, embodied human-making God."[3]

Embodied Knowledge and the Leader

Much of what leaders do can be described as "knowledge work." In other words, leaders are professional thinkers. For some, that means hours spent pouring over data so that we can make decisions that track with personnel needs, productivity concerns, market shifts, and so on. For others, it means walking slowly through the crowd and gathering soft data as we get to know our people and the human needs of our organization. As we'll see below, thinking well embraces both these aspects and more.

In any case, thinking is one of the leader's most important tools. The problem is, too many of us treat thinking as a disembodied exercise—a pure act of the mind. But if knowledge is embodied, then we have to be careful not to disconnect our thinking from its bodily context. As we saw with Dave Ramsey in chapter 17, an employee could make perfect sense on paper and still fail the "gut" test. This is the everyday mode of human knowledge we all grew up with, yet we lost it somewhere along the line when we came to believe that the only valid form of knowledge is the kind you can demonstrate on paper. If we're going to become better leaders and knowers, we need to think a little more broadly.

Taking Back Monday: Leadership and Primal Emotion

If we accept the bodily component of our knowing, then we need to pay careful attention to what actions and emotions have to do with the way we lead. Emotions in particular have garnered significant attention from experts in leadership development. According to Daniel Goleman, the bestselling author of *Emotional Intelligence*, our emotions impact our thinking so much that it's as if we have two minds: "Our emotional mind will harness the rational mind to its purposes, for our feelings and reactions—rationalizations—justifying them in terms of the present moment, without realizing the influence of our emotional memory."[4] More often than we are willing to admit, our head plays second fiddle to whatever's going on in our heart.

Thus Goleman emphasizes the *primal* cast of the emotions in leadership.[5] Throughout history humans have fallen in line behind whoever best wielded emotion to inspire others. All we have to do is peek at the latest political campaign, red or blue, to see how winning candidates seldom *convince* with arguments but *compel* with emotion and rhetoric. In modern organizations, the primal role of emotional leadership may be invisible, yet it "remains foremost among the many jobs of leadership: driving the collective emotions in a positive direction and clearing the smog, created by toxic emotions."[6] The most effective leaders don't persuade us with rational arguments aimed at our heads. Instead, they find a way to speak directly to our *hearts*.

Biblical Cardiology: The Nexus of Thinking, Feeling, and Doing

An overemphasis on thinking will turn us into pointy-headed leaders with meager influence over actual *human* beings. Too much touchy-feely stuff, though, and our strategic judgment won't be worth the Hallmark card it's printed on. Worse, we might learn to *manipulate* others with our emotions rather than *lead* them. Really, what we need is a balance between thinking, feeling, and (as we'll see) doing. The best way to find that balance is to look closely at how the Bible brings these three elements together under one heading: the *heart*.

In Scripture, the heart is something more than a mass of ventricles and atria. Instead, it's the center of our being—our essence as thinking, feeling, and doing creatures. We're used to talking about the heart in strictly emotional terms. And that's one biblical way to think about it. We love with our hearts (Matt 22:37; cf. Deut 6:5). We suffer the reproaches of others as heartbreak (Ps 69:20). The heart is where we experience sorrow and anguish (Rom 9:2). But that's not *all* we should say. We also *think, understand,* and *ponder* with our hearts (Isa 6:10; Matt 13:15; Luke 2:19; cf. Gen 37:11). With our hearts, we *believe* and are justified (Rom 10:10). More than that, our hearts are the center of *action* in our lives. We *bring forth* good deeds out of the good treasure in our hearts (Matt 12:35). The gospel sets us free from sin and makes us "obedient from the heart" to biblical teaching (Rom 6:17 ESV). In Proverbs, it's the heart—not the head—that keeps wise commandments (Prov 3:1).

Part of what it means to live an integrated life is to *act* on what we *feel* in our hearts and *know* to be true. Each part overlaps, making it impossible to say we know what it means to love our neighbor when our apathy prevents us from acting in the world. Heart-healthy Christianity requires being "doers of the word," not only hearers (Jas 1:22 ESV). All the analytic rigor in the world isn't enough to overcome the hardening of our emotional and practical arteries.

Conclusion: Tuning Our Hearts to Think, Feel, and Do

The relationship between thinking, feeling, and doing is complex. What are you supposed to do when you think you need to fire an employee but can't get past the emotional hurdles involved? What course of action should you take when you think a deal looks great on paper, but your emotions tell you to walk away? In some cases, you trust your gut and give your employee another chance. In others, you trust your due diligence and move forward with the deal. Whatever the scenario, you have to *do something*. Doing nothing is itself a form of action—whether it's enabling an incompetent employee or neglecting a solid opportunity. As I'll pick up in the next chapter, the way you respond to decision points like these is never a matter of cold, detached logic. Whether we admit it or not, our choices flow from the practiced habits of our hearts, not merely the thoughts in our heads. If we're going to think, feel, and act moving forward, then we need to spend time training our hearts and bodies to think, feel, and do what God has created us to do.

Learning to Think with Your Heart

Principle: Knowledge is about more than using your head. Embodied presence demands closer attention to the *heart* and the willingness not only to *think* but to *feel* and *act*.

Practice: Give yourself thirty minutes to reflect on your last major decision. What steps did you take to decide? Take stock of the precise moments when a gut feeling, an angry reaction, or a sense of peace influenced the process. Did those emotions help or hinder you? How can you account for them in future decisions?

CHAPTER 20

Practice Makes Permanent

Hitting a major league fastball should be physically impossible.[1] The average fastball travels about ninety to ninety-five miles per hour. At that speed, it takes the ball around 400 milliseconds to travel from the pitcher's hand to the catcher's glove. If you factor in the 100 milliseconds it takes the brain to process visual imagery, that leaves the hitter a mere 300 milliseconds to put his Louisville Slugger on the ball. Of course, he's got to get the bat around in time—there go another 175 milliseconds. All told, the batter has about 125 milliseconds to gauge the pitch and decide whether and where to swing. To put that in perspective, that's roughly one third the amount of time it takes to blink your eyes. No sweat, right?

How can anyone even see a fastball, let alone hit the thing? What it comes down to is this: major league batters can see into the future . . . sort of. The human brain is remarkable at reading patterns and anticipating what comes next. When a seasoned hitter sees that pitcher's arm come across, he can tap into a lifetime's worth of experience to judge the angle of the pitch and make a decision before the ball ever leaves the pitcher's hand. This is the batter's form of embodied knowing (see chapter 19). If you asked him to explain it, he'd probably be dumbfounded. How did he get here? Well, how do you get to Carnegie Hall? Practice. Countless hours in the batting cages have made batters into the kind of people who just *know* how to hit a fastball.

The Power of Practice

The Christian life is very much like what we saw above. We *practice* the faith by taking part in the ordinary means of grace, such as reading Scripture, participating in worship, and spending time with God in prayer. In all this, the Father is forming and re-forming us into the image of his Son by the power of the Holy Spirit (Rom 8:29; 2 Cor 3:18; Col 3:10). In Christ, Paul says, you have "taken off your old self with its practices and have put on the new self" (Col 3:9–10). What do the practices of the new self look like? Here are a few: compassion, kindness, gentleness, forbearance, and forgiveness (Col 3:12–13). In sum, God forms us through all the Christian virtues, the most important of which is love.

Human beings are what James K. A. Smith calls "liturgical animals."[2] We are constantly being formed in and through our everyday actions—the "liturgies" that constitute our existence. Whether I'm standing up and saluting the flag at a football game or ordering something on the internet, I'm training my body to engage the world in a certain way (patriotism or consumerism). I "put on" a form of life by engaging in the practices that correspond to it. This is why Paul so often writes in the imperative, charging his readers to *do* the right thing regardless of whether they *feel* like it or not.

We've all been formed in one way or another. Whether it was by the case studies we read in grad school or the decades of experience in our industry, we are the products of our practice—most of which we've forgotten. The way we conduct a staff meeting, our reflexive contempt for a less-than-competent colleague, our built-in risk aversion—these are just a tiny sampling of the array of embodied actions we engage in as leaders, and they're all deeply ingrained products of our formation. We can read as many books on leadership as we like, but readjusting our leadership mindset is never enough to replace our negative habits (contempt, anger, dismissiveness, and so on) with virtues. We can't outrun our shoddy thinking with more thinking. Instead, we need to get into the cage and start swinging.

Ground Yourself: Lift Up Your Eyes (Ps 121)

Begin by recalling an emotionally charged event. Then setting a timer to chime at two one-minute intervals, do the following to connect the emotional and the physical:

- Close your eyes and see yourself in the situation with all the emotions and all the details.
- Wrap your arms around yourself, put your head down, and allow whatever emotions you have to flow in until you hear the bell chime.
- After you hear the chime, open your eyes, sit up, and place your hands palms up on your thighs.
- Practice holding a half-smile.
- Keep your eyes open, lift your eyebrows, and breathe deeply.
- Continue recalling the emotionally charged event until you hear the chime again.

Practicing Better Leadership

In the last chapter, we saw how closely our thinking connects with our feeling and doing. What we left hanging, however, was how to train ourselves to connect those three elements so that we could grow as fully integrated, fully present leaders. This is where practice comes in as a way to *train* our embodied presence as thinkers, feelers, and doers. How do we do that? Here are three ways to start:

Feel your thoughts. We're not computers. God doesn't want us to move through the world like a brain on a stick. If we take the Bible's teaching on the heart seriously, then we can't be content with a strictly rational approach to leadership. Next time you face a difficult decision, engage your heart as well as your head. Gather the facts, analyze the data, and do your due diligence, but don't forget to stop and check your gut.

Mind your emotions. Emotions aren't sins; they are a barometer. They tell us what we value most. Still, sin crouches at the door, waiting to cloud our judgment at every level. Next time you face a decision, prayerfully observe your emotions. What matters most to you, and how might your emotions signal a sinful blind spot?

Do it. Knowledge demands action. I can't say I *know* what it means to lay my life down for my wife if I've never seen the inside of our laundry room. That's true whether or not I *feel* like doing my part at home. While "going through the motions" is a bad place to live, we need to realize that our emotions often *follow* actions. Next time you find yourself sidelined by the paralysis of analysis, force yourself to *act*.

As any major league hitter will tell you, practice is worthless if it's done apart from a coach's watchful eye. You can swing away at your thoughts, feelings, and actions, but without an experienced guide to let you know how you're doing, you'll never know whether you've made genuine progress. That said, seek out an accountability partner or a mentor to be *your* batting coach. Set goals together, schedule a weekly debriefing, and make sure that coach holds you accountable. As we'll soon see, the practice that makes permanent doesn't work in isolation.

Conclusion

In this chapter, we've learned that practice has a deeply formative influence on everything we do as humans. This seems almost too simple to say, but I'll be the first to admit that I too often think of leadership in purely *mental* terms. Mindset is important, but that stack of leadership books on your desk won't help a bit until you put that material into practice. Transformation is about more than deciding to change our lives; it's about "putting on" our new selves through a Spirit-enlivened commitment to *do* what God calls us to do in order to become who he wants us to be. It's time to stop living inside our own heads and start enjoying fully embodied lives.

Practice Makes Permanent

Principle: Thoughts and intentions alone will never transform our leadership. We need practice—a lot of it—to "put on" the virtues of presence and humanity in our everyday lives.

Practice: Choose a virtue and list the everyday actions you can take to cultivate it. Then commit to *practice* some of those actions daily for the next month. For example, to cultivate selflessness, make a daily habit of buying coffee for a team member. Simple acts like this one will train you to put others first.

CHAPTER 21

The Blessing of Beingfulness

So there's Bill, sitting in his psychologist's office. His back is on fire, his headache hasn't gone away, and he still can't seem to catch his breath. As much as he'd like to find a way back to work, his body won't cooperate. For years, he has treated it like a teenager's first car—his tank is empty and the oil hasn't been changed in eight thousand miles. Can Bill just suck it up, bury the pain, and *will* himself back to work? Can his determined mind overcome the broken-down matter of his fifty-five-year-old body? Or will he end up losing himself in the obscurity of early retirement?

From Disembodiment to Embodiment

Bill's years of disembodied living have robbed him of the deep human resources God gives us to do his will. Bill, by treating his body as an instrument, has left himself worn out and defeated. By compartmentalizing, he has neglected his body's store of performance-enhancing drugs. He has dehumanized himself, and more likely than not, he has done the same to his employees. Sure, Bill's been "in" his body for fifty-five years, but as far as beingfulness is concerned, he's been completely absent. What's the moral of the story? Don't be like Bill. Instead, let his story serve as an invitation to learn presence in, with, and through your body.

Quit Ignoring Your Body

What's going on in your body right now? Are you in pain? Tired? Anxious? In chapter 18, we learned there's an intense link between our emotions, our bodies, and our thoughts. As the psychiatrist Bessel van der Kolk showed in his book *The Body Keeps the Score*, unresolved trauma can't help but manifest itself in individual and organizational dysfunction.[1] We may not carry the specific scars of childhood abuse or posttraumatic stress, but our emotions carry the same potential for harm. It's on us to appraise and reappraise our emotions, to name them for what they are, and bring them to God in prayer so that *he* can provide the holistic healing we need. When David's bones "wasted away" under the emotional weight of his sin, he took it to God in confession (Ps 32:3–5). There, David found healing for his soul and his body. What would change in your life if you really believed God could do the same for you?

Start Thinking with Your Heart

As the Proverb says:

> Above all else, guard your heart,
>> for everything you do flows from it. (Prov 4:23)

For too long, we've lived as though this Proverb meant to say everything flows from our *minds*. As we learned in chapter 19, the Bible paints a much more holistic picture of the connection between our thinking, feeling, and doing. Our bodies know more than we think, and our feelings impact our decisions and actions more than we're willing to admit. It's time to stop denying our emotions and pretending as though we're guided by nothing more than cool, detached logic. Don't let your emotions usurp your better judgment. Instead, learn to listen to them as a faithful guide, and trust your analytically tempered, prayerfully attuned *gut* to faithfully guide your decision making.

Practice Embodied Leadership

"Change your thinking, change your life!" I get that, but I'm tired of all the self-help hucksters who paint "mindset" as the universal cure for every leadership ailment. We are embodied thinkers, feelers, and knowers, and our leadership depends on much more than head knowledge. In chapter 20, we learned how we are deeply formed by the innumerable swathe of practice sessions we've engaged in, from infancy to the present. All the leadership books, TED talks, and inspiring podcasts in the world won't change anything if we don't include their central insights into our daily lives. The only way our people will see the fruit of our embodied presence is if we lay down deep roots through deliberate practice.

Imagine Yourself: Your Future Is in Your Body

Consider this: Your mind will lie to you but your body never will. Beingfulness has tremendous benefits as it makes you constantly aware of your environment. Imagine that your body—with its signals, nudges, aches, and pains—is speaking the truth. How could you benefit from this awareness in your daily interactions?

Sabbath: Deep Rest for Your Body

God made each of us—heart, mind, soul, and *body*. We've only gestured toward the many ways in which a deep sense of bodily presence can dramatically enhance your life and leadership. But in all our striving for performance, we can't neglect the bodily rest that God holds out for us. That said, here are three practices to work into your regular rhythms of rest and sabbath.

Stop: Acknowledge your body's need for sabbath by unplugging from the demands of your everyday life. Paradoxically, a good run might be the retreat your body needs from the trauma of sitting behind a desk for forty hours a week.

Trust: Stop burning the candle at both ends and get a good night's rest. Use times of solitude to reconnect with your bodily state. Prayerfully meditate on what God might be trying to say through your physical and emotional pain.

Enjoy: Celebrate the fact that God has given you this body as your point of contact with the world. Practice well to play the game of life faithfully, offering up praise to God for the good gift of our embodied reality.

The Brain and the Body

Our brains have more neural connections than there are stars in the Milky Way galaxy. In Psalm 8, David responds in wonder not only to the universe but also to God's care for humanity:

> When I consider your heavens,
>   the work of your fingers,
> the moon and the stars,
>   which you have set in place,
> what is mankind that you are mindful of them,
>   human beings that you care for them? (Ps 8:3–4)

Oswald Chambers says, "This is not humanity's calamity but its peculiar dignity. We do not further our spiritual lives in spite of our bodies, but in and by means of our bodies."[1] Although Chambers was not of a generation that was "body conscious" or in a time that validated emotions and sensations, he understood that we are not simply spiritual or ethereal beings but bodily creatures.

If God is mindful of us, we certainly need to be mindful of ourselves.

The Body Doesn't Lie

Our bodies are wired for balance. They will do anything they can to make up for depletions in other parts of us (spiritually, emotionally, and mentally). For example, when stress becomes intolerable, we may experience physical symptoms such as a pounding heart, sweating, shaking, chest pain, nausea, stomach troubles, feeling dizzy or light-headed, or intense fear.[2]

Being mindful of our bodies directly relates to our experience of the world. God has designed us to interpret the world through sensations, urges, movements, emotions, images, memories, and thoughts. Once we become mindful of how these physical aspects are processed in our bodies, we can begin to balance our bodies' interpretations of the information.

Wired for Connection

The human nervous system is built around the balance of two opposing actions. The sympathetic nervous system is associated with the fight-or-flight response that is the result of the release of cortisol (stress chemicals) throughout the bloodstream. The parasympathetic nervous system is associated with relaxation, digestion, and regeneration. These two parts are meant to work in a rhythmic alternation that supports healthy rhythms of alertness and restfulness, thereby benefitting physical and mental health.

Neurobiologist Stephen Porges, who has done significant research on the nervous system, has identified the vagus nerve as the largest nerve in our body. This nerve controls our body's ability to detect danger, sense safety, experience rest, and connect socially. Nerves are the conductors of sensory information from the body to the brain. The nervous system (which Proges refers to as the polyvagal system) is refined through connection and stimulated by touch, which means our bodies are hardwired for connection starting from birth.

According to Porges's research, an overabundance of physical or emotional stress—which the body receives as if it were danger—can lead to high blood pressure, heart attacks, migraines, anxiety, panic attacks, and high cholesterol, as well as gut problems (irritable bowel syndrome), autoimmune disorders (fibromyalgia, Crohn's,

Hashimoto's), chronic pain, and inflammation, some of which Bill experienced (see chapter 16).

The body keeps score. Healthy and refined nervous systems sort new information appropriately. Unhealthy and unrefined systems take information and experiences that would normally be perceived as safe and files them as dangerous. When our nervous systems are out of balance, we experience our lives as dangerous and distressing.

Good Stress, Bad Stress

Eustress is different than *distress*. Eustress occurs when the body doesn't perceive something as life threatening but still notes that it causes pressure. Typically, this pressure can be met with resources that push us through. *Distress* is a stress that comes from experiencing a lack of nourishment, rescue, or resources in response to a cry for help.

People who grow up in abusive environments become normalized to these negative stressors. Often CEOs or other highly productive people are energized by constant stress, although they will hit a wall at some point because we aren't designed to feel safety from stress. Among those who have suffered childhood abuse, their bodies warn them of danger if things are going well in their marriages or relationships. Sometimes, one person in the relationship will disturb the status quo in order to return the relationship to its "normal." Other times, victims of childhood abuse will choose an abusive person to be in relationship with because their body has been wired to handle it.

Rewiring

Our universal needs are those that, no matter who you are in the world, you will have in varying degrees and at various times of your development. Thomas Keating, a Catholic priest and pioneer of the contemplative movement, often speaks about the universal needs of

- Safety
- Security

• Affection
• Pleasure
• Esteem
• Power
• Control

Each of these needs has a direct effect on the body's ability to connect and relate to ourselves, others, and God.

For instance, when we experience pleasure in a healthy way, we develop our identity and our autonomy. We can find pleasure being alone. Unhealthy experiences or a lack of pleasure creates a jealous, insecure, clingy person with body shame. Keating says that when we do not have healthy development of these needs, we do not create healthy emotional programs that define happiness.

As those created by God, we need safety, pleasure, and esteem. These aren't evil. We need affection and a sense of power or control. Because we are made in God's image, we need to be able to create. We also need to rest in order to feel complete.

Our bodies need sabbath rest. It's a universal cosmic principal. Everything has a sabbath rhythm. Everything must take a rest, or it will be forced into one. When we refuse to rest, there will be a limit enforced on us. The fall promised that.

We are wired for balance. The more you are able to bring awareness to your body, the easier it will be to find balance. God is calling you on a transformational journey—from a mindless separation between your body and mind to embodied mindfulness, from being disconnected from yourself and others to being connected through listening to your body for indications that you need connection. True rest comes from connection, which is found by having our universal needs met.

We were created with bodies. God wants us to be connected to our bodies. As Richard Rohr asserts, *Everything Belongs.*[3] Our need for rest belongs. Our need for connection belongs. Our need for balance belongs. Our need for safety belongs. Our need for security, affection, esteem, pleasure, control, and power belong. Our bodies belong.

DISMEM-
BERED

INDIVIDUAL

OTHER-
FUL-
NESS

COLLECTIVE

MEM-
BERED

CHAPTER 22

The Loneliest Job in the World

On February 10, 1961, George Tames walked into the Oval Office and snapped one of the most iconic photographs of John F. Kennedy. In the black-and-white shot, we see the newly minted president alone, hunched over his desk, facing the south window. Later, the *New York Times* affixed the caption "The loneliest job in the world" in order to describe the intense burden Kennedy had to bear during the Cuban Missile Crisis.[1] Bill Clinton so admired the photo that he had it hung in his private office on the second floor of the White House. *The West Wing* even re-created the picture with Josiah Bartlett (Martin Sheen) mimicking Kennedy's pose during the show's opening credits.

As leaders, we often feel like we're standing alone with the fate of an entire organization weighing down on our shoulders. According to the *Harvard Business Review*, 61 percent of CEOs struggle with loneliness to the extent that their job performance actually suffers.[2] I've personally counseled leaders like these. They spend their days surrounded by hundreds of people yet feel as though they're stranded on a deserted island. They say things like

- Nobody talks to me unless there's a problem.
- I'm just another cog in a machine of my own making.

- There's not a single person here who understands what I'm dealing with.

From the outside, leaders may look like the charismatic center of the universe. But on the inside, the pain of social isolation keeps them from being fully present among the crowd.

I know these leaders because I *am* them. I became a lead pastor at twenty-three years old. Whatever people saw on the outside, on the inside I had no idea who I was or what I was doing. For years, I struggled to harmonize my internal insecurity with my external need to lead with confidence and authority. Although I was always surrounded by close friends and people I love, I couldn't help but feel isolated. When you only let people see a fraction of your true self, you come to feel like nobody knows *you*—only the sanitized version you present.

Like me, many leaders treat loneliness as an unwelcome visitor. Others, however, welcome it as a professional necessity in a corporate world dominated by ambition and competition. Thanks to years of practiced detachment and the relational fallout that comes with climbing the ladder, these leaders have drifted into a state of disconnected absence at work. At home, they experience more of the same. Sure, their families are still kicking around the house. But after years of playing second fiddle to Mom's or Dad's career, their kids and spouses might as well be living in another zip code. The dining room is quiet, the bedroom is frigid, and everybody goes about their own business. Home used to be a place to reconnect and engage; now it's a nonplace where they go to disengage their hearts and disconnect their minds. They want to reach out to that partner sitting on the other end of the couch, but they've either forgotten how or they lack the energy to even try. Leaders who find themselves here say things like

- My spouse doesn't understand what I put up with every day.
- My kids don't care whether I'm home or I'm gone.
- My house doesn't feel like a home anymore.

Of all the crowds to feel lonely in, this one hurts the most.

The Irony of Isolation

In December 2018, more than 2.3 billion people logged into Facebook. On average, users spend more than thirty minutes a day on the platform. If multiplied out over a lifetime, the average user will spend one year and seven months of their life on Facebook.[3] During that time, users are inundated with the billions of photos, videos, and posts shared every day. Thanks to Facebook, everybody's got an endless fount of opportunities to connect with friends, family, and that guy they ran track with in 1992.

Yet for all the connection we find on social media, we are in the midst of what former US Surgeon General Vivek H. Murthy calls a "loneliness epidemic." According to Murthy, "We live in the most technologically connected age in the history of civilization, yet rates of loneliness have doubled since the 1980s."[4] Social networks like Facebook are something of a false friend in this epidemic. According to a survey of nearly 2,000 young adults, increased social media usage tracked with *higher* levels of loneliness.[5] While more research needs to be done before we can positively say that social media *causes* loneliness, these numbers do highlight a troubling paradox: we're more connected than we've ever been, yet we still feel like we're all alone.

Shepherd, Heal Thyself?

Nowhere is our sense of isolation more pressing than in the church. As someone who spent the better part of two decades leading a multisite church movement and building a nationwide church network, I know exactly what it's like to sit in a crowded pew or stand in the spotlight and still feel as though you're alone. As I mentioned above, I have witnessed the pain of lonely leadership—in myself and others. I see it in its most acute form when another pastor's suicide hits the news. Often they are godly pastors who served their churches and families well. On the outside, they were surrounded by spouses and kids who adored them, elders who supported them, and congregants who clung to their every word. On the inside, they were just like the rest of us—broken, isolated, and afraid.

Scott Sauls, pastor of Christ Community Church in Nashville, provides a vivid example of a leader who decided to come out of hiding and describe the "nightmare" of living with debilitating anxiety:

> How bad was the living nightmare? I could not fall asleep for two weeks straight. Even sleeping pills could not calm the adrenaline and knock me out, which only made things worse. At night I was terrified of the quiet, knowing I was in for another all-night battle with insomnia that I was likely to lose. The sunrise also terrified me, an unwelcome reminder that another day of impossible struggle was ahead of me. I lost nearly thirty-five pounds in two months. I could not concentrate in conversations with people. I found no comfort in God's promises from Scripture. I was unable to pray anything but "Help" and "Please end this."
>
> Why would I tell you this part of my story? Because I believe—no, I am certain—that anxiety and depression hits ministers disproportionately. And a minister who suffers with this affliction, especially in isolation, is a person at risk. When I was in seminary, two pastors committed suicide because they could not imagine going on another day having to face their anxiety and depression. Both suffered with the affliction in silence. One wrote in his suicide note that if a minister tells anyone about his depression, he will lose his ministry, because nobody wants to be pastored by a damaged person.[6]

Pastors struggle mightily under the expectations of those they lead. Whether or not it's true of every congregation, the sense that nobody wants a damaged leader drives pastors into hiding from the very people God has given to help shepherd *them*. According to a 2015 study conducted by the Francis A. Schaeffer Institute of

Church Leadership Development, 52 percent of pastors surveyed felt they were unable to keep up with their church's expectations.[7] Roughly a third said they regularly contended with discouragement, depression, and despair. Fewer than half said they had at least one true friend whom they could trust. If this is true for "professional Christians," how much more should Christian professionals worry about isolation. The loneliness epidemic is real, and Christians are not exempt. If we're going to survive, we need to rediscover the deep human connection for which we were made.

Check Yourself: Current State of Vulnerability

As I will discuss further at the end of this section, vulnerability can be good. For now, let's look at some of your patterns and connections as they relate to vulnerability.

- When you feel shame, how do you disconnect from others? By withdrawing? Pretending that nothing happened? Refusing invitations to see friends? Making up excuses to stay away?
- What does connection look like for you? Joy? Duty? Obligation? Initiating events and activities?
- How have you defined safety? Where are your safe places?
- How have you defined security? Who makes you feel secure?

Conclusion: From Disconnection to Connection

In the next several chapters, we're going to look at what I describe as *otherfulness*. As we'll see in the coming chapters, human beings were made for others. Created in the image of God, we are wired for connection. We see that not only in Scripture but also in studies that show the harmful biological and sociological effects of isolation. Disconnected living is disembodied living; it violates our design. When God made the world, the only "not good" thing he saw was lonely Adam lumping about in the garden (Gen 2:18). So God made him a bride (Gen 2:21–22). When the Second Adam came into the world, God prepared him a bride as well: the church (Rev 19:6–10). In our new creation (2 Cor 5:17), God has removed the sinful barriers to connection and is stitching redeemed humanity back together (Eph 2:11–22). Because that's true, we can give up our rugged independence, rediscover the gift of interdependence, and lean into the blessing of tribes without succumbing to the idol of tribalism.

Otherfulness is our gift, but it's also a deep struggle for those who feel like they have the loneliest jobs in the world. I often meet with clients during the most difficult times of their professional lives. They're usually godly men and women—strong leaders at home, work, and church. More often than not, they regularly meet with peers for encouragement, accountability, and support. Yet as I soon learn in conversation, they tend to hold those groups at arm's length. The profound anxieties they carry with them seem off-limits in those spaces. They live in fear of being exposed, and for that reason they struggle to find the freedom offered in true otherfulness.

St. Augustine famously prayed, "You have made us for yourself, and our heart is restless until it rests in you."[8] We might say God has created us for each other as well. Our hearts are restless until they join others in the safety and security of our Father's loving embrace. We can't afford to hide any longer. We were never meant to live on our own. Leaders should know this better than anyone, for we rally people around a cause and shepherd them *together* toward a common vision of goodness and success. Too many of us have lost sight of our need for human connection. Only otherfulness can release us from this prison of our own making.

CHAPTER 23

The Case for Otherfulness

In the previous chapter, I mentioned the "epidemic of loneliness." According to a survey of more than 20,000 adults, alarming numbers of people struggle with loneliness (47 percent), isolation (43 percent), and a lack of meaningful relationships (43 percent). And 18 percent say they have *no one* they can talk to.[1] For public and personal health, research has shown that loneliness "is more harmful than not exercising, twice as bad as being obese, and about as bad as being an alcoholic or smoking a pack of cigarettes a day."[2] As if that weren't bad enough, loneliness is also considered a strong predictor of premature death.[3] Even if loneliness doesn't kill us as individuals, it might bankrupt our nation. According to AARP, Medicare spends an estimated $6.7 billion a year on expenses related to social isolation among older adults.[4]

The price and prevalence of loneliness should prompt us all to make a new friend today. But for leaders, this isn't just a personal problem. A recent survey from Totaljobs reports that three out of five employees feel lonely at work.[5] That means you don't have to head down to the neighborhood parish to find Eleanor Rigby; she's working in the office right next door. And the numbers say her loneliness is probably stressing her out (68 percent) and keeping her up at night (56 percent). To cap it off, there's only about a 10 percent shot she'd actually be willing to talk to you about her problem.

As Christians, that should bother us on a human level. As leaders, it should bother us on an organizational level as well. For one thing, loneliness and loyalty do not go hand in hand.[6] Disconnected employees are more likely to disengage and leave than their well-connected peers. Even if they don't bail on us, researchers from California State University, Sacramento, and Wharton have found that loneliness can impair job performance.[7] Whether or not we ourselves struggle with loneliness, our employees do. If we want to rehumanize the workplace and win the war on disengagement, then loneliness just might be our Bunker Hill.

A Friend Loves at All Times

Not a single reality TV show goes by without some contestant uttering, "I'm not here to make friends; I'm here to win." The workplace too has no shortage of rugged individuals who'd just as soon leave their social lives at the door. As great as professional detachment sounds in theory, the numbers suggest otherwise. According to Gallup's "State of the American Workplace," only 20 percent of employees have a best friend at work.[8] If that number were to jump to 60 percent, "organizations could realize 36 percent fewer safety incidents, 7 percent more engaged customers, and 12 percent higher profit."[9]

Gallup's numbers suggest that loyalty to the team means loyalty to the team's *members*: "When employees possess a deep sense of affiliation with their team members, they are driven to take positive actions that benefit the business—actions they may not otherwise even consider."[10] Interestingly, Gallup couches its findings not only in the data but in human nature: "To ignore friendships is to ignore human nature. Yet, many organizations continue to abide by policies that dissuade or flat out discourage people from socializing or becoming friends."[11] Once again, secular research is telling us something our Bibles have been telling us all along. When you dehumanize yourself and others by denying everyone's *social* nature, you cut people off from the *human* resources God has provided for everyone.

The Power of Peers

As we'll explore further in the next chapter, human beings are made for relationship. That's what Gallup "discovered." Guess what, leader. You're human too. The trouble is, leaders often stand apart from the organization by virtue of their unique position. If you're the only CEO, there's nobody else for you to lean on, not just for connection but for counsel and support. According to Leon Shapiro and Leo Bottary, "CEOs are faced with a singular reality: There are very few people they can rely upon for impartial advice."[12] While that's true, I wouldn't limit it to CEOs. Whether you lead from a traditional executive role or you occupy a singular role in a nonprofit or church, you might struggle to find someone to relate to.

In *The Power of Peers*, Shapiro and Bottary tell the story of Paul Caskey.[13] Fresh out of college, Caskey went to work for the struggling cosmetics manufacturer CCP. Within a few years, Caskey helped build the company up from $640,000 to $4 million in sales and, as his reward, earned the position of CEO. Not long after, CCP hit a production ceiling. Due to climate, the company had to shut down every summer. Unsure of what to do, Caskey approached his CEO advisory group. Upon hearing the problem, one of his peers raised a simple question: Is there anything else you could make during that time? Sure enough, there was. Long story short, Caskey expanded CCP's product line, eliminated the annual shutdown, and grew sales to $12.5 million. In all, Caskey's recognition that he needed *others* to help him both tripled his company's revenue and created 110 jobs in his community.

Missed Connections

Connecting is human, but not all connections are as they should be—especially when individual responsibility is sacrificed for the "wisdom" of a particular tribe. We only need to look to the Great Recession to see the perils of connection done wrong. Looking back, it's hard to fathom how *everyone* could have missed the shenanigans going on in the secondary mortgage market. The signs were written on the wall: sketchy mortgage lenders, poorly underwritten loans, the bundling of toxic assets. Yet it wasn't until the economy cooled, interest rates spiked, and whole swathes of homeowners began to default on their mortgages that people began to realize that an entire industry had collectively lost its mind in one of the worst cases of *groupthink* ever.

Groupthink is the inevitable result when people let their God-given desire for tribal connection devolve into tribalism (more on that in chapter 26). The opposite of *synergy*, groupthink happens when people seek harmony at the expense of creativity and competence. We expect group members to lift one another up, but as Cass Sunstein and Reid Hastie have argued, group members tend to *amplify* one another's errors rather than correct them.[14] The snowball effect looms large. Once the group latches on to one course of action, the momentum of the majority bowls over the cautious wisdom of the minority.

Conclusion

In the award-winning article, "The Psychological Price of Entrepreneurship," Jessica Bruder dispels the mythology around building a modern business: "Successful entrepreneurs achieve hero status in our culture. We idolize the Mark Zuckerbergs and the Elon Musks."[15] What we don't see, however, are the secret demons that hound many of our entrepreneurial heroes. Bruder goes on: "Before they made it big, they struggled through moments of near-debilitating anxiety and despair—times when it seemed everything might crumble." Every burgeoning leader's favorite slogan seems to be "Fake it till you make it," but in the daily practice of "faking it," we train ourselves to hold others at arm's length.

My friend and vulnerability partner Ryan West shared Bruder's article with me as we were both ramping up our businesses. When he did, Ryan made me promise that we'd always tell the truth in and about our work. Here's the truth: we all need friendships marked by commitment, trust, and authenticity. These core elements of otherfulness are the relational glue that not only wards off debilitating loneliness but also enables us to perform at our highest level. We probably didn't need social scientists to tell us as much, but the most obvious features of life often slip by unnoticed until someone points them out. Now that we've reminded ourselves of the "obvious" truths that loneliness is bad and the *right* kind of connection is good, it's time to discover *why* connection is good and what otherfulness looks like in the context of work and life.

CHAPTER 24

You Are Never Alone

There's nothing us red-blooded Americans love more than an inspiring yarn about our independence and the power of the individual. From Benjamin Franklin to Oprah Winfrey, our culture tends to idolize people who defy the odds, pull themselves up by their bootstraps, and climb the ladder from rags to riches. As a result, something in us bristles at any attempt to rob our heroes of their credit. When naysayers attribute our heroes' successes to lucky breaks or shady deals, we quickly defend them. When political candidates suggest that some program had more to do with their rise to the top than skill, we take offense. "Yes, they *did* build that," we protest. And when we look at our own lives and businesses, we too are their architects.

That's all good and true, but when we take responsibility and elevate our stories to the level of mythology, we trade the truth for a lie. We trick ourselves into believing we've gone it alone this whole time and that the only way forward is to stick to the solitary path. But as Joshua Wolf Shenk demonstrates in his book *Powers of Two*, the idea of the "lone genius" is a myth that has been dominate so long that we no longer question it.[1] But as Shenk convincingly shows, every Warren Buffett has his Charlie Munger, and without John Lennon, Paul McCartney would have been just another teenager with a goofy haircut. We're right to admire exceptional individuals, but we're crazy to think they made it to the top on their own.

The same is true for each one of us. Think about

- that coach who pushed you to run the extra mile,
- that professor who took the time to make sure you got the material,
- that boss who encouraged you to set your sights higher, and
- that friend who wouldn't let you give up.

From the parents who gave us life to the customers or congregants who consistently show up and everyone in between, there's no such thing as a self-made man or woman. And there's no shame in that. It's a basic part of what makes us human.

We're Made for Each Other

When the Bible talks about our creation in the image of God, it doesn't single out an individual and say, "*That one* is my image." Instead, Genesis says that male *and* female together are created in the image of God (Gen 1:27). There's an organic relation here; while we can refer to an individual as one of God's images, it's only in connection with others that the image is most fully and truly expressed. Relationship is at the heart of what it means to be human. It bears repeating: the only not-good thing God saw in his creation was Adam *sans* Eve. Similarly in the New Testament, salvation is a *corporate* reality: we are made and *remade* for communion with God and one another. Our myths of self-making run contrary to our creaturely design.

The consequences of that myth aren't just damaging to our spiritual lives; they are reflected in our bodies as well. In *The Power of the Other*, Henry Cloud tells the story of a Navy SEAL who nearly drowned in training.[2] It was the end of "Hell Week," and Bryce was on the last leg of an ocean swim when his body hit a wall. His spirit was willing, but the sailor's flesh was weakened by the intense demands of training. As he began to sink, Bryce caught eyes with Cloud's brother-in-law Mark, pumping his fist from the shore. In that wordless exchange, *something* happened, and Bryce found the strength to continue. Reflecting on the story, Cloud asks, "How can something as immaterial, invisible, and mystical as an emotional connection with a buddy have what amounts to a material, measurable, and physical effect like fueling a body across space and physical boundaries?"[3] This, Cloud says, is "the power of the other," and it's one of the most mysterious facts of life.

Check Yourself: Self-Compassion Scale

Dr. Kristin Neff and Dr. Christopher Germer have done work on self-compassion. To begin provoking deeper self-compassion and creating stronger ties with people, answer these questions daily and plan your day with them in mind:

- How can I be more mindful today (e.g., balanced in my emotions and thoughts)?
- How can I be less fixated and obsessive today in my feelings, thoughts, and actions?
- How do I remind myself that I am a part of a community and that I have a place in it?
- How can I recognize my common humanity and that everyone fails?
- How can I practice being kind to myself?
- How can I be less judgmental of my experiences?

What Our Bodies Think about Disconnection

In the book *Loneliness*, neuroscientist John T. Cacioppo offers an account of embodied social connection.[4] Loneliness, he says, is a biological trigger. Just as hunger pains get us to make a sandwich, loneliness tells us to find a friend. But why should our bodies care whether we're lonely? According to Cacioppo, the loneliness trigger kept our earliest ancestors from getting picked off by wild animals and rival tribesmen. Like a biological Jack Shephard, the trigger speaks this practical truth: "If we can't live together, we're going to die alone."[5] The cortisol released by this trigger revs our engines into "the red zone." That's a good place to be when we're in danger of being eaten or beaten. But if we stay fully revved, our immune systems, sleep patterns, and cognitive functions begin to decline.

Christians may want to think carefully about Cacioppo's evolutionary narrative about prowling sabretooth tigers and prehistoric herding. Even so, his jumping-off point is the observable effect of loneliness on our bodies. If human beings are made for relationship, then why wouldn't we expect our bodies to react adversely in the absence of meaningful connection? If we set aside forms of dualism in which the "real me" is an immaterial soul trapped inside this material body, then we might realize that loneliness truly is "bad for us" in every physical, spiritual, and psychological sense of those words.

Otherful Connection: To Speak and Be Spoken To

The loneliness trigger warns us that something has gone wrong; we've wandered from the "herd" and need to find our way back. In God's design, however, otherfulness has to do with far more than strength in numbers. Unlike animals, we are made to communicate with one another. From the same Latin root where we get the word *community*, communication literally means to make something (a thought, emotion, perspective, etc.) common between two or more people. While chimps and dogs can certainly communicate in a plethora of audible and inaudible ways, only human beings can share (i.e., make common) one another's longings, fears, anxieties, and joys in prose, poetry, and song. Overcoming loneliness, then, is about more than simply getting around other people. Every leader who has felt alone in a crowded room can tell you that. Otherfulness is about communication—the *sine qua non* of human existence.

We encounter this from the very beginning. Unlike the animals, God created human beings with a unique capacity to speak.

In naming the animals, Adam takes his first stab at communication (Gen 2:19–20). Only, in that project, we learn that Adam couldn't find himself a true dialogue partner among the animals. For that, he needed another image bearer (Gen 2:21–22). As the story unfolds, the dialogue goes horribly wrong. God had spoken a good word: "Don't eat from the tree." But when the Serpent showed up and spoke a twisted word, everything began to unravel. Instead of listening to God by way of her husband, Eve followed the Serpent's darkened advice. And rather than listening to God and speaking up for what he knew was right, Adam listened to the Serpent by way of his wife. The rest, we could say, is history.

If the fall is our primordial breakdown in communication, then Jesus is the incarnate Word who permanently restores both humanity's dialogue with God and our individual communication with one another. The confusion of Babel has been mended by the Spirit of Pentecost. Over and over, the New Testament calls us not merely to imbibe the truth but to recite it *in community* (see, e.g., Eph 5:15–20). In our holy conversation we experience saintly communion. By "speaking the truth in love," we grow into the mature body of Christ (Eph 4:15–16). As image bearers, we were made for it. As Christians, we're called to live in the embodied otherfulness of restored humanity as the world watches.

Conclusion

Speaking the truth in love sounds good on Sunday mornings, but how can leaders embody otherfulness outside the church? We find an apt example in the well-known encounter between King David and the prophet Nathan (2 Sam 12). After David slept with Bathsheba and sent her husband Uriah to be killed in battle, God appointed Nathan to rebuke the king. Rather than burst into his chamber with a prophetic ribbing, Nathan told his adulterous friend a story. By the end of Nathan's tale, David's eyes were opened to what he had done. Like Jesus, Nathan embodied the truth and spoke it in love, holding David to account in the best way he could.

Like David, we're all prone to isolation and self-justification, especially when we've strayed from the straight and narrow. And like David, we all need someone to not only speak the truth to us but to help us get up when we've fallen. We need that buddy standing far off on the shore, pumping his fist to spur us on just as we start to sink. It's time to fight back against the myth of self-making and embrace otherfulness in community as the path to full presence in this world.

You Are Never Alone

Principle: The myth of self-making contradicts God's relational design for human beings. Leaders can't learn humanity and presence in isolation. We *need* others to know and love us even as we know and love them.

Practice: Jot down a list of five friends you can call at any time of the day. Embrace these names as your lifeline to otherfulness. Call them often, if only for a few minutes at a time. Share your struggles. Invite their correction. Solicit their prayer. These are the people who've made you. They're the ones who will gently remind you of the truth: "*I* didn't build that. By the grace of God, *we* did."

CHAPTER 25

The Journey from Dependence to Interdependence

M eet Jill. Ten years ago, Jill started a custom screen printing company. Today, her company does over $8 million in annual revenue and employs more than fifty people. Even so, Jill isn't what you'd call a model leader. Working upward of eighty hours a week, she lives on the edge of burnout. Work friends are few and far between. In fact, her employees have learned to steer clear of her as much as possible. Jill doesn't mind; she prefers to be alone. Staff meetings are as terse as they are tense: "Hurry up so I can get back to my desk." The business is doing great, but Jill is exhausted. She knows she can't keep this up, but she doesn't know what to do or who to talk to.

Jill came by her independence honestly. Her dad left when she was too young to remember, and her mom spent most of her time struggling just to keep food on the table. Thanks to her mother's three jobs, Jill learned how to survive on her own. She never asked for help because she knew it would never come. At home and in school, she simply found a way to continue. In college, she kept to herself and carved out her own path to the top of the class. Business school was more of the same. If the idea of the "self-made woman" wasn't a myth (see chapter 24), Jill would be a prime example.

Dependence: Humans in Immature Relation

Jill is strong and independent—traits we generally admire in leaders. But in her learned independence, she's forgotten what it means for human beings to depend on one another. She needs a reminder, and the best place to find it just might be in a bit of *literal* navel-gazing. Have you ever considered what your belly button might have to say about the fabric of human existence? Strange question, I know. But that little notch in our bellies shows us that we are radically dependent beings. From the moment of conception, we have relied entirely on someone else. Even outside the womb, infant cries testify to that inescapable dependence. While all this seems patently obvious at the level of bubble baths and baby formula, we often miss the impact of relationships on developing infants. When the bond between a baby and caregiver is broken, the child will not only fail to thrive physically, but the seeds of otherlessness will take root as the brain prepares to cope with a life of social isolation.

The intimacy of mother and newborn reminds us that God made us to live in relationship. The neurological trauma of that severed bond reminds us that, in this fallen world, all is not as it should be. As we'll see below, human beings were made to rely upon one another (interdependence), but our brokenness complicates that reality. On one end of the spectrum, broken bonds sever our healthy sense of dependence and, like Jill, predispose us for a life of unhealthy independence. On the other end, we settle into our dependence and fail to launch out on our own. A three-year-old's reliance on his parents for food and shelter is as it should be. A thirty-year-old's refusal to leave their basement is a travesty. A five-year-old's need for parental approval is a normal feature of natural development. A fifty-year-old's inability to construct a stable identity—ideally in Christ—is a tragic falling-short of all she was made to be.

Check Your Dependence

As a leader, who and what do you depend on to satisfy your physical, spiritual, and emotional needs? Do you treat your spouse like a glorified servant? Are you looking to your pastor or small group leader to do your "spiritual work" for you? Do you need your subordinates to approve of everything you say in order to validate your worth as a leader? Is your sense of identity wrapped up in the market's response to your latest launch? Are you looking to your children to provide you with your ultimate sense of meaning? If any of these things are true, then it's possible that sin and brokenness have taken the blessing of otherful connection and deformed it into otherless dependence.

Independence: Humans in Isolation

So far, Jill has served as an example of independence prompted by a broken childhood home. But what about those who grew up with parents they could depend on? How can an unbalanced sense of independence grow out of a "normal" upbringing? One answer to that question comes from teenage brain chemistry research. According to psychiatrist Daniel Siegel, the impulsiveness, addictive behavior, and hyperrationality that mark out the quintessentially American teenager come from "shifts in the brain's structure and function during the adolescent period."[1] While dopamine plays an important role in this process, the behavior has less to do with "raging hormones" and more to do with teenagers' attempts to navigate the neurochemical realities of developing cognition, sociality, and creativity. Their brains are telling them they're ready for independence even though their actions scream otherwise.

We misinterpret teenagers' brain chemistry, says Siegel, when we take adolescence as a trial to be endured rather than a teaching moment to be embraced. Instead of being told to "grow up," teenagers need us to put on our best Solomon impression, inviting them to listen to their fathers' instruction and not forsake their mothers' teaching (Prov 1:8). This means accepting their adolescence as the fumbling attempt at adulthood that it is. It also means recognizing that a driver's license, summer job, and a college admissions letter does not prove that they are ready to strike out on their own—at least not entirely. Rather, teenagers need to learn what it looks like to differentiate themselves without losing a sense of that healthy dependence that marks every human relationship.

Like too many teenagers in our country, Jill had to grow up too fast—at home and at work. In many ways, so have we. At work especially, the state of leadership development highlights a sad reality: junior leaders are being thrown into the fire with little to no mentorship. This is a real problem among businesses right now; one of the top requests Leadership Reality gets is to help organizations identify and develop emerging talent. While you'd be hard-pressed to find an executive who doesn't admit the crucial need for leadership-pipeline development, studies show that only 19 percent of organizations would say they're "very effective" at growing young leaders.[2] Like a pack of dopamine-laced teenagers, the next generation of leadership is being unleashed into the workforce and encouraged to figure everything out on their own. They're being trained for independence but have no real sense of when and how to depend on others.

Check Your Independence

Throughout this section, we've looked at the ironic pain of isolation (chapter 22), the human and business costs of loneliness (chapter 23), and the myth of our rugged individualism (chapter 24). Jill is a common example of what it looks like when we wall ourselves off from human connection and commit ourselves to independence and isolation. How have you isolated yourself? Where have you cut ties instead of cementing bonds? What secrets are you keeping that need to be told? Do you have people you can call when life seems to be going off the rails? Recall the advice I gave at the end of the last chapter: Who can you talk to *right now*? If you don't have a list of five people you can chat with for five minutes to help you reconnect, then now is the time to begin cultivating those friendships.

Interdependence: Humans in Mature Relation

Human beings are made for connection; that's the essence of otherfulness. But what does that connection entail? Surely, we don't want to be *that* guy or gal who can't make a single decision without picking up the phone to call Mom and Dad. At the same time, we want to honor and value our parents' opinions highly enough to realize we should probably pick up the phone more often than we do. The myth of self-making tells us to cherish independence and cast off every restraint as we charge to the top. But if we cut a path alone, we'll soon realize that the top is incredibly lonely. There, where we need others the most, we'll learn that a lifetime of self-reliance has rendered us wholly incapable of finding the help we desperately need from others.

As a community being remade together in the image of God by the power of the Spirit, Christians are called to resist a life of otherless independence. The many "one another" passages sprinkled throughout the New Testament presuppose a living and loving relationship of giving and taking. We are members of one another, called to bear with one another in love, kindness, tenderheartedness, and forgiveness (Eph 4:1–32). But even as we bear each other's burdens, we recognize that we will each have to bear our own burden before the Lord in the end (Gal 6:1–5). Healthy dependence doesn't mean codependence; we have a responsibility to one another and to ourselves. In sum, we're called to interdependence—a life of communal participation that knows when to stand apart and when to sit within.

Conclusion: Cultivate Interdependence

For most leaders, dependence isn't the struggle; "dependent leader" almost seems like a contradiction. If you're reading this book, then I'd guess something in you resonates with Jill's story. At this point, I hope you've seen that isolation contradicts your God-given design. The following chapter looks at a concrete way to practice otherfulness in the workplace. But cultivating interdependence requires more than a trick here and a tactic there. Otherfulness is a skill learned in the ebb and flow of ordinary life in connection with others.

What's your life like at home? Can you and your spouse depend on one another? How connected are you to a church? How often do you share your needs or ask for help? On the flip side, are you hearing the needs of others and offering your time and resources to fulfill them? These everyday acts of mutual dependence challenge our ingrained penchant for independence and train our hearts, minds, and bodies to reach out to others. There's no better way to cultivate the interdependence for which we were made and remade than to participate in the body of Christ. In the next chapter, we'll consider what that might look like for a leader today.

The Journey from Dependence to Interdependence

Principle: Unbalanced dependence and independence distorts our social reality. God made us for both: to lean on and be leaned on in otherful interdependence. We do that by loving others through concrete acts of service and allowing them to serve us in return.

Practice: Find an opportunity to serve someone this week. Mow the neighbor's lawn, bring a meal to an elderly member of your congregation, or volunteer at a rescue mission. When you do, take time to connect with the people you're serving. Let these moments remind you how much we all need one another.

CHAPTER 26

Tribes Without Tribalism

In Okinawa, Japan, the average life expectancy for a woman is about ninety years. That's eight years longer than the average American female.[1] Not only do Okinawans live longer, but they live *better* into old age,[2] enjoying late-life independence and low rates of heart disease, cancer, diabetes, and stroke.[3] Dan Buettner—a National Geographic fellow devoted to understanding the world's longest-living people groups—attributes a good part of the Okinawans' longevity to a distinct social practice called *moai*.[4] The word *moai* means something like "meeting for a common purpose," and it describes small groups of Okinawans assembled into communities. Unlike your home group Bible study, the *moai* stretches from the cradle to the grave. Traditionally, children are put into a group shortly after their birth. About half of the people on the island participate in a *moai*, and many have more than one. Some groups have lasted as long as ninety years with members meeting regularly for social, financial, and emotional support.[5]

Another word for the *moai* is "tribe." Whether it's our nuclear family or a group of college friends, we all belong to one tribe or another. There's no avoiding it; for as long as there have been people, there have been tribes. For the majority of human existence, these have centered on biology and geography. But thanks to the internet, people can now form tribes around *anything*—from ethnic identity to a mutual admiration for the '90s movie *Hackers*. This boundlessness is both a blessing and a curse. For leaders specifically, tribal insight is crucial to understanding how creating a leadership tribe can drastically impact our lives and performance. But before we can learn how that works, we need to learn what tribes are, how we screw them up, and what we can do better.

Ground Yourself: Who's in Your Tribe?

Take in slow cleansing breaths as you think about your tribe.

- Notice what needs you have today. How would you ask for help meeting those needs?
- How do you think your tribe would respond to your needs?
- Would they meet your needs or blow them off?
- Do you need to add others to your community so that you have people in your life who are attentive to your needs?
- Who in your tribe needs something that you can help with?
- Are you offering help? If so, how does it feel?

The Power of Tribes

In the book *Tribes*, Seth Godin draws on the power of the tribe to describe leadership. According to Godin, "One of the most powerful of our survival mechanisms is to be part of a tribe, to contribute to (and take from) a group of like-minded people."[6] This desire for belonging explains why people rally around charismatic leaders, especially when the ideas they present are new and exciting: "Heretics are the new leaders. The ones who challenge the status quo, who get out in front of their tribes, who create movements."[7] When it comes to competition between ideas, "the best one doesn't necessarily win. No, the idea that wins is the one with the most fearless heretic behind it."[8] The thought is much the same as the one behind primal leadership (see chapter 19): ideas matter, but the most effective leaders are those who capture people's hearts.

For Godin, all that is meant as an encouragement for leaders to embrace their sense of purpose, form a tribe of passionate believers around their cause, and change the world for the better. A decade after it's writing, though, the tribal idea has become dangerous. Thanks to increased polarization, identity politics, and the rise of domestic terrorism, tribes have come to represent the fringes of society led by some of the most detestable characters. When we think of tribes, we can't help but think of *tribalism* and the weaponization of social identity. On cable news, tribalism is the source of endless bickering, name-calling, and cynicism. In the real world, it's the source of outright racism, campus censorship, and lone-wolf terrorism. Okinawan *moai* notwithstanding, it seems we'd be better off if we just let the idea of the "tribe" go.

Redeeming the Tribe

It's easy enough to see tribalism at work in the internet troll who hurls racial epithets on Facebook. It's not so easy to see it in our own leadership. In chapter 2, I shared the story of Ron Johnson's meteoric rise at Apple followed by his catastrophic fall at JCPenney. As we saw, Johnson strutted into the retail space with the absolute confidence that what worked for Apple would work for JCPenney. Well, he came from the tribe of Apple located in the heart of Silicon Valley, and as far as he was concerned, his tribe knew best. It wasn't long before Johnson learned that the outsized influence of his tribe had put him completely out of touch with market reality.

So far, things aren't looking good for the tribe. But, whether we call it by that name or another, the idea of a tribe drives us back toward the social nature of human existence. The error of tribalism is that it tends to dehumanize whoever exists outside the tribe. The opposite, yet equal error would be to deny the impact of tribes and pretend as though we could discipline ourselves into some mythical tribeless existence—as if we were the only truly unbiased and neutral observer in the world. Sorry, folks, but that isn't going to happen. We all come from *somewhere*, and we can't help but see the world from our own social and cultural vantage point. That's not a bad thing; it's a *human* thing.

The question isn't whether tribes are a good thing or not. The question is: do we do tribes well? Taking this all the way down into your personal life as a leader, what tribes are you a member of? Beyond your family, where do you go to belong? Is it your church, small group, or that group of guys you watch football with on Sundays? Maybe it's that handful of people you volunteer with down at the rescue mission on Saturday mornings. Or maybe it's that circle of younger women you've been mentoring. Whoever it is, these tribes are essential to rounding out your life as a *human*. And, as we're about to see, they're the key to bringing out your best as a *leader*.

Find or Create Your Own Leadership Tribe

I'm going to keep banging this tribal drum because it's *that* important. Whether you call it a tribe, a peer-to-peer group, or a coaching network, every leader needs a crew of fellow travelers to grow, challenge, and support us. To become our best selves at home and at work, we need the safety, vulnerability, and accountability these kinds of groups provide. Unfortunately, when I ask leaders about their crew, the answer I often hear is, "I don't have one." Look, I'm all for more coaching, advising, and development, but even the best coach or consultant can never replace a tight-knit crew.

At its most basic level, I'm talking about friendship here. Friendships are grounded in trust, authenticity, and commitment. They're forged through a sense of mutual safety; we can be real with one another without fear of rejection. A true friend is loyal; they stick by your side in the best of times and the worst of times. With your crew, you can take off your mask and *be* who you are, when you are, where you are, and how you are. Your husband or wife can't do that work—at least, not all on his or her own. Whenever somebody tells me their spouse is the only friend they need, I bristle. Spouses are perhaps our most important friends, but they can't be our *only* friends.

Leaders need friends at both the personal and professional level. As we saw in chapter 23 with the case of Paul Caskey and his CEO advisory group, every leader needs his or her own leadership tribe. Friends are indispensable, but you need a group of people who know what it's like to lead and how specifically to encourage you, lend support, and hold your feet to the fire. In this intentional setting, "you'll be asked the hard questions—questions from people who know what it's like to sit in the CEO's chair, are blind to sacred cows and have no tangible self-interest in the outcome."[9] The critical distance involved in a leadership tribe like this allows you to get vulnerable without fear and to receive *real* advice without having to worry about organizational politics.

If you don't already have this tribe, either find or make one. Look for people you can trust to share your experience. In *The Power of the Other*, Henry Cloud describes the ideal partner for this tribe in terms of a "Corner Four" relationship. Unlike corners one, two, and three, which respectively describe leaders who isolate, self-flagellate, or self-congratulate, a corner four leader seeks out true and meaningful connections (i.e., interdependence). These relationships, Cloud says, are marked by mutual understanding, intentional support, ability to help, firm character, and a demonstrable record of positive results. Who are the people in your life who fit that description? Grab your phone right now, invite them to lunch, and start working out a plan for how you can team up to encourage and support one another in the future.

Conclusion

In this chapter, we've taken a brief look at tribes—the good, the bad, and the ugly. We can't escape our tribal reality. It's up to us, however, to embrace the power of the tribe as a force for good in our lives as well as the lives of the people we lead. Tribes are a social venue for human flourishing; it's only when the tribe descends into trib-alism that we turn something God-given and good into something inhuman and vicious. If we refuse to turn our tribes into a venue for dehumanization, we can redeem the tribe and lean into it as an on-ramp to fuller, more *human* living.

Tribes Without Tribalism

Principle: Humans are tribal creatures. Leaders need to understand their tribal relationships and leverage them for their good and the flourishing of those they desire to lead.

Practice: Write up an inventory of fellow leaders from *outside* your company who meet Cloud's requirements for a corner four relationship. Invite them out to breakfast for an informal mastermind. Gauging their interest, see if you can formalize the gathering into an advisory group that meets once a month.

CHAPTER 27

The Blessing of Otherfulness

Are you tired? Lonely? Stressed out? Has your drive for independence cut you off from the world? Are you lacking a deep connection with the people around you? When we met Jill in chapter 25, her answer to all those questions was definitely yes. Schooled by years of fierce independence, she found herself walking a plank of her own making, ready to plunge into the abyss of complete and utter breakdown. What would change if Jill stopped going it alone?

From Otherlessness to Otherfulness

In this section, we've learned that God has created us for otherfulness—a relationship of vibrant interdependence with the people around us. When we go it alone, we force ourselves to do something we were never designed to do, and we deny the blessings found in human collaboration. We tell ourselves we can survive better alone, but in reality we cut ourselves off from the social resources we need to perform our best. Then we reap the physiological consequences of otherlessness in our bodies. What will we do? Will we allow ourselves to drift toward isolation, or will we fight back?

You Were Made for Others

What does your social life look like right now? Do you have one? Or do you feel like you're living and working on a desert island? If that's you, don't try to knuckle through it alone. If you're drowning, you need a buddy to pump his fist from the shore. Who is that faithful friend? Even if it's been a while, pick up the phone and reach out. Grab on to your Nathan and hold on for dear life. If you don't know who that is or if you can't find someone, start by *being* that person yourself. If you were made for others, then others were made for you. Somebody needs your words as much as you need theirs. Come out from the shadows.

Depend and Be Depended Upon

As strong, independent leaders, we tend to value self-reliance above all else. As a result, we often don't know what to do with dependence. At best, we strive to be reliable to everyone else—even while we refuse to ask for help. At worse, we project our independence onto everyone else and create a culture where *help* becomes a four-letter word. In chapter 25, we learned that the authentic, connected life for which we were made includes both dependence and independence in healthy measure. As human beings, we discover our truest freedom in interdependence. One of the best gifts you could give an employee is the encouragement to discover his or her limits in an environment where asking for help is not only encouraged but celebrated.

Lean On Your Tribe

Life is tribal. We can never transcend the circles of friends, family, neighbors, and coworkers who've made us into the people we are today. The question is: Do we do tribes well? Do we see the effect our tribes have on us, and do we value the goodness of those tribes to which we don't belong? As leaders, we must shepherd our organizational tribe, along with all its little subtribes, toward excellence. For that, we need help, not just from the people in our everyday lives but from other leaders who've been where we've been and seen what we've seen. Do you have a group like that? If not, then for the sake of yourself and the people you lead, get one.

Imagine Yourself: Perception Is Reality

You can impact your reality by changing your perception of reality. To see how, walk through this exercise:

- Consider how you would like to be perceived in an ideal relationship. List the characteristics you'd like someone to use to describe you.

- How do you not want to be perceived? List the ways you do not want to be described.

- Choose someone in your family or at work that you have a hard time relying on. Now imagine that person telling friends about you with all the positive characteristics you listed.

Sabbath: Rest in the Presence of the Other

God has made us for one another. More importantly, God has made us for himself. God is the ultimate other, our heavenly Father who wants nothing more than to call us into fellowship with him through the preeminent otherfulness of his Son and the ministry of his Spirit. In Christ's self-sacrifice, we see the epitome of love and connection. In communion with his body, we have the demolition of every social, cultural, racial, and political wall that would divide us from our brothers and sisters. By his Spirit, we are being made and remade for love in perfect community. This is more than a common project for God's people; it is his covenant promise and gift of his grace.

> **Stop:** Embrace sabbath as an invitation to quit trying so hard to make it on your own. Unplug from the pressures that encourage you to hide. Retreat from isolation and find solace in the company of people you can trust.
>
> **Trust:** Stop trying to be the "lone genius," and rest in the fact that you were never meant to go it alone. Don't treat solitude as a permanent way of life. Instead, use it as a temporary retreat to meditate and contemplate your radical dependence.
>
> **Enjoy:** Celebrate the fact that God has made you for others and others for you. The game of life isn't meant to be played alone. Give praise to God for the gift of community and his invitation to live in the company of faithful friends.

Our Sabbath Feast

Last year, I sat down with my family on New Year's Day to discuss rhythms and goals for the coming year. As we talked about places to visit, restaurants to try, and technological boundaries to observe, my kids all spoke up for a tradition we'd let slide in recent years: "We want to throw more parties!"

So we started putting together what we call "sabbath feasts." We set aside one Sunday per month and invited fifteen or twenty families over to the Montgomery house. Each month, we picked a theme connected to the liturgical calendar—with the exception of a Kentucky Derby/Cinco de Mayo mashup in May. Every dinner began with a few liturgical readings, prayer, and communion. Once we were done feasting on Christ together, we'd open up the party for hours of food, conversation, and laughter.

At each sabbath feast, we set ground rules for all our guests: (1) stop working, (2) unplug from technology, and (3) bring something to share. Why the rules? As much as these feasts were about having a good time, they were also about disconnecting from the digital and analog pressures of modern life. Selfishly, I needed to get real with people—to engage in otherful presence without the constant temptation to drift back into worldly absence. It turns out, others needed the exact same thing. After a recent feast, a friend and fellow entrepreneur sent me this message: "Just wanted to say that this last week was one of the crappiest weeks I've had in a while. Was pretty depressed, but after tonight I feel like I'm ready to take on Everest (or maybe a 2-mile trail run). Either way, I'm ready to go. Thank you."

We can't go it alone, no matter how hard we try. More often than we realize, the thing we need most isn't a thing at all; it's a person. God has made us for himself and for others. Our hearts will always be restless until we find rest in him. In our darkest moments of anxiety, fear, and worry, we can *rest* in knowing the Lord of the sabbath has bound himself to us for all of eternity. We are never alone; it's time to start living like it.

Mindfulness of Others

After two DUIs in three months, James, a successful finance executive, called my office hoping to expunge his record by pursuing treatment and therapy. During our first appointment, James admitted that he couldn't tell anyone besides his wife and business partner what had happened.

Like many others, James's life didn't start out this way. He grew up on a farm, and as an adult he was committed to living near extended family, work, his kids' school, and his neighborhood. But as his business, wealth, and collection of vintage hot rods grew, he justified moving across town to a gated community with neighbors he never had the time to meet. James's daily life slowly drifted away from family get-togethers to late nights at work while his kids shuttled themselves around to activities and social events. The exchange seemed sensible until James was forced to reevaluate his isolated state and saw how unmanageable his life had become.

Are you like James, feeling like you never have enough time for yourself, your work, *and* meaningful connections?

Vulnerability Is a Strength

If American individualism leads us to isolation, what guides us toward mindful and meaningful relationships? How do you measure who is a healthy, autonomous, securely attached adult?

The framework we will use to track healthy development has

three main stages. In *dependence*, from birth to age eleven, our survival depends completely on others. Next, in *independence*, from ages twelve to twenty-four, children move toward autonomy, self-definition, and new attachments outside the home. Finally, *interdependence*, the end goal of human development, is a blend of dependence and independence. A healthy individual knows when help is needed and what can be done independently.

We see many Americans stuck in the second stage, independence, including many business leaders, because independence has become a cultural virtue and therefore has been promoted as a sign of strong leadership. In interdependence, however, vulnerability is no longer perceived as a weakness.

Let's talk a little more about vulnerability. Why do we believe having needs is bad? Why are we afraid to ask for help? Why do we think that being vulnerable is a weakness?

We come by our beliefs regarding vulnerability honestly, but we can change those beliefs by practicing vulnerability with others who we trust to offer attention and respond with nourishment. Vulnerability is very difficult for performance-driven types. Our society celebrates the expert and the perfectionist, which means we celebrate the invulnerable. This is how we, like James, drift into isolation. No one wants to admit their incompetence.

Yet we are wired for relationships. Everyone needs people to feel safe with, people from whom we can learn. Who are those people for you? If you don't have these people around you, eventually your false sense of competence will be exposed, and you will feel like a fraud.

Healthy vulnerability and true competence leads to healthy, secure relationship with those around you. Answer the following questions to help you identify the relationships you have in which it is safe to practice being vulnerable:

- Who do you keep close?
- Who is in your inner circle?
- Who do you go to for safe harbor?

- When you feel threatened, who can you go to?
- Who do you find a face-to-face connection with? (Who sharpens you? Someone who challenges you without it being threatening.)
- Who do you find a side-by-side connection with? (These are your ride-or-die friends, those who will walk with you no matter the consequences.)

Being in these vulnerable relationships requires saying no to some things to be present to those around you. Attune yourself to be mindful of overreactions or underreactions. We can't know the thoughts of others, but we can pay close attention to them.

Practicing Self-Compassion

Being present with others begins with practicing self-compassion. Knowing and being present to your body, emotions, and thoughts leads you to empathy. Naming how you suffer enables you to move from being a victim of your story to a survivor that can grow, heal, and build bridges of compassion for others.

Self-compassion leads to deeper connections with others. And when you approach relationships mindful of yourself and others, it leads to compassion, which in turn leads to kindness and, ultimately, to genuine connection.

STORY

ENCHANTED

STORY-
FUL-
NESS

DISEN-
CHANTED

DATA

CHAPTER 28

What's Your Story?

A young boy nestles into bed beside his mom as she tells him a story about a veterinarian named Harry Colebourn. World War I was raging in Europe, and Harry had volunteered to serve. On his way there, he came across an old trapper with a young bear. Concerned, Harry bought the cub and named her Winnie—short for Winnipeg. Before long, Winnie captured the hearts of Harry's entire company. But when the time came to head to the front, Harry knew what he had to do. So he took Winnie to the London Zoo where she would be safe. Soon enough, a little boy came to visit, and the two became fast friends. The boy's name was Christopher Robin Milne, and his friendship with that little black bear—along with a stuffed bear of his own, of course—is what inspired his father to create everyone's favorite bruin: Winnie-the-Pooh.

This is the story Lindsey Mattick tells in her children's book *Finding Winnie*. What makes the book so charming is the fact that *she's* the mother in bed at the beginning of it, and the little boy is her son Cole, named after his great-great-grandfather: Harry Colebourn. That makes this more than just a story about our favorite Bear of Very Little Brain. Rather, *Finding Winnie* is a story about legacy and identity. In it, we learn how the kindheartedness of one man ultimately brought joy to children around the world. More than that, we get to follow along as Cole learns his place in the story. Harry's future is Cole's past; Harry's legacy is Cole's identity. Those two poles—past and future—come together in the present when Lindsey snuggles with her little boy and uses a captivating "smackerel" of a story to tell him who he is.

What Does Pooh Have to Do with You?

Leadership development is a booming industry. Businesses spend more than $24.5 billion a year on an endless stream of counsel, advice, and tactics—all meant to train leaders for success.[1] As much as my team depends on the latest and best leadership tools, profiles, and assessments, I've found nothing more transformative than this simple question: What's your story?

Our stories define our reality. A leader's past shapes his or her sense of what's fake and what's real. The anticipated future invites leaders to imagine a reality not yet realized. Shaped by the past and imagined for the future, stories enable leaders to live and lead in the present. The mission of Leadership Reality is to help leaders give thanks for that three-dimensional story, use it to define their reality with hope, and empower others to do the same.

Every leader wants to tell a better story—to live a full and meaningful life. Like Harry, they want the choices they make to have a lasting impact. At the same time, they feel stuck. They're focused on the future, but their past won't stop rearing its ugly head. Their stories are full of guilt and shame, and they're not sure what to do with those emotions. They want to leave a legacy every bit as rich as Harry's, but they can't figure out who they are. In helping leaders wade through this complexity, I almost always find two existential questions swirling beneath the surface:

1. **Who am I?** This complicated question brings together a leader's entire life story. In an important sense, the project of this book has been to help leaders answer the who question in the most holistically human way possible.
2. **Why am I here?** Just as our actions reveal our hearts (Matt

12:35), our purposes flow from our personal identities. Until we discover who we are, we'll never grasp what we're meant to *do* at home, at work, and in our communities.

As I said early on, the central aim of this book is to help us become true "entrepreneurs of identity." But how do we do it? So far, we've considered the many ways time, place, body, and relationships make us who we are. But how in the world are we supposed to hold together all that complexity in our daily lives? How can we possibly keep track of when and where we are, what our bodies are saying, and what role our relationships play in the whole process? If you feel a bit dizzy right now, I don't blame you. As we'll see in this final section of the book, the answer to these questions is story. By embracing the shaping influence of our past and the imaginative power of the future, we can live and lead in the present for the glory of God and the good of everyone who comes into contact with the story he's telling in and through us all.

The Story We Live and the Story We Leave

Like little Cole, our stories tell us who we are. They are informed by the words others speak into our lives: "You've always been so creative," "You're a born leader," or "You were made to succeed." But really, our story is *our* story; the words of others contribute to the story we tell ourselves. Sometimes that story is positive and powerful. Other times, not so much. The stories we tell about ourselves and others have the power to shape and define our reality. If the primary story you tell is "I've always been a loser," then your interpretive framework will work against you. Unreturned phone calls, sideways glances, failed projects—they'll never point to anything but the simple fact that you're a loser, never mind the actual reasons behind those circumstances. If guilt and shame dominate your story, no amount of creative rewriting will get you past your past and into the future.

We need to own our life stories—to bring them into the light of day instead of hiding them in the shadows. Until we do, we will inevitably distance ourselves from the people around us and lead from a place of inauthenticity and fragmentation. Stepping out of the darkness is hard, but doing so enables us to walk in a light that not only shines in us but through us. These brilliant stories enlighten others' lives and end up getting told long after we're gone. As Brené Brown says,

> Owning our story can be hard but not nearly as difficult as spending our lives running from it. Embracing our vulnerabilities is risky but not nearly as dangerous as giving up on love and belonging and joy—the experiences that make us the most vulnerable. Only when we are brave enough to explore the darkness will we discover the infinite power of our light.[2]

Check Yourself: Stages of Acceptance

Reflect on the hard parts of your story. Where are you in the process (adapted from Kübler-Ross's five stages of grief) of accepting that these times are part of your story?

- **Denial:** not wanting to believe it's real
- **Anger:** feeling that it is unjust and should not have happened or be happening
- **Bargaining:** trying to make a deal to escape the reality
- **Depression:** having reality set in and feeling the impact
- **Acceptance:** acknowledging the reality of "what is"

The Authority and the Author

Brené Brown is right. We need to own our stories and let out that infinite light that dwells within. Paul had something similar to say to the Ephesians when they found themselves surrounded and enticed by darkness: "You were once darkness, but now you are light in the Lord. Live as children of light" (Eph 5:8). The key words are "in the Lord." As Christians, we confess that we're not the primary authors of our story. Like the moon reflecting the sun, the light we reflect must first come from another. We live, move, and have our being in God, the one who knit us together in our mothers' wombs and sketched out our lives before we took our first breaths (Ps 139).

As easy as it is to think of God as a cosmic authority, we forget that he is the *author* of all things—from the grand narrative of the entire universe down to the individual stories we live on earth (Ps 139:13–16). Not a sparrow falls to the ground without the Father's say-so (Matt 10:29). Our entire story—past, present, and future—is not a mystery to God but a gift of his creative goodwill. Our lives aren't "a series of random scenes that pile up like shoes in a closet."[3] They're a cohesive narrative of carefully crafted moments held together by the inscrutable wisdom of God. Because God is the true and proper author of our stories, we are called to lay our lives at his feet and trust him with our narrative. When we do that, as Dan Allender says, we can finally begin to "join God as a coauthor" in the story he's written, is writing, and will write through us.[4]

Step Into the Fullness of Your Story

In this section, I want to invite you into what I call *storyfulness*. On the one hand, storyfulness means a wholehearted embrace of our narrative. We don't revel in guilt or shame, nor do we run from it. Instead, we acknowledge the darkness, give it a place in our story, and offer it as evidence that we are no longer who we once were. On the other hand, storyfulness envisions the future. It recognizes that life is full of both pain and possibility and that it's just as pathological to disregard possibility as it is to avoid pain. In owning the past and anticipating the future, we're set free to live in the present. We don't obsess over what's already been written or experience crippling anxiety worrying over what's coming up ahead. Instead, we live in our story now, confident that our heavenly Author is working it out according to his perfect plan.

What's your story? What are your regrets? Which wounds do you carry? Which weakness crops up over and over again? How have you failed, and what have your failures taught you? What are your great victories? Which strength has carried you thus far? What do you value most? Why do you think God has you here now, and where do you think he's leading you next? These are *story* questions, and our answers to them can never be anything more than provisional so long as we still find ourselves in the middle of the story. In this section, we're going to descend deeper into narrative and, through it, discover why and how storyfulness will not only improve our lives but also benefit the people in our lives.

Ground Yourself: Everything Is as It Should Be

The creator of Dialectical Behavior Therapy (DBT), Marsha Linehan, defines suffering as the refusal to accept the pain in our lives. Most of our suffering is caused by the phrase we repeat in our minds, "This shouldn't be happening." However, if we can accept logically, given everything we know about life, our past, and so on, that life is as it *should* be, then we are able to accept the pain of it more easily. What is happening in your life now that feels like it shouldn't be happening? Has it caused you to suffer?

Here is a mindfulness practice that will help you accept life as it is and not as you think it should be:

- Focus on an object in the room.
- Breathe.
- As thoughts, emotions, sensations, or feelings emerge, silently repeat, "Everything is as it should be."

- Do this for three minutes.

This exercise demonstrates how easily your mind will drift away from the present and into the past or future. We must learn how to remain in the present with our whole being. Living in the past or future only increases our suffering, as we cannot control our circumstances in those realms. The past is complete, and the future is only influenced by present behaviors.

Conclusion

Who are you and why are you here? No two questions have ever been so simple yet so complex. We all want to be the hero of our own story. Like Harry Colebourn, we want to be the kind of people whose ordinary actions have such an extraordinary impact that their effects echo down the corridors of history. We want to be comfortable in our skin, to know who we are, where we've been, and what we offer the world. We want our legacy to help create someone else's identity. We want our story to not just be remembered but told and retold. But the only way to do that is first to remember it ourselves, to find our identity in the midst of our story.

In the book *To Be Told*, Dan Allender describes the power of story in his life. At the age of nineteen, Allender discovered that the man he grew up believing was his father was actually someone else. If you've read the opening chapter of this book, then you won't be surprised *why* I resonate so deeply with Allender. What matters most, however, is the fact that in finding peace with his story and its Author, Allender discovered *who* he was and *why* God put him on this planet. It's only fitting that this chapter closes with his stirring invitation to storyfulness:

Your story has power in your own life, and it has power and meaning to bring to others. I want your story to stir me, draw me to tears, compel me to ask hard questions. But your story can't do these things if you can't tell it. You can't tell your story until you know it. And you can't truly know it without owning your part in writing it. And you won't write a really glorious story until you've wrestled with the Author who has already written long chapters of your life, many of them not to your liking. We resist telling a story we don't like, and we don't like our own stories. But consider this: if you don't like your story, then you must not like the Author. Or conversely: if you love the Author, then you must love the story he has written for your life.[5]

CHAPTER 29

The Case for Storyfulness

Coury Deeb is a long-time friend, a fellow adventurer, and an award-winning documentary filmmaker. For fifteen years, his company, Nadus Films, has scoured the world looking for stories worth telling. "Good stories," Coury says, "are the byproducts of good leaders doing good." Retired Navy SEALs, Maasai warriors in Tanzania, fearless executives of Fortune 500 companies—these are just a few examples of leaders who risked everything to write the kind of story Nadus strives to tell. When leaders like these own their stories and tell them well, they invite others to see who they are, why they're here, and what they have to offer. Through Coury's cinematic eye, their stories become compelling films that impact lives, transform cultures, and drive financial returns.

As Nadus has proven time and again, a story well told is powerful beyond words. One of the easiest ways to glimpse that power is to look at the marketplace. Stories sell, and the stories that sell best invite us to find ourselves within them. People don't storm the Apple Store to buy their newest smartphone or tablet because last year's model suddenly stopped working. No, Apple tells a story about progress and identity, packaged in a sleek finish that screams status. We want the cool gadget, but even more, we want the story it helps us tell about ourselves. That's true whether we're talking about an iPhone, a BMW, or a Rolex.

If you're a leader, then your job is to influence people, to "sell" them a vision of the world and their place in it. Like a dishonest salesman, you *could* use the power of story to press emotional buttons and lead people wherever you want. However, a good leader knows that the best stories don't manipulate people but open their eyes to see what we can accomplish together. In business especially, stories inspire and unite us. They challenge us to embrace the truth about who we are as individuals and what we can do together. The leaders who own their stories and tell them with conviction have the power to improve people's lives—starting with their own.

The Stories We Embody

In 2002, a team of researchers from Yale published a study on the link between longevity and self-perception. From twenty-three years' worth of research, they found that participants who had a positive view of their aging lived 7.5 years longer than those who didn't.[1] In fact, they discovered that "self-perceptions of aging had a greater impact on survival than did gender, socioeconomic status, loneliness, and functional health."[2] Positive self-perception did more to impact longevity than low blood pressure and cholesterol, lower body mass index, nonsmoking, and exercise. The stories we tell ourselves about "getting older" affect how we experience old age—let alone whether we get there!

This isn't to say that we can add years to our lives by whistling a happy tune every time we spot a new wrinkle in the mirror. We don't create reality; only God can do that. But the stories we tell can either promote healthy contact with what's real or plunge us into a diseased form of virtual reality. As we see in Scripture, God has long given his people stories as a means of embracing the former while combating the latter. "Who are we and why are we here?" is the question every Israelite kid asked as his family gathered to slaughter their best lamb for Passover. God told their parents to answer with a story: "It is the Passover sacrifice to the LORD, who passed over the houses of the Israelites in Egypt and spared our homes when he struck down the Egyptians" (Exod 12:27). With these words, the strange imagery of hacked-up lambs, bloodied doorposts, and flattened bread made sense. The parents could say, "This is what it was like when God saved us. This is our story, and the ritualism is how we're stickin' with it."

In Israel, the yearly Passover wasn't merely about remembering the past but allowing it to shape the present. It was to be a sign on their hands and a memorial between their eyes "that the law of the Lord may be in your mouth. For with a strong hand the LORD has brought you out of Egypt" (Exod 13:9 ESV). On the night when Jesus was betrayed, he stood before his disciples and, in what would become the church's new Passover celebration, held up a sign, "This is my body. . . . This cup is the new covenant in my blood" (1 Cor 11:24–25). Once again, God was giving his people a symbol, a sign to participate in with their bodies and a story to tell one another until Jesus comes back. To this day, the Lord's Supper is a ritual and a story that defines our reality and empowers us to live as those redeemed.

Story as the Great Simplifier

In chapter 24, we looked at the story of David and Nathan (2 Sam 12:1–15). After David had impregnated another man's wife and tried to cover it up by sending him to his death, the prophet would've been well within his rights to berate his wayward king. He could've launched into a full-blown covenant lawsuit, laying out the Mosaic laws about adultery, murder, and godly kingship. But he didn't. Instead, Nathan told David a story, and by the conclusion, the king knew that he'd done wrong and what needed to happen next.

Stories are the most powerful communication tool we have. That's why, at its heart, the Bible isn't a divine handbook so much as it is a collection of narratives that all tell "one Big Story. The Story of how God loves his children and comes to rescue them."[3] But the communicative power of story isn't limited to the religious or the emotional sphere. If you run a quick search on Amazon, you'll find a raft of titles focused on the power of story as a communication tool in business. As Seth Godin has pointed out, the best marketers are storytellers—a point demonstrated by Apple, as I noted above.[4] But storytelling isn't only about selling; it's about communicating—using narrative to "make common" that which matters most. Like Nathan and David, stories enable us to convey more than we ever could in a mission statement or a corporate memo. In our work with executives, entrepreneurs, and small business owners, we've found that stories are the great simplifier. As we'll unpack in the following chapters, stories

- bring clarity out of complexity,
- translate our losses into lessons,
- turn our failures into findings,
- move strategy into reality, and
- create safety and vulnerability.

Leading with Reality

In *Leadership Mosaic*, I tell the story of Brené Brown and her 2010 talk at TEDxHouston.[5] As a shame and vulnerability researcher, Brown decided to take a chance and get personal. Despite a few reservations, she shared candidly about her nervous breakdown, spiritual awakening, and the time she spent in therapy. The next morning, Brown felt hungover: *"What did I do? Five hundred people officially think I'm crazy and it totally sucks."*[6] Much to her surprise, Brown's talk, "The Power of Vulnerability," created a viral frenzy online. As I write this, the video sits on TED's top five list with nearly forty million views.[7]

When I talk about vulnerability and getting real with stories, leaders often push back for fear that I want them to become touchy-feely with their workforce. Nothing could be further from the truth. Vulnerability isn't about emotional exhibitionism; it's about integrity. It's about getting straight on who you are and where you come from so you can lead from a place of convictional authenticity.

Owning our stories empowers us to be *who* we are, *when* we are, and *where* we are. Storyful leaders are eminently comfortable in their skin, and everyone around them knows it. These are the leaders who inspire, unite, and drive their organizations toward excellence.

When I walk leaders through their story, I challenge them to get honest about their past, excited about their future, and strategic about integrating those two perspectives to better live in the present. The tangible product of that intensive process is an executive presentation that reminds leaders exactly who they are and why they're here. As I've witnessed repeatedly, this process is business changing and life changing. Reconnecting leaders with their story and giving them the language to communicate that reality is the most powerful thing a coach could do for his executives.

Conclusion

Recently, our team met with a client to work out the agenda for a company-wide leadership development workshop. Early in the meeting, we learned our client was in the midst of an incredibly difficult season. They had just lost a handful of major accounts, profits had fallen through the floor, and positions were being eliminated left and right. Understandably, senior management wasn't as interested in working on leadership development as they had been when we initially signed our contract.

We knew we had to pivot, so I looked the CEO in the eye and asked him, "Have you been here before?" He blinked and nodded; this wasn't the first time he and his company had sailed through turbulent waters. I challenged him and his team to lean into the pain instead of running from or minimizing it. Doing so recast this difficult moment as just another episode in a decade-long, unfolding story. My team ditched most of our original material and crafted an executive storytelling session. When that CEO stood before his embattled workforce and shared the story of all the company had been through over the previous decade, the mood change was palpable. Despair gave way to resolve as employees reconnected with the bigger picture. They'd been here before, and together they could find the courage and resilience not only to make it through but to grow in the process.

Like a stone falling through a spider's web, stories cut through the tangled mess of life and business. They simplify complexity, clarify mission, and amplify engagement. They allow us to transcend the limitations of corporate doublespeak and cut straight to the heart of the matter. But before we can inspire and transform others, we need to see how the story we tell ourselves impacts the stories we tell others.

CHAPTER 30

The Stories We Tell Ourselves

W"ho are you?" is a question vague enough to irritate yet deep enough to send us into an existential tailspin. How do you answer that question? Maybe you rattle off a few words about your job. But is that really who you are? When you're gone, do you want your grown kids to remember you as executive vice president or as Grandpa? So maybe you have a few words to say about your family. Maybe that's who you are. But does that really pass the legacy test? We all want to be remembered for the mark we leave on those closest to us, but something in us longs to make a difference that goes beyond that.

The question "Who are you?" reaches deep into a mass of complexity that we can never sort out for ourselves. What brings together the many disparate strands of our identity—spouse, parent, sibling, leader, executive, volunteer, neighbor, friend—into one cohesive whole? By now, you can guess my answer: story. But as we'll see in this chapter, the stories we tell ourselves are often darkened and distorted by those parts of our narrative that we can't seem to get over.

Identifying The Contamination Narrative

In *The Power of Story*, Jim Loehr talks about the faulty assumptions we make that sabotage our lives. When many people tell their life story, it contains what Loehr calls "the contamination narrative."[1] It goes something like this: life was going great, something negative happened (divorce, illness, failure), and then everything fell apart. For many, the contamination narrative swallows up the rest of the story. Rather than owning that moment in the narrative, they spin out alternate plotlines to deflect the blame (she stopped trying, my employees just couldn't execute my vision) or to excuse themselves from the hard work of getting up off the mat (I'm damaged goods, I'll never get over this, I'm finished).

As Christians, we believe that everyone shares a primordial contamination narrative. Adam and Eve failed to listen to God, they lost their place in the garden, and we all ended up cursed in the process (Gen 3; Rom 5). Beyond that universal story, we each have a particular version of the contamination narrative, that moment or season when everything took a wrong turn. Many of us have more than one. Often, we look back and see it as a testimony to God's faithfulness. But for too many of us, we're still trying to get beyond the pain. We're in the thick of our contamination narrative, and no matter how much time we spend in the shower, we can't seem to get clean.

Ground Yourself: Name It to Tame It

Is there a story you have not told? Why have you been afraid to tell it? Can you write it down? Can you organize it by telling your thoughts, movements, urges, emotions, imagery, and sensations? Share it with someone safe.

A Pattern of High-Stakes Contamination

Earlier in the book (chapter 19), I introduced you to my friend Larry, to the run of health problems he and his wife faced, and to his realization that his body could no longer sustain his intense lifestyle. What caused Larry to push himself so hard on the bike and in his business? Part of the answer was a recurring contamination narrative. In seventh grade,

Larry learned the value of hard work when he helped with his father's construction business. He carried that work ethic with him to college and through his early career, consistently working longer hours than his peers. When he was twenty-seven, Larry went back to work with his father. Overleveraged and oppressed by high interest rates, the company needed a savior, and Larry thought he was the man for the job.

For the next three years, he managed construction projects by day and mastered the tax code by night. He sacrificed sleep to work on a financial model until finally it began to pay off in 1990. With his capital in place, Larry went on to build an empire. His company developed four thousand apartment units and expanded its staff to over three hundred employees. They were making money hand over fist, clearing out bad debts, and shoring up some of their shakier investments. But in 2003 Larry's armor began to crack. Several of his apartments began to underperform, and the management load became more than he could bear. Throughout his life, he'd taken to extreme sports as a way to manage the pain, but his body started to break down. Worse, so did his marriage.

Thanks to counseling, Larry and Janet survived this difficult season. Larry's company, on the other hand, did not. To avoid bankruptcy, he was forced to wind down the family business, dissolve more than twenty strategic relationships, and take an interim job until he could figure out what to do next. Although he didn't intend for it to happen, Larry soon found himself at the helm of another high-stakes development company, repeating the cycle of hard work and intense exercise that eventually led to our first meeting. He was broken down and ready to quit.

Redeemed to Tell a Better Story

Larry's story is like that of so many other leaders, contaminated by recurring cycles of intensity, anxiety, self-doubt, and addiction. He was a Christian during this time, but his drug of choice—adrenaline—kept him from identifying the contamination and bringing it into redemptive contact with God and God's story. In Jesus's encounter with the woman at the well, we get a paradigm example of what that redemptive contact looks like (John 4). Even though God knows our failures, he still invites us to take a swig of his living water. Later in John's Gospel, we learn that the living water Jesus has for us is none other than the Holy Spirit (John 7:39). By the blood of the cross, Jesus takes our contamination upon himself, sprinkles our hearts to cleanse us, and washes our bodies with pure water (Heb 10:22). Through the gift of the Spirit, he not only invites us to begin a new chapter in our story but also gives us the *power* to live that story for his glory and our good.

There is more light in Christ's story than there is darkness in yours. The Father has taken a personal interest in your story by sending Jesus to die for it and the Spirit to bring it back to life. That's who you are. That's what holds together our complicated narratives and keeps the past from contaminating the present. Does that mean we should forget the past? Of course not. The Bible often reminds us of who we *were* so it can point out who we *are* in Christ. And though freedom from the contamination is ours in principle, the realization of that freedom is a long battle fought alongside a faithful army of brothers, sisters, pastors, mentors, and counselors. But that's all part of the story, a story we're called to tell. When we tell it well—with authenticity and vulnerability—it empowers others to tell a better story as well.

Imagine Yourself: Safe Storytelling

Although it is difficult, there is great freedom in telling stories about our hurts, failures, and losses. Start with imagining safe storytelling.

- Recall a time that you shared your most vulnerable secret and it was honored.
- Now, imagine sharing your "shame" story with a safe community.
- Write a eulogy that you want to hear and imagine the

redemptive end to your story. (e.g. If your story was a movie, how would it end?)

After you imagine these, consider telling someone—verbally or in writing—one of your hard stories.

Conclusion

Every morning, real estate agents gather into their respective Keller Williams offices for a morning "power hour." These morning meetings are designed to whip agents up into a frenzy before they spend the next two hours on the phone. An important part of that routine is self-affirmation. Agents are taught to spend five to ten minutes in front of a mirror talking themselves up before they spend the next two hours getting shot down. In practice, the whole thing often comes off like a bad SNL skit: "I'm good enough, I'm smart enough, and doggone it, people like me."[2] In principle, there's little more powerful than looking yourself in the mirror and speaking the truth. So tell yourself the truth today. This is your story. This is your song. Now get up, praise your Savior, and stop letting your darkened past try to tell you who you are.

The Stories We Tell Ourselves

Principle: We are storytelling animals; the stories we tell ourselves either make or break us. To lead with presence and authority, we need to bring those stories out of the darkness and into the light.

Practice: Write out a fifteen-minute version of your life story. Where are the "contamination narratives," and how do they affect what follows? What would change if you were to recast the contamination as a catalyst for growth through adversity? How would that alter the story you tell about who you are?

CHAPTER 31

The Stories We Tell Each Other

In *Wake Me Up When the Data Is Over*, Lori Silverman tells her readers about a group of strategists at Bristol-Myers Squibb who used story to sell visionary strategy to their no-nonsense president.[1] Rather than drafting a fifty-page document they knew he'd never read, the team worked up an article about what the company would eventually look like if they implemented their strategy. Then they printed the story in a mock copy of the *Financial Times* dated three years in the future. Above the fold, the headline read: "Bristol-Myers Squibb Named Top-Ranked Global Pharmaceutical Company." After reading that story, something clicked, and the president decided it was time to move forward. In all, a 1,500-word article "sold" the vision better than a 15,000-word memo ever could.

Tell Me the Truth

When we want to draw someone in and speak words that *actually* make a difference, there's no more powerful medium than story. Jesus modeled this well, using parables drawn from everyday life to bring deep truths up to the surface where ordinary people could grab them. However, Jesus did more than simply illustrate the truth. On Jesus's lips, stories invited listeners to step out of themselves and into reality. For those with ears to hear and eyes to see, these stories embodied a reality they longed to be part of. For those without, Jesus's stories confirmed what was already true about their hardened hearts and their desire to live in a reality of their own small making.

I'm not Jesus and neither are you, but the prophetic weight our stories carry is profound. Stories do more than just illustrate the world; they open up reality and invite others to step in. As leaders, this makes story an incredibly powerful tool for either creating a workplace culture or destroying one. What stories are we telling, and what worlds are we opening up? Are we inviting people to get a glimpse of the truth about us and our role in the world? Or are we telling a darker story, one that projects a world marked by fear and isolation? In the following pages, we'll consider how our stories shape one another and how they help us foster a unified culture that not only includes but values people from diverse backgrounds.

The Stories We Tell Our Kids

According to a group of researchers at Princeton, good storytelling engenders successful communication by creating something like a "mind meld" between speakers and listeners. According to Matthew D. Lieberman, director of UCLA's social cognitive neuroscience lab and author of *Social: Why Our Brains Are Wired to Connect*, "This is what our brains were wired for: reaching out and interacting with others."[2] Stories are among the most powerful tools our brains have for putting us in contact with other human beings. This is what makes storytelling so potent—and so dangerous.

One of the easiest ways to grasp the formative power of story is to examine our children. Kids love stories. Heck, we all love stories. But with great storied power comes great responsibility. The stories we tell our kids don't just get their attention; they shape our kids' lives. We see that from the stories we read to our children. *The Little Engine That Could*, for example, has long served to embed the virtue of perseverance in our little ones' minds and hearts. Moving from written to oral, stories about our experiences and family history fill out our kids' sense of identity—much like Lindsey and Cole (chapter 28) or the Israelites and Passover (chapter 29). Less easy to recognize are the unarticulated stories we tell our kids. These include our everyday words, actions, and attitudes toward them—the stories that tell our kids whether we think they're an insufferable little brat or a precious gift from God. All these stories—written and unwritten, spoken and unspoken—deeply impact our kids for good or for ill.

Check Yourself: Family Myths and Oral Traditions

Every family has a canon of stories that come out at meals, celebrations, funerals, or when looking at pictures.

- What were the stories repeated in your childhood?
- What stories do you want your children to know and hear?
- How can we add the elements that create good stories, evoking emotion, provoking thought, and promoting replication?

The Stories We Tell Our Employees

Too often, leaders use stories as a way to fabricate rather than communicate. Faced with constant pressure to perform, they project an image of perfection when, really, they're just as scared and broken as everyone else. In a recent workshop, we had a leader share six true stories of success and failure: three victories to build the vision and three losses that could become lessons. The effect was powerful. His team learned how those stories had shaped their leader. By listening, the team felt as though they'd gained a new window into his heart and mind. More than that, leader and followers alike learned that perfection was an ideal they could no longer afford to pursue. The truth of a leader's story set that organization free.

As a leader, the stories you tell employees, volunteers, and colleagues have formative power. More than that, the stories you invite them to tell one another are crucial to forming a cohesive organization centered on the company's core values. One of our clients takes advantage of this reality by sending a monthly newsletter. Each month, they invite their team members to nominate one another for exemplifying the company's values. When the newsletter goes out, everyone has the chance to see how their peers have embodied the company's spirit that month. Simple as it may seem, telling one another's stories has fostered a deep commitment to one another and to the business.

Northwestern Mutual offers a fantastic example of this kind of formative storytelling. Consider this story from their website:

> The year was 1859. An ox and a passenger train collided just outside Johnson Creek, Wisconsin, and two of our policy owners were killed in the wreck. The claims totaled $3,500, which was $1,500 more than our two-year-old company had on hand. Then President Samuel S. Daggett and his fellow trustees personally borrowed the money to settle the claims, proving that our dedication to our clients is as old as the company itself.[3]

Since 1859, leaders at Northwestern have used this story to demonstrate the company's commitment to its customers as the heartbeat of its culture. Trainers use this story to inscribe the company's values deep within the hearts of all its advisors and employees. It'd be easy enough to list those values in a handbook and admonish everyone to "go the extra mile," but the train wreck story does something far more powerful. It invites employees to assume their place in the company's narrative, to become the kind of person who embodies that 1859 commitment. That kind of transformation drives the personal engagement that leaders so desperately need to see.

Stories That Cross Boundaries

Ron Hall was a wealthy art dealer with little concern for anyone but himself when he met Denver Moore at the Union Gospel Mission in Fort Worth, Texas. In Hall and Moore's coauthored bestseller *Same Kind of Different as Me*, the two tell the story of their unlikely friendship. The book pings back and forth, telling each man's life story on its own terms. Hall grew up in a 1950s lower-middle-class white family in Texas, surrounded by subtle racism that he never really recognized. A few decades older than Hall, Moore grew up in a family of black sharecroppers in 1930s Louisiana. Rather than glimpsing it from the outside, he experienced racism firsthand working on a plantation. In one harrowing example, Moore describes a time he was attacked by three white men, lassoed, and dragged down the road.

The two stories Hall and Moore tell are starkly different, yet eerily similar. As Moore describes it, we're all "homeless" in this world and on a journey to our final "home" with God:

> I used to spend a lotta time worryin that I was different from other people, even from other homeless folks. Then, after I met Miss Debbie and Mr. Ron, I worried that I was so different from them that we wadn't ever gon' have no kind a' future. But I found out everybody's different—the same kind of different as me. We're all just regular folks walkin down the road God done set in front of us. The truth about it is, whether we is rich or poor or somethin in between, this earth ain't no final restin place. So in a way, we is all homeless—just workin our way toward home.[4]

Both Hall and Moore had versions of the contamination narrative (see chapter 30). Hall's was a time of suffering and doubt after his wife died from cancer. Moore's was his oppressive upbringing and the years he'd spent in prison and on the streets. Together, however, they learned to tell their stories in the context of a lived friendship. Without sacrificing their individual stories, they realized they were part of a larger story—God's story—that brought them together. Within that story, much more united them than divided them.

Stories That Turn Enemies into Friends

On Sept. 16, 2017, a group of Donald Trump supporters organized a rally on the National Mall in Washington, DC.[5] When a group of protestors from "Black Lives Matter of Greater New York" showed up, things began to turn ugly. In an unexpected turn of events, however, the rally's organizer invited the protest group's leader, Hawk Newsome, on stage to say his piece. When Newsome got up, he led with a simple identity claim, "I am an American." Then he built on that common identity to remind the audience of their national story: "And the beauty of America is that when you see something broke in your country, you can mobilize to fix it." By the end of his speech, the crowd was cheering and rally participants were asking Newsome to pose with their kids for photographs. A man they'd perceived as an "other" or an "enemy" turned out to be a brother and a friend.

The stories Hall, Moore, and Newsome tell are important for leaders on two levels. First, they show us how the power of our story can transcend even the sharpest barriers. When we rally around a common story, our differences don't disappear but find their place in a larger narrative. Second, these stories serve as a model for how we can do the same. If leaders are going to move intentionally toward diversity and inclusion, they need to create a broader narrative space in which individuals feel free to share their stories in all their grit and glory. In the telling of those stories, they'll see that much more unites than divides them. Together, they'll take up their place in the company's narrative.

Conclusion

The stories we tell are powerful beyond words. They open up reality and invite others to become who *we* say they might be. This is both an awesome privilege and a heavy responsibility. Do we tell true stories that give life, inspire hope, and unite our hearers around a common cause, or do we spin tales that take life, instill despair, and tear people apart? Do we use our stories to humanize or to dehumanize, to create culture or to destroy it? Have we given our employees the tools to tell their stories well? None of us can afford to avoid these questions any longer. The stories we tell each other do more to impact our organizations than any strategic analysis or mission statement ever could.

The Stories We Tell Each Other

Principle: Storytelling is the most powerful way to bind scattered individuals into a tight crew. Leaders who encourage communal storytelling inspire employees to be present *together*.

Practice: Send out a company-wide email soliciting stories about when your employees saw one of their coworkers embody the spirit of your organization. Pick three of the most compelling stories, package them up in written form, and send them to everyone in the company.

CHAPTER 32

The Stories We Tell Together

O ne of the most powerful exercises we use in our workshops involves a few hundred images and a roll of Scotch tape. These images run the gamut from everyday office objects to abstract art. We prepare for the exercise by posting the images around the room. Then we give participants fifteen minutes to look around and answer three questions:

- Which picture captures leadership in this organization today?
- Which picture illustrates where you'd like to be this time next year?
- What is it going to take, in specific terms, to bring those two images together?

When the time expires and we invite participants to share and expand upon their answers, the responses from other people in the room are always remarkable: "I never knew that about you," "I didn't know you cared so much," "I'd love to hear more of your story," and so on.

What's the point? In *The Fearless Organization*, Amy C. Edmondson, professor of leadership and management at Harvard, argues that fearless companies create environments where leaders are free to confess their ignorance, admit their wrongs, and ask for help. In inviting people to think visually and share their perceptions of the company in its past, present, and future dimensions, we do more than bond and strategize. We create a safe environment where leaders can get real. In that vulnerable space, we don't just sit around and sing "Kumbayah." We encourage leaders to collaborate and begin constructing a shared narrative around who they are, where they've been, and where they're going.

As we've seen, there are the stories we tell ourselves and those we tell one another. In this chapter, we're going to look at the stories we tell together—the shared narrative about who *we* are and why anyone should care. Here, your job as a leader is to be the chief storyteller. Like an Israelite father or Christian preacher, your job is to stand before the "congregation" and give storied meaning to their activity. More than that, it's your duty to massage that narrative into the deep tissues of the company, using the power of story to form a people who own that narrative. When that happens, there's no stopping the lengths to which your employees will go to spread that story in the marketplace.

Leading with a Story

In family systems therapy, individuals are treated as a part of the whole; whatever happens to one of us happens to all of us. Mature leaders embody that dynamic. They understand intuitively that an organization isn't a collection of atomized individuals; it's an organic whole that is always greater than the sum of its parts. The web that connects employee to employee, employee to team, and team to organization is more complex than we could ever grasp. How do you account for that complexity? How do you unite an organization of 150 human actors and the relationships between them?

Once again, my answer is story. Storytelling leaders unify the diverse strands of their organization by telling true stories, first about themselves and then about others—their team, the company, and the market. Annette Simmons, an expert in helping business leaders wield the power of narrative, lists the six types of story every leader needs to be a good storyteller:

1. **Who I am:** This is the leader's origin story. From a place of vulnerability, this story describes who the leader is, where they come from, and why people should care.
2. **Why I am here:** This story conveys passion for the work and the organization. It connects with employees at the level of purpose, value, and meaning.
3. **Vision:** Every leader needs to paint an image of the future with colorful, moving, and inspiring words. These stories help them create that image.
4. **Teaching stories:** Whether they communicate events that happened to us or to others, teaching stories use concrete examples (like Jesus's parables) to enflesh important truths about how things get done in our company.
5. **Values in action:** These human stories—examples of customer service done well or community outreach—demonstrate what you value most.
6. **I know what you are thinking:** These stories connect with people. They show empathy and critical thinking, letting others know you've considered their position and want what's best for them and the company.[1]

The Stories That Make Us

Leading with a story isn't about manipulating people with emotions and rhetoric. Instead, it's about fostering human connection and challenging people to step into something bigger than themselves. This is especially important with respect to cultural values. Whether it's a story about a little blue train or young George Washington cutting down his father's cherry tree, stories embed values in our hearts and minds better than any platitude ever could. As we saw with Northwestern Mutual in the previous chapter, stories can shape individuals and business cultures. Without them, employees lose sight of who they're supposed to be and, as a result, how they're meant to contribute.

According to Paul Smith, "If you don't have strong company value stories, then in the minds of your employees (where it matters most) you probably don't have strong company values."[2] People don't know who they're supposed to be or what they're supposed to do unless you give them a story to grab hold of. As the philosopher Alasdair MacIntyre said, "I can only answer the question 'What am I to do?' if I can answer the prior question 'Of what story or stories do I find myself a part?'"[3] To put it in more business-minded terms, "An organization's culture is defined by the behavior of its members and reinforced by the stories they tell."[4]

The Stories We Make

Steve Clayton is the chief storyteller and general manager of Microsoft's Innovation, Culture and Stories Team. A computer engineer by training, Clayton got his start at Microsoft in 1997. As a presales consultant, he quickly learned he had a knack for translating technical jargon into everyday language. Others realized this too, and soon he was traveling around the globe, speaking about the magic of technology. Eventually, Clayton started the *Geek in Disguise* blog as a way to narrate his adventures at Microsoft. When the blog blew up in popularity, the company took notice and promoted him to chief storyteller.

Clayton's charge was to transform Microsoft from an opaque, technical juggernaut to an open and transparently human enterprise. Today, the Microsoft Story Labs website he helped to create is lauded as one of the best content hubs on the web. On it, contributors share stories about the ways Microsoft's technology is being deployed across the globe—from creating renewable energy in Spain to feeding malnourished children in India. In telling these stories, Clayton has found a way to cut through all the cultural noise and secure a hearing for his company. In the process, he's highlighted the real value Microsoft provides to the world: "It's very easy to slip into celebrating yourself and celebrating your product, but it's a lot more rewarding to go and find stories of where those products actually have an impact."[5]

Conclusion

As a leader, your job isn't merely to make sure all the trains run on time but to craft and communicate an engrossing story about where those trains come from, where they're going, and why every employee should invest in making sure they arrive. Using all the tools of a storyteller, leaders can weave together the diverse strands of their organizations and orient them toward a common goal. These stories provide a common vision that holds the company together. More than that, they shape the stories we tell outwardly. Wielding the power of a storyteller and equipping your employees to do the same will empower your organizational story to be heard in the market and in the world. As Clayton puts it,

> We believe there is an appetite for people who want to read a story, and we think we have great stories to tell. Stories have stood the test of time. No one goes into a pub and says, 'I want to tell you some data.' They say, 'Let me tell you about a movie I saw, or a book I read, or a journey I took, or person I met.' Stories get embellished and they get retold, and that's why some of the greatest stories have stood the test of time.[6]

Do you want your company's story to stand the test of time? Then it's time to own your corporate story, tell it well, and invite your employees to join you in doing the same.

The Stories We Tell Together

Principle: The best leaders own their organization's story and communicate it with passion. They invite others to write themselves into that narrative and, in turn, communicate it to the world. Stories build cultures, and storied cultures rise to the top of their class.

Practice: Set aside two hours to tell Simmons's six types of stories. Record your voice, dictate your thoughts, or jot ideas down on a yellow legal pad—whatever works. Once you've got your ideas down, coordinate with your communications department to polish the narrative. Drill those stories into your mind, and start telling them every chance you get.

CHAPTER 33

The Blessing of Storyfulness

L eadership is exhausting. We constantly feel as though we're being
pulled in every direction, and there's an endless amount of stuff
for us to keep up with. At work, employees from every department
and pressures from the market stretch our strategic minds to their
breaking point. At home, our spouses and kids ask more of us than
we know how to deliver. In our churches and communities, more
and more people make demands on us. We try to manage our time,
but our schedules end up managing us. We try to be present, but
our minds often end up somewhere else. We try to take care of our
bodies, but fourteen-hour workdays leave little room for a healthy,
home-cooked meal. We try to make time for relationships, but there's
just too much on our plate.

If we don't find our place within this complexity, the omnidi-
rectional pull of leadership will eventually rip us apart. How then
can we knit our world together? How can we rediscover the unified whole that makes sense of all our striving? How can we leave
behind our fragmented existence and live as integrated wholes? As
I've argued in this section, the answer to that question is storyfulness. By owning our story, living it, and inviting others to do
likewise, we find the unifying power we desperately need in our
chaotic lives.

From Disenchantment to Enchantment

What is it about modern life that makes it so difficult to find our story within the chaos? Part of the answer to that question is that we've lost sight of the larger story—the metanarrative—that holds reality together. Max Weber calls it *disenchantment*, the movement of human history from the mystical to the scientific and back again. According to the theory, for a long time, monotheism gave the world a cohesive story, but modern science rid us of that religious baggage and sought to tell a new story about what holds the world together. But science was thoroughly unequipped to do that, and the result is fragmentation. People tell a million different stories, each of which provides meaning. In the end, we're back in a reenchanted world of angels and demons, Titans and Olympians, each vying with one another for ultimate significance.

Against modern fragmentation, we need a reenchanted story at both the individual and the global level. We don't find this story in fairy tales, Greek mythology, or daily horoscopes. Rather, we find it in the story God tells about his good creation, the fall of his treasured images, the redemption won for them in his Son, and the work he's doing through his Spirit to create a new world that is wonderfully diverse in its complex intricacy yet perfectly united in its relation to the triune God. God dwells in storied fullness, holding together the past, present, and future in a perfect plan for all things. And to the extent that we rediscover our individual stories within that larger story, we see what holds together our messy lives. But what does that mean for you as a leader? How do you bring that reality to bear on your life and business?

Tell Yourself a Better Story

Who are you? By now, you've probably thought more about that question than you have in a while. As we've seen in this section, our stories—understood in light of God's story—are the only things comprehensive enough to weave together the various threads of our personal identities into a meaningful tapestry. If story can serve such a central, unifying role in our lives, then we must pay close attention to the story we tell ourselves. If we don't, we'll allow the negativity to crowd in and distort everything that comes along. So tell yourself a better story today. Fight for the truth about who you are in Christ, what that means, and start living the story that he died to secure for you.

Use Foundational Stories to Bring People Together

In 2018, two policemen handcuffed and escorted a pair of black men out of a Philadelphia Starbucks. Within hours, the incident went viral on social media, only to be quelled by an apology from Starbucks and mandatory unconscious bias training for its employees. For many leaders, this incident was a wake-up call; there is absolutely no margin for error when it comes to diversity and inclusion. Bottom-line reasons aside, Christian leaders should want workplaces to reflect the diversity of God's creation. But how do you do that without sticking your foot in your mouth? In the book *Inclusion*, Jennifer Brown discusses her strategy in helping Fortune 500 clients: the founding story.[1] Just as organizations have founding stories, so do people. By tapping into and sharing the moments in our stories when we've been unfairly treated, excluded, or marginalized, we can both demonstrate the value we place on diversity and inclusion and model how our employees show that same respect to others.

Tell a Better Story . . . Together

Do people know what you do at work? This seems like an obvious question, but it's one we often miss. As Steve Clayton showed us with Microsoft in the previous chapter, stories connect the work we do with its real-world consequences. By telling stories, we show the world that we're not just some money-making machine but a value-creating force to be reckoned with. In a noisy, distracted world where attention is precious and hard to come by, stories make people stop and take notice. So don't just tell your personal story today; tell your organizational story as well. More than that, equip your employees to share that story with everyone they meet, within and outside the company. Seek individual success stories—the customer you helped overcome a significant problem, for example—and use them to internally and externally reflect the mission and values you hold.

Sabbath: Rest in the Midst of Your Story

Recently we facilitated a retreat for a company whose leaders truly understood the power of story. At the beginning of the day, we had each executive check in personally and professionally. One VP leaned into the moment, sharing his anxiety and fear about the company's current season. When he stepped out onto that limb, not a single person tried to fix him. Instead, the CEO acknowledged his legitimate anxiety given the weight of the challenges they were facing. She thanked him for his vulnerability and followed with her own, sharing her sense that they all needed better attunement for the future.

Storyfulness isn't about unicorns and rainbows. It's about real people with real vulnerabilities living and leading out of our frail humanity. Leadership is exhausting, and we're all looking for time and space to rest from the cacophony of personal and professional noise. When Jesus walked the earth, he was constantly surrounded by needy people and messy circumstances. Even in the midst of that, he made it a point to retreat to a solitary place to rest and commune with God, often in the face of ongoing, unfulfilled needs. Why wasn't he consumed by the needs before him? Why didn't he work harder to serve every need that was brought his way? In short, the answer is story. Jesus knew who he was and why he'd been sent, and he wasn't about to let all the things he *could* do distract him from what he was *supposed to* do. In what story do you find yourself? If

God's story is the metanarrative that makes sense of our individual narratives, then we can trust him to weave together the loose ends as we stop and take a breath.

> **Stop:** Enter into sabbath as a much-needed intermission. Unplug from your constant attempts to author the story on your own terms, and receive the grace of God instead. Retreat from whatever contradicts the story he's telling.
>
> **Trust:** Own your story and rest in the truth that God in Christ has cleansed you of the contamination. Pursue solitude as an intentional space in which you can meditate on God's story of redemption and your place within it.
>
> **Enjoy:** Celebrate what God has done in your story. Play the scenes of his faithfulness over in your head. Give praise to him for his authorial goodness.

Learning to Tell Our Stories

When scuba divers become disoriented, a sign of nitrogen narcosis, they cannot trust their perceptions, which is why divers are educated on preventative tactics before they ever enter the water. They are told to "follow the bubbles" and "check the compass." Like these divers, in order to understand your purpose, you first must know where you've been, where you are, and where you are going.

Our stories are our GPSs or our trail of bubbles—the goal is orientation. How did I get here? Where am I going? Stories help teach us and bring us to the surface.

Identity

The first step an author often takes in writing a story is to find the identity of the main character. When we think of telling our story, we must ask a similar question: Who am I? Our identity can be defined by culture, nationality, ethnicity, religion, or sexuality. What parts of your identity are you ignoring, denying, or lying about? Can you clearly describe these parts of your identity? Are these defining characteristics interwoven into the story you tell about yourself? Why or why not?

Maybe you have had bad experiences. "It happened" and "It

happened to me" are some of the most powerful words a person can speak. In a therapeutic environment, they are a sign of health.

Trauma is a disintegration of the self. The parts of ourselves that are wounded become fractured and disorganized. Reintegration comes in the telling of our disintegration.

Several experiences can cause disintegration of identity—a one-time traumatic event or even a chronic cultural message that disintegrates your self-identity. Notice how your past always matters. One of my client's uncle likes to say, "Issues tissues!" This is a light-hearted yet still insidious shaming strategy to dissuade conversations about the painful disintegrations that have occurred. Here are some lies you may be telling yourself or others that push our stories into the shadows:

- The past is the past.
- That had no effect on me.
- Oh, I hadn't thought about that in years. It is not important.
- I am not going to be like one of those poor saps on Dr. Phil.
- I don't have time for all that woo-woo, feel-good stuff.
- Back in my day, everyone just did what they needed to do. They didn't dwell on all their issues. They turned out fine.
- Jesus healed it all. I don't need to talk incessantly about it.

The last lie is especially dangerous. Using your present-day faith to deny your past or any part of your story is called "spiritual bypass," and it doesn't work.

These lies are a natural survival defense to protect ourselves. Fear is a natural instinct used for self-preservation. However, if we remain in denial or lie to ourselves and do not name the fear, our bodies still believe the dangers continue to be present. Biologically, we react to a tiger in the room unless we tell ourselves, "The tiger is no longer there. I do not have to be afraid." And when you can't tell yourself this truth, others can speak it to you.

No, not everyone is worthy of your story, and I'm certainly not asking you to post your past traumas or mistakes on Facebook. But you need a safe space to speak your story, and you need to be cautious of being around others that reinforce your defensive excuses.

The Results of Organized Storytelling

Good stories evoke emotion, provoke thought, and promote replication. Important things happen when you tell your story in an integrated way, each part of the story adding to the next and gathering strength along the way. What are those important things? Vulnerability, authenticity, accuracy, connection/resonance, countering shame, and building bridges.

Before bed, we tell our children stories. Stories take our minds from cyclical or unproductive thoughts and give us a place to rest. Stories provide rest, even if they are difficult to tell.

Leadership and legacy are always about moving forward. You wonder why you are stuck. You are experiencing a roadblock. You're too tired to move forward. It no longer feels worth the effort. Silence immobilizes. Break the silence. Tell your story.

Good or bad, successes and failures, know your story—sense it, feel it, and speak it so that you can change it. Be conscious of your story. We tell our stories because we want to understand ourselves, learn from the past, and expand our compassion toward others who are suffering.

Storytelling that integrates your past, present, and future creates legacies that are worth repeating.

con-
clu-
sion

CHAPTER 34

Providence, Identity, and Performance

WORKING OUT WHAT GOD WORKS WITHIN

I magine," Warren Buffett said to a room full of shareholders in 1997, "it is 24 hours before you are going to be born and a genie comes to you."[1] Channeling the philosopher John Rawls, Buffett explained that the genie would let this room full of Aladdins design the world into which each one would be born. But there was a catch. Nobody gets to decide who they'll be: rich or poor; black or white; American or Armenian; healthy or infirm. Buffett called this the "ovarian lottery," and the point of this riff was to highlight the responsibilities of wealthy Americans toward those who came from less privileged stock.

In a 2014 letter to shareholders, Buffett had more to say about how well he had fared in the ovarian lottery. In short, Buffett considered it "dumb luck" that he and his business partner were born in the United States, "and we are forever grateful for the staggering advantages this accident of birth has given us."[2] Not exactly the "I built that" message you'd expect to hear from a guy who's made $80 billion off the stock market.

We'll have some things to say about Buffett's "dumb luck" below. For now, let's look at the nugget of truth in what he said.

Throughout this book, we've been trying to rediscover our humanity and become "entrepreneurs of identity" in the dimensions of time, place, body, community, and story. If we're honest about it, these elements have much more to do with the "ovarian lottery" than we care to admit. Why do I get to live in the twenty-first century rather than the first? Why was I born in California instead of Columbia? Why am I the olive-skinned son of a Peruvian rather than the pasty-white son of a Cornhusker? Why did I get to fall in love with a beautiful double major in French and international business with a mind and heart for business, social impact, and missions? Why did a "chance" encounter with the church planting guru Ed Stetzer on one Sunday afternoon twenty years ago set me in a direction I'd never dreamed for myself? Why am I a part of this story and not another one?

If I'm honest, I can't take credit for any of these identity-defining moments or constraints in my life. I didn't will myself into existence. Nor did I decide who I'd meet and when. So, again, why *this* story? If God is the author of our lives, then the answer to this question seems simple: he wrote my story this way. But what does that mean? Does that make me a spectator, watching from the outside as God does whatever he wants in my life? Should I settle into the story God has written for me, accepting my identity in time and space as a bit of divine luck? Not exactly.

An Old School Dilemma

In the past few years, I've had the privilege of working with my long-time friend Bert Guinn and his team at the Greater Louisville Medical Society (GLMS). Long before we started working together, Bert and I served together at Sojourn. Bert has been the embodiment of hard work and grit for as long as I've known him. I've watched him bust his tail in an entry-level position, knock out an MBA, and climb his way through the ranks to become the CEO of GLMS. All the while, he's loved his family as a stellar husband and father and led his church as a faithful elder.

When Bert took over the top executive spot, GLMS's eighty-thousand-square-foot headquarters was in dire need of repair, and the organization lacked the necessary capital. They needed to move into a more efficient space, but Bert couldn't just sell off the property. Built in 1892, the Old Medical School that housed GLMS was a local treasure. Three decades earlier, Bert's predecessor and mentor had joined with countless others to rescue the building from the wrecking ball. When he stepped down, Bert felt as though his mentor had literally handed him "the keys to the kingdom." It was up to Bert to ensure it didn't fall into the wrong hands or, worse, get torn down.

The situation spiraled from bad to worse. When a long-time tenant ended their lease, GLMS waved goodbye to over $200,000 in annual revenue. At a loss, Bert coined the phrase "Commitment reveals providence." Every day, he repeated this mantra for himself and his coworkers, quelling their doubts with the firm conviction that if they stuck with their commitment to hard work and prayer, God's good plans would surely be unveiled. Within a few weeks, there was a knock at the door. A local nonprofit that cared for sick children and their families told Bert they had outgrown their space and were interested in purchasing theirs. A couple of months later, that nonprofit moved into the newly renovated Old Medical School. And GLMS? They moved into a much more efficient and affordable space in a better location.

Winner, Winner, Chicken Dinner

You might call Bert's story a miracle of timing. As we unpacked in chapter 7, timing is incredibly important to the success of organizations and leaders. But as anyone who's ever tried to time the stock market—or any market—will tell you, there's "something more" to timing than analyzing the data, running your forecasts, and choosing when to go. As we saw in the 2014 letter, Warren Buffett attributed that "something more" to a notion you wouldn't expect from the most successful investor to ever walk the earth: luck.[3]

A common adage in the business world is that success follows hard work and good luck. Buffett worked feverishly for Hathaway's shareholders, but he's humble enough to admit that he never would've made it without luck.[4] Some might consider his positive attitude toward luck a liability, but we'll let his eleven-digit net worth speak for itself. In fact, it's possible that Buffett's attitude has made him even "luckier" than he would have been if he were a bit more sensible. According to the authors of *Heart, Smarts, Guts, and Luck*, "Some people believe in Luck—and this belief makes them luckier. Luck is a part of their optimistic outlook and openness to new things. They embrace that there are other forces beyond themselves and their own understanding as well as serendipitous encounters that play a critical role to their success."[5] Other forces? Yes. Serendipity? I'm not so sure.

Did Bert Get Lucky?

I hesitate to question Warren Buffett, and I've found that the *Heart, Smarts, Guts, and Luck* authors present a fantastic exploration of entrepreneurship and business building. Still, for Christians who believe in a God who "works out everything in conformity with the purpose of his will," luck is a four-letter word (Eph 1:11). If God is the author, then nothing in this world happens by chance. Not even a creature as insignificant as the sparrow falls to the ground without his divine say-so (Matt 10:29). The perfect buyers didn't come along because Bert got lucky; they came along because God was at work in his and his organization's story.

To describe what happens in God's world, we need a ten-letter word: providence. The Westminster Shorter Catechism defines providence as God's "most holy, wise, and powerful preserving and governing all his creatures and all their actions."[6] In that dense little phrase, we learn that

- God's motives are always pure and without reproach (holy).
- God skillfully weaves together everything that happens in the universe (wise).

- God is not limited by anything in all of creation (powerful).
- God sustains all things under his Fatherly care (preserving).
- God governs all things by his kingly might (governing).
- No creature, not even a sparrow, escapes God's providence (all his creatures).
- No act, big or small, occurs apart from God's control (all their actions).

Dumb luck has no place in God's world. God appoints our times and places (Acts 17:26). He forms our bodies in our mothers' wombs (Ps 139:13). He sovereignly determines not just the when, where, and how of our existence but also the *who*—the family, friends, colleagues, and employees we come into contact with every day. This world is, as the Protestant Reformer John Calvin said, the theater of God's glory. God is the divine playwright, purposefully crafting a cosmic drama in which human actors are called to play their part.

Becoming an entrepreneur of identity is less about cranking up our productivity to eleven (job performance) and more about stepping into the role God has written for each of us (*theo*-performance). When we're driven by productivity, every action we take becomes a desperate grab for identity. We work to prove our worth. We earn to convince others of our value. We strive to portray an image we think others will admire. But when we drop our anxious need to synthesize our self-worth and instead step into the reality God has graciously made *for us*, we realize our true freedom as performers in God's cosmic drama. We don't work to earn our identity. Instead, we receive it as God's good gift. From our God-given identities, we work. And, as we do, we grow more fully into the men and women God is calling us to become.

God Works and We Work

So what's left for us to do? If God is writing the script, doesn't that make us his puppets? Why work when God's already working everything out according to his plan? Surely, we are in the realm of mystery here. The same Bible that says God works all things according to his deliberate plan also says that evildoers bear the responsibility for their sins (Acts 2:23). The same Jesus who says *we* must come to him also says that unless his Father draws us, we never will (Matt 11:28; John 5:40; 6:44). The same redemption that God works in us is also meant to be worked out by us (Phil 2:12–13). This is only a glimpse of the real yet glorious tension we see in the Bible: God works and we work.

On my desk, I have a sign that reads *Ora et Labora* ("work and pray")—a formula used in the ancient monasteries. In those three Latin words, we catch something of the dramatic tension in our performance. Even as we work our tails off, we pray that God would "establish the work of our hands" (Ps 90:17). As difficult as it is to wrap our heads around this idea, God's work establishes our work. There's no contradiction here. Just as wind resistance establishes an eagle's flight, so too does God's constraining will create the free air in which we're called to soar. If he doesn't move, we don't move. If he doesn't make us, we don't make ourselves. If he doesn't pick up his pen, we don't pick up ours.

Conclusion

Have you ever called something a "God thing"? I hear Christian leaders say those words all the time when something big goes their way. At one level, I want to affirm their desire to give God all the glory. At another, I want to shake them out of their Christianese-induced slumber. Sure, it was a "God thing" when you closed that huge account and saved the business last week. But have you stopped to consider that God may have been doing his "thing" over the past three months you spent nurturing that account? To be sure, God doesn't *need* us to accomplish his will. Still, he *wants* us, and part of his desire is that he would work *through* us, not without us or against us.

By all accounts, the story I shared about Bert qualifies as a "God thing." But God's thing didn't happen apart from Bert's thing.

Remember the motto he repeated with his team: "Commitment reveals providence." Under Bert's leadership, GLMS did what it took to position themselves for a quick sale to a motivated buyer. Even in the midst of God's work, they worked to assemble the pieces so the move could go off without a hitch. When it was all said and done, the staff presented Bert with a gift. It was their way of thanking him for reminding them to trust that God will show up in and through their work. He carries it with him to this day—a leather keychain with a single word emblazoned on the side: providence.

I consider myself a winner of the "ovarian lottery," and I hope you do too. The contest was rigged. Why am I the olive-skinned son of a Peruvian man, raised in California and rooted in Louisville? As I've said all along, this is the story God has written for me—the performance he's called me to give on the world stage. Yet to perform in his drama isn't merely to parrot a dead script but to embody his living word, to live in light of what he's said about me, the world, and everything in it. Becoming an entrepreneur of identity is work, but it's a job none of us would have if God hadn't done the work first. Not by good luck, but by the providential grace of God, we are what we are (see 1 Cor 15:10). And by the redeeming grace of God in Christ, we are set free to become who he's designed us to become.

CHAPTER 35

The Fight for Identity on God's Playground

In chapter 14, I mentioned the walks my daughter Georgia and I took around the neighborhood. "I'm an explorer," she would exclaim as we ambled down the streets of Louisville, looking for new and interesting things to discover. What I failed to mention, though, was that my young Georgia wasn't just an explorer. She was much more. Some days, she was an artist, waving her paintbrush around the house. Other days, she was a scientist, experimenting on and hypothesizing about the "treasures" we had discovered on our walks. My favorite part of these "childish" attempts to become an entrepreneur of identity: whenever Georgia decided who she wanted to be that day, she'd ask me, "Am I a scientist, Daddy?" All it took was, "Absolutely, G," for my daughter to take off and let the rest of the family know who she had become.

Unless You Become like Children

Jesus said that unless we become like children, we will never enter the kingdom of God (Matt 18:3). Fiona Gardner has reflected deeply on what Jesus's words might entail for our walk with God, pointing to three central aspects of a child's spirituality: relational consciousness, play, and powerlessness. As kids grow, they become increasingly aware of their *relationships* with God, people, and the world. The need for *play* arises as they learn to manipulate their circumstances and imagine the possibilities beyond them. Their sense of *powerlessness* develops as they begin to realize that to survive they depend upon others—ultimately God. Taking these three aspects into account, Gardner offers her sense of what Jesus had in mind:

> Jesus asks us, his disciples, to journey in life towards a condition of complete simplicity and where all impediments to this are stripped away. It is a journey to become free in our relationship with God. It is an ongoing journey towards a potential state of mind and a way of being truly alive. It is not about going backwards to a state of pre-verbal impotency, but rather a way forward into being attentive in our present relationship with God.[1]

To discover who she was, Georgia first needed to discover how she fit in relation to the world around her. Every walk down the street, stroke of the brush, and silly game she played was another foray into her identity. It wasn't until Georgia received her validation from me, however, that she felt free to own her identity and declare it to others. She was powerless to identify herself in that way; she needed the words of love and affirmation that I, her father, was more than happy to provide.

God is calling us to live and lead like Georgia. He wants us to offer him our childlike attempts to discover who we are. Whether we realize it or not, our hearts' deepest longing is to hear his fatherly "Absolutely." Where human identity and divine approval meet, we will find the freedom to live and lead from a place of redeemed and restored humanity. One day, we will hear Jesus say, "Well done, good and faithful servant," as we finally enter into the deep rest of his divine presence. Until then, we live in a fallen world in which entrepreneurship of identity is less like child's play and more like war—an all-out struggle between competing interests, rival claims to identity, and the constant pressures of the marketplace.

Searching for Ourselves on the Battleground

Jesus is calling us to step onto the playground of identity, but we can't seem to escape the battleground of life and business in a broken world. Consider these words from Kevin O'Leary, successful investor and popular fixture on the reality show *Shark Tank*: "Business is war. I go out there, I want to kill the competitors. I want to make their lives miserable. I want to steal their market share. I want them to fear me and I want everyone on my team thinking we're going to win."[2] Even though I'm sure he was playing to the camera, O'Leary's words ring true for most leaders. Business is war. Sink or swim, win or lose, kill or be killed, eat or be eaten. I'm sorry to say that, in my experience, nonprofits and churches aren't always that different.

Don't get me wrong. Short of killing our competitors or making their lives miserable, the battleground metaphor is extremely valuable. Business is competitive. If we're not diligent, somebody like O'Leary is going to show up and eat our lunch. There are seasons of leadership when it feels like we've been deployed overseas: battling for market share, downsizing the company, shipping a new product. In those seasons, what your people need isn't a pastor but a general.

Still, we need to recognize that metaphors are powerful beyond words. Metaphors are like compact stories; they shape our reality. The war metaphor can lock us into an overly narrow view of life, identity, and business. If every negotiation is a battle, then you will never learn the value of give-and-take. If every employee is a cog in the war machine, then other people become means to an end. If you're only a general, then you'll be oblivious to those moments when your people really do need someone more like a pastor. To do justice to the reality of leadership, we need to broaden our metaphorical vision.

Save a Tank, Rent a Cottage?

In *Rest*, Alex Soojung-Kim Pang tells the story of Dwight Eisenhower and his first major command during World War II.[3] As the newly appointed Commanding General of the European Theater of Operations, Eisenhower was tasked with planning the largest American campaign in the Atlantic theater to date. Working fifteen to eighteen hours a day and struggling to sleep at night, Eisenhower found himself in desperate need of a retreat. So he sent his aide Harry Butcher to find him a getaway. Soon enough, an unassuming little house in the woods named Telegraph Cottage would become the refuge where Eisenhower could escape to play golf, read cowboy novels, and go horseback riding. While some might see that as a dereliction of his duty, Eisenhower understood it to be vital to American success. He was right. According to the people closest to him, Telegraph Cottage didn't just save Eisenhower's sanity; it helped him plan the operation that would launch American troops into the theater and usher the future president into the limelight.

As Eisenhower demonstrates, we need a healthy dose of "play to win" to balance out the "fight to kill" tendency in our lives. The playground and battleground live in dynamic tension. The former is the place where we experiment; the latter is where we implement. The former is where we write our story; the latter is where we tell it. The former is where we discover who we are; the latter is where we put our identity to work. There are seasons when life takes place mostly on the playground; there are others when we dig in for a long, hard battle. In either case, we can never wrench these two metaphors apart. In the war for identity, we play our way to victory. On the playground of personal discovery, we're going to get into a fight or two.

Learning to Play the Game

What does life look like on God's playground? What game are we playing? Dallas Willard often referred to life on this side of heaven as a school of eternal living.[4] In this place, with these bodies, and in the company of others, we are living a time-bound story with eternal consequences. This school is a place of nonjudgment—a gracious institution in which our registration has been paid in full by the blood of Christ. A cosmic battle rages around us, but our foe has already been defeated on Calvary. The battle has already been won. Therefore, so has the game. We are who we are in Christ, and nothing could ever take that away.

For leaders, that's all wonderful, but what does it have to say about the game we're playing at work—a game that focuses less on personal identity formation and more on human resources, marketing strategy, and management technology? In *Mastering Leadership*, Robert J. Anderson and William A. Adams approach this concern by drawing an important distinction between a leader's outer and inner games.[5] The former refers to all those technical competencies you'd expect to see in a good leader, like managerial and communication skills. The latter refers to everything going on beneath the surface. Most leaders focus on the outer game—that is, gearing up to win the battle. However, as Anderson and Adams point out, the outer game is rarely what we identify with greatness: "When we describe *great leadership*, we describe something beyond skill, capability, and competence. We use words like *integrity, honesty, passion, vision, risk-taking, fearlessness, compassion, courage, authenticity, collaboration, self-awareness, selflessness, purposefulness, humility, intuition,* and *wisdom*."[6] These qualities all belong to the inner game.

There are two more dimensions to consider in the game leaders play: short-term and long-term. Everything in our society is geared toward the former. From text messages to value meals to same-day delivery, we are constantly looking for ways to get what we want when we want it. Instant gratification is the name of our modern game. Our culture is forming us to be the kind of leaders who live and lead in the short term. In the short-term, entrepreneurship of identity is a long-term luxury real leaders can't afford. As a consequence, we ignore our emotional lives, lead out of a sense of command and control, and measure performance in dollars and minutes rather than prayer and providence. However, the long-term fruits of our shortened roots leave us with a sense of soulless self-loathing as we realize we've sacrificed our long-term impact for the sake of a few short-term wins.

Playing to Win

Short-term leaders live on the battleground of *today*, focusing all their energy on winning petty battles instead of setting their sights on long-term victory. Or worse, they refuse to set foot on the playground at all, rejecting the entrepreneurship of identity as a frivolous game. Who can think about time when a battle is raging? Why should we care about our bodies beyond their ability to launch us into the fight? Does it really matter where the battle is taking place or who we're fighting alongside? What's the point of searching for storyfulness when the enemy is one account away from ending our story? Even if we know that the best thing we can do for our organizations is learn to show up, pay attention, and become more human, the real-time demands of leadership militate against every attempt to slow down and discover who we are.

The burden of this book hasn't simply been to show you how to discover your identity and level up your leadership but to make the case for why becoming more human will help you win in the marketplace. Christians sometimes get squirrelly with the notion of winning in business. But competition isn't inherently evil. In the end, the leaders and companies who win aren't necessarily those who game the system or lay waste to the marketplace. Instead, they're often those who do better work for customers, employees, communities, and the world. In a word, they're more fully *human*. Humanity is inherently valuable in every sense of the word, and *human* businesses are the most valuable of all.

The best leaders sacrifice instant gratification for the sake of lasting impact. They don't neglect their outer game, but with Anderson and Adams, they realize the inner game runs the show and are willing to spend time cultivating self-awareness and presence. They step onto the playground to become entrepreneurs of identity, not because they're afraid to fight but because they know the path to victory runs straight through Telegraph Cottage. They refuse to sacrifice people or places for the sake of profit. It's not that they don't believe in turning a buck. Instead, they've grasped that a *human* approach to value surpasses even the most lucrative forms of dehumanization.

Great leaders show up physically, psychologically, and spiritually. They pay attention to themselves, their employees, and their surroundings. Most important, they embrace their humanity in the fullest sense as they seek to cultivate a better world for the people they serve. To put it in a single word, they're *present*. In a dehumanized and dehumanizing world, this kind of presence takes intense focus and hard work. Even so, this is a game that leaders can't afford to lose.

Conclusion

At the outset of this book, I shared my story of absence and presence. While most men struggle to escape the shadow of their fathers' presence, I lived the first forty years of my life trying to reckon with the *absence* of mine. Like my daughter, I longed to present myself before a loving father, to show him who I'd become and to hear him say in his most affirming voice: "Absolutely." When we finally found each other, his presence was more than I could bear, yet less than could truly satisfy my deepest longing.

It took twelve years for me to finally ask my father to take a paternity test. Sure enough, we were a match. Six months after he read the results, I found myself back in California. With healthy encouragement from a friend, I picked up the phone. I couldn't believe what I heard when my father answered: "I've been waiting for you to call!" Over lunch the next day, my father welcomed me into his life with a warm embrace and a raft of family photos—"strangers" that I could immediately see myself in. An hour later, his wife walked in, and as I shared my story with her, I found the moment to be more than I could handle. Tears welling up in our eyes, we sat together in that moment—fully present, fully engaged, fully alive. A few months later, my four kids welcomed their new "Mimi" and "Pops" into our home in Louisville. I was so obviously overwhelmed by their presence that my wife, Mandy, had to pull me out of myself: "Stop trying to process all of this at once, just be with him."

As Christians, we believe in a story of absence and presence. We once were estranged from our heavenly Father, but he sent his only Son so that we could be ushered back into his fatherly presence. If forty years of absence was too much for me to process, how much more overwhelming should life in the presence of our heavenly Father be? That's why presence is ultimately a matter of grace. God has made human beings for life with him. That's what the Christian life is—eternity in the Father's presence through the sacrifice of the Son and in the power of the Holy Spirit. It's from that place of perfect presence that God wants us to engage our world as leaders. God is whispering to us in our pain, calling his people to stand up and lead out of our redeemed and restored humanity.

Sooner or later, all our earthly fathers will let us go. While our hearts' deepest longing is to hear them affirm our childlike attempts to find ourselves, there is only one Father who can fully give us what we seek. In his presence, we can finally discover when we are (time), where we are (place), what we are (body), who we're with (others), and what we're meant to do with our lives (story). These are the givens of our creaturely reality, the hallmarks of human existence into which God himself set foot in the incarnation of Jesus Christ. When the *time* had fully come, God sent forth his Son to take on an earthly *body* and inhabit this earthly *place*. Born of a woman, he came from *others* as a son and for them as a servant. His *story* came to intersect with our own—to redeem us from the curse of the law, adopt us into his heavenly family, and invite us to sit before our Father in heaven (cf. Gal 4:4–5).

These are the boundaries that God has marked out for us—time, place, body, others, and story. They are the ground on which he's called us to come and play as the war rages around. This is where life happens. This is where leaders discover who they are and, out of that deep sense of identity, inspire others to discover who they are as well. It's a place of safety and self-awareness, where we're called into something better than simple mindfulness. Here, we're called to put on the mind of Christ and take our every thought of life and leadership captive to him—the only true human who ever walked the earth. In him, we find everything we need to show up, pay attention, and become fully human.

Breathe in: *Abba Father.*

Breath out: *I'm home, right now, right here.*

Acknowledgments

Writing a book is unlike any other venture. The initial excitement and vision for the project propels you forward. You're sure you're going to change the world. Then reality comes crashing down. You realize that putting words on paper is hard work. Reading over those words and making them better is even harder. Doubt—in yourself and in the project—seems ever-present. Showing up to the blank page, once a symbol of boundless creative possibility, becomes a harrowing grind.

To be honest, it would have been much worse if I had bought into the myth that the writing life requires a solitary genius agonizing over a keyboard day after day. When the seed of this book was planted well over twenty years ago, I already knew that I was going to need as much help as I could get. By God's grace, this has been a collaborative effort from day one.

I began meeting with Eboni in a coffee shop in Nashville. Our scheduled hour-long meetings turned into three-hour heart-to-hearts as we discovered we were kindred spirits. We've been collaborating ever since. Eboni, you are a gift for leaders and an advocate for the broken. The precision of your care continues to astound and inspire me. Thank you.

Kenny, you are a wizard with words and a gifted theologian. Nothing less than God's strange providence could have taken a leader like you out of the business world and brought him into the church, just as I was leaving full-time ministry to join the business world. Our respective talents and transitions galvanized our ability to work together. You are a gift to the realms of church and business alike, and I am thankful to partner with you.

To Sarah Braud: your gift of storytelling and your keen editor's eye have ensured that this book is the best it can be. Unlike most writers can report of their editors, I am happy to say that your presence and insight always bring me joy.

To Lauren Tharp, who waded into the complexity of epic writing retreats and helped keep us on track, and who is grounded in the realities and brutalities of the business world: thank you for keeping this book and our business real and alive.

To Melinda, our first editor on this project and our editor at Leadership Reality: you owned this project—and an absolutely unreasonable deadline—from day one.

To Hatfield Media: thanks to Shayne Hiles and Jeff Dehut, this book's visuals took on new life. Thank you for your critical help in shaping this message through your gift for design.

I also want to thank the team at Zondervan—Ryan Pazdur, Nate Kroeze, and Matthew Estel—for taking the time to consider this project and for giving us the freedom and encouragement to explore these difficult topics critically and constructively.

To all the companies that have gifted us with work: I never imagined entering the business world could be so thrilling, horrifying, and challenging—often all at the same time. Those who have let me look behind the curtain, opening their businesses and lives to my counsel, have trusted me in ways that are hard to fathom. It's even harder to distill my gratitude into a simple word of thanks. This work has refined me, shaped me, and made me a better human—a better Christian—in the process. I am nothing less than honored by every one of you.

Finally, I come to my own tribe. I believe that every good finding in this book grew out of an failure; every lesson emerged from an initial loss. I cannot imagine my life without the company of the good friends who loved me well through all those failures, shouldering me in my discouragement and knowing that, in the end, coal makes diamonds.

Last, and most of all, I thank my family. Mandy, you are my love and the soil for my roots. These past few years have been by far some of the most painful and challenging for both of us. You have endured with me through every moment. Without you by my side, I would be living a very different story.

To my children—Elijah, Stella, Levi, and Georgia—thank you for helping me every day to show up, to pay attention, and to believe I can become a better and more human father in this crazy, breakneck world. I love you.

A Case for Mindfulness

Fully present leaders engage employees, maximize productivity, and create energy where there was none before. We're not alone on this point. Corporate America has grown increasingly enamored with the bottom-line benefits of a present and engaged workforce. How have they gone about cultivating that presence? One word: mindfulness. In recent years, mindfulness has become "Corporate America's Strange New Gospel."[1] A well-known case study illustrates why. During Mark Bertolini's first five years as CEO of Aetna, the insurance giant put 13,000 of its employees through mindfulness training.[2] As a result, the participants enjoyed a 28 percent drop in stress levels, 20 percent improvement in quality of sleep, and 19 percent drop in physical pain. Here's the kicker: mindfulness contributed to 62 minutes of recovered productivity per employee per week. That adds up to $3,000 a head, not to mention costs saved on healthcare for overly stressed employees. Multiply that out, and you've got about $40 million in recaptured productivity—all from a little meditation and yoga during the workday.

Google, Apple, Nike, General Mills, and Goldman Sachs represent just a handful of the Fortune 500 companies who've bought into the mindfulness revolution. It isn't just in our businesses; mindfulness is spreading out into American culture at large. Public schools across the United States are embracing it as a way to reduce student anxiety, promote mental health, and encourage positive behavior.

All told, the mindfulness and meditation industry generated $1.2 billion in 2017. Already a full 7 percent of America's alternative care market, that number is projected to top $2 billion by 2022.[3]

Eastern Religion in Disguise?

What is mindfulness anyway? We'll get to our definition below, but for now it's important we look at mindfulness from popular perspective. According to Virginia Heffernan of the *New York Times*, the word "has come to comprise a dizzying range of meanings for popular audiences."[4] For some, mindfulness is a way of life; for others, it's a useful set of practices for helping them to cope with reality. The term itself dates back to the late nineteenth century when a former British magistrate named Thomas William Rhys Davids coined the term *mindfulness* as a way to sell his countrymen on the Buddhist practice of *sati*, a form of meditation that brings together memory, recollection, awareness, and temporal presence.[5] Nearly a century later, the Hippie culture of the sixties and seventies went bananas over all things Eastern, including *sati*. As those young idealists grew into middle-aged pragmatists, much of their spirituality began to fade. Still, secular people wanted to hang on to the self-improvement of Buddhism without any of the religiousness.

So along came a molecular biologist named Jon Kabat-Zinn. As someone trained in Zen Buddhism, Kabat-Zinn found in mindfulness the opportunity to strip meditation of its religious husk and repackage it for the masses. In 1979, Kabat-Zinn opened the Stress Reduction Clinic at the University of Massachusetts Medical School and developed an eight-week stress-reduction program called Mindfulness-Based Stress Reduction. He went on to publish a spate of mindfulness-related books, culminating in his 1994 release, *Wherever You Go, There You Are: Mindfulness Meditation in Everyday Life*. Over time, through Kabat-Zinn and others like Daniel Goleman and Richard Davidson, mindfulness entered America's consciousness.

Sati vs. Zakar

The genius of Kabat-Zinn's approach was his ability to wrap Eastern spirituality in Western scientific research. That's precisely what makes most Christians nervous. Should they be? Bhante Henepola Gunaratana defines mindfulness as "present-moment awareness" cultivated by *sati*, or "bare attention."[6] When you're fixated on last week's screw-up or plagued with anxiety about the future, mindfulness equips you to step back, notice what's going on inside of you, and regain clarity—that is, presence. In the corporate environment, this is as far as the story goes: learn a few mindfulness exercises, pepper them throughout your day, and enjoy the benefits. In that minimal way, it's hard to imagine what Christians would have to fuss about.

However, many (not all) Buddhists would argue that *sati* shows us how everything changes, nothing is permanent, our worldly longings are futile, and the "self" is just an illusion. As Christians, we must reject this vision of reality. In Scripture, we learn that there's more to reality than change (Jas 1:17). As Adam learned when he was cast out of Eden, futility is a product of the fall (Gen 3:17–19). Humanity isn't an abstract collective consciousness. Each of us is an individual made for communion with God and with one another (Eph 2:18).

From a Christian perspective, mindfulness needs to focus less on *sati* and more on *zakar*—the Hebrew verb for remembering. Whereas *sati* calls us to abstract ourselves from the past in order to rediscover the present, *zakar* reminds us that we exist within the broader framework of God's redemptive story. We are all created to inhabit a particular time and space within history (Acts 17:26), and we are created anew in Christ to carry the specific work that God has placed before us (Eph 2:10). *Sati* says we need to let go of our past; *zakar* calls us to embrace it as a gift. *Sati* says life is ultimately futile; *zakar* reminds us that God has rescued us according to his purpose. *Sati* robs us of our individuality, *zakar* reclaims it for the sake of relationship.

If you're looking for a take-down of mindfulness, this isn't it. On the flip side, we're not constructing a baptized version of mindfulness. Instead, we offer a practical guide to reclaiming your presence as a leader in five dimensions: time, place, body, other, and story. For some, mindfulness is the worldview that makes presence possible. For others, it's nothing more than a useful technology. For us, it's a challenge for Christian leaders to put on the mind of Christ (1 Cor 2:16; cf. Phil 2:5).

Principles and Practices

The following is a collection of the fifteen principles and practices you'll find distributed across this book. For more information, consult the associated chapter.

Chapter 6: The Gift of Time

Principle: Time isn't a resource to be manipulated but a gift to be received. Because God has numbered our days, we can live in the freedom of knowing that he has given us all the time we need to do what he's calling us to do.

Practice: Set aside fifteen minutes each morning to pray over your schedule. Ask God to free you from anxiety over all there is to accomplish and for the faith to trust that he has already gone before you into your day.

Chapter 7: Leadership at the Speed of When

Principle: The best leaders don't let the urgency of leadership short-circuit their own embodied sense of timing. Always in tune with the present, they know when to jog and when to sprint as they lead people toward the finish line.

Practice: Fit restorative breaks into your schedule this week. Every hour, on the hour, get up and take a five minute walk around the halls. Remember, you're not slacking; you're ramping up your impact for the next hour.

Chapter 8: You're Going to Die

Principle: Death is the common lot of humanity in this fallen world. Knowing our days are numbered, present leaders resolve to live each moment for the glory of God and the good of others.

Practice: Put thirty minutes on your calendar to reflect on your own inevitable end. Who do you want by your side in your final moments? Who will be there when they lay you in the ground? What will they put on your tombstone? How will you be remembered?

Chapter 12: There's a Place for Us

Principle: Without a place, leaders flame out. We need to *make* and *protect* our homes and neighborhoods so they can become spaces of love, joy, peace, rest, and presence.

Practice: Plan a one-day, in-home retreat. Shut off every connection to the outside world and commit your family to a day of full presence. Read books, play games, cook a meal together, and *talk* to one another. If you don't have a family to do this with, invite a good friend or significant other to join you.

Chapter 13: Out of the Shadows

Principle: Displacement lurks in the space between *official* and *shadow* cultures. Placefulness at work and in the community bridges that gap. It enables us and others to live, lead, and work at our highest levels.

Practice: Gather your senior leadership. Put up a whiteboard and brainstorm your ideal work environment. Prompt your team with positive descriptors: high-energy, collaboration, productivity, and so on. Dream up a space that embodies those characteristics.

Plot out what it'll take to move from your current space to that ideal environment and commit to incremental action.

Do you lead a distributed workforce? If so, encourage each employee to envision his or her own space. How can they cultivate placefulness where they are?

Chapter 14: Rediscovering Your Place in Nature

Principle: God made us for this world, and he made this world for us. To be all he made us to be, and to perform in the way he designed us to perform, we need to get back to nature.

Practice: Go for a stroll in the woods. Stop to appreciate *everything*: the bubbling brook, the tall tree, the bright sky. When you do, praise God for that specific beauty. Ask him to cultivate in you a deep sense of wonder over all he has made.

Chapter 18: Embodied Stress: An Unexpected Friend

Principle: When we write stress and anxiety off as sin, we ignore what our bodies are trying to tell us. We need to acknowledge and befriend these responses, even as we take them to God to hear what *he* would say through them.

Practice: Next time you feel your heart rate quickening and your blood pressure rising, stop and notice your circumstances. What triggered this stress? Was it a person? A deadline? A daunting task? Take a deep breath and offer up that trigger to God in prayer.

Chapter 19: Learning to Think with Your Heart

Principle: Knowledge is about more than using your head. Embodied presence demands closer attention to the *heart* and the willingness not only to *think* but to *feel* and *act*.

Practice: Give yourself thirty minutes to reflect on your last major decision. What steps did you take to decide? Take stock of the precise moments when a gut feeling, an angry reaction, or a sense of peace influenced the process. Did those emotions help or hinder you? How can you account for them in future decisions?

Chapter 20: Practice Makes Permanent

Principle: Thoughts and intentions alone will never transform our leadership. We need practice—a lot of it—to "put on" the virtues of presence and humanity in our everyday lives.

Practice: Choose a virtue and list the everyday actions you can take to cultivate it. Then commit to *practice* some of those actions daily for the next month. For example, to cultivate selflessness, make a daily habit of buying coffee for a team member. Simple acts like this one will train you to put others first.

Chapter 24: You Are Never Alone

Principle: The myth of self-making undercuts God's relational design for human beings. Leadership can't learn humanity and presence in isolation. We *need* others to know and love us even as we know and love them.

Practice: Jot down a list of five friends you can call at any time of the day. Embrace these names as your lifeline to otherfulness. Call them often, if only for a few minutes at a time. Share your struggles. Invite their correction. Solicit their prayer. These are the people who've made you. They're the ones who will gently remind you of the truth: "*I* didn't build that. By the grace of God, *we* did."

Chapter 25: The Journey from Dependence to Interdependence

Principle: Unbalanced dependence or independence distorts our social reality. God has made us for both: to lean on and be leaned on in otherful interdependence. We do that by loving others through concrete acts of service and allowing them to serve us in return.

Practice: Find an opportunity to serve someone this week. Mow the neighbor's lawn, bring a meal to an elderly member of your congregation, or volunteer at a rescue mission. When you do, take time to connect with the people you're serving. Let these moments remind you how much we all need one another.

Chapter 26: Tribes Without Tribalism

Principle: Humans are tribal creatures. Leaders need to understand their tribal relationships and leverage them for their good and the flourishing of the people they lead.

Practice: Write up an inventory of fellow leaders from *outside* your company who meet Cloud's requirements for a corner four relationship. Invite them out to breakfast for an informal mastermind. Gauging their interest, see if you can formalize the gathering into an advisory group that meets once a month.

Chapter 30: The Stories We Tell Ourselves

Principle: We are storytelling animals; the stories we tell ourselves will either make or break us. To lead with presence and authority, we need to bring those stories out of the darkness and into the light.

Practice: Write out a fifteen-minute version of your life story. Where are the "contamination narratives," and how do they affect what follows? What would change if you were to recast the contamination as a catalyst for growth through adversity? How would that alter the story you tell about who you are?

Chapter 31: The Stories We Tell Each Other

Principle: Storytelling is the most powerful way to bind scattered individuals into a tight crew. Leaders who encourage communal storytelling inspire employees to be present *together*.

Practice: Send out a company-wide email asking for stories about when your employees saw one of their coworkers embody the spirit of your organization. Pick three of the most compelling stories, package them up in written form, and send them to everyone in the company.

Chapter 32: The Stories We Tell Together

Principle: The best leaders own the organization's story and communicate it with passion. They invite others to write themselves into that narrative and, in turn, communicate it to the world. Stories build cultures, and storied cultures rise to the top of their class.

Practice: Set aside two hours to tell Simmons's six types of stories. Record your voice, dictate your thoughts, or jot ideas down on a yellow legal pad—whatever works. Once you've got your ideas down, coordinate with your communications department to polish the narrative. Drill those stories into your mind, and start telling them every chance you get.

Notes

Chapter 1: How Long Can You Keep This Up?

1. Mindfulness is a difficult concept to pin down in modern usage. In this book, we're not taking a hard line for or against it. Rather, we're treating mindfulness as a way to apply the mind of Christ (1 Cor 2:16; cf. Phil 2:5) to every dimension of our humanity. For more on what mindfulness is and how we intend to work with it, see appendix A.

2. Anxiety and Depression Association of America, "Facts and Statistics," ADAA, https://adaa.org/about-adaa/press-room/facts-statistics.

3. National Institute of Mental Health, "Major Depression," NIMH, most recently updated February 2019, https://www.nimh.nih.gov/health/statistics/major-depression.shtml.

4. For a brief introduction to the problem, see Jeanne Sahadi, "Depression in the C-suite," CNN Business, August 7, 2018, https://www.cnn.com/2018/09/30/success/ceos-depression/index.html.

Chapter 2: The Case for Presence

1. Pascal-Emmanuel Gobry, "Apple's Amazing New Grand Central Store Could Generate Half-A-Billion Of Sales A Year," *Business Insider*, July 26, 2011, https://www.businessinsider.com/apple-grand-central-store-revenue-2011-7.

2. As of May 9, 2019, JCPenney is trading at just above $1.00. Compare that to its $43 value in January 2012 immediately after Johnson announced his bold new vision.

3. Gardiner Morse, "What Ron Johnson Got Right," *Harvard Business Review*, April 11, 2013, https://hbr.org/2013/04/what-ron-johnson-got-right.

4. Evgeny Morozov, *To Save Everything, Click Here: The Folly of Technological Solutionism* (New York: Public Affairs, 2014).

5. Tasha Eurich, *Insight: The Surprising Truth about How Others See Us, How We See Ourselves, and Why the Answers Matter More than We Think* (New York: Currency, 2018).

6. Ibid.

7. Kathryn Schulz, "Being Wrong," *The New York Times*, June 10, 2010, https://www.nytimes.com/2010/06/11/books/excerpt-being-wrong.html.

8. Gallup, "State of the American Workplace, 2017," Gallup.com, https://www.gallup.com/workplace/238085/state-american-workplace-report-2017.aspx.

9. Ibid., 2.

10. Christine Porath, "Creating a More Human Workplace Where Employees and Business Thrive," Effective Practice Guidelines Series (SHRM Foundation, 2016), https://www.shrm.org/hr-today/trends-and-forecasting/special-reports-and-expert-views/Documents/Human-Workplace.pdf.

11. American Management Association, "New Study Shows Nice Guys Finish First," AMA, January 24, 2019, https://www.amanet.org//articles/new-study-shows-nice-guys-finish-first/.

12. Ibid.

13. For a quick way into Eurich's research, see Tasha Eurich, "What Self-Awareness Really Is (and How to Cultivate It)," *Harvard Business Review*, January 4, 2018, https://hbr.org/2018/01/what-self-awareness-really-is-and-how-to-cultivate-it.

14. Matthew Lippincott, "Effective Leadership Starts with Self-Awareness," Association for Talent Development, April 17, 2018, https://www.td.org/insights/effective-leadership-starts-with-self-awareness.

15. Travis Bradberry, "Emotional Intelligence—EQ," *Forbes*, January 9, 2014, https://www.forbes.com/sites/travisbradberry/2014/01/09/emotional-intelligence/.

16. Geetu Bharwaney, Reuven Bar-On, and Adèle MacKinlay, "EQ and the Bottom Line: Emotional Intelligence Increases Individual Occupational Performance, Leadership and Organisational Productivity" (Ei World Limited, 2011).

Chapter 3: How Do We Get Our Humanity Back?

1. Andrew Sullivan, "I Used to Be a Human Being," *New York Magazine*, September 18, 2016, http://nymag.com/intelligencer/2016/09/andrew-sullivan-my-distraction-sickness-and-yours.html.

2. Ibid.

3. Ibid.
4. Anthony A. Hoekema, *Created in God's Image* (Grand Rapids: Eerdmans, 1994), 52.
5. Thomas Merton, *The Intimate Merton: His Life from His Journals* (San Francisco: HarperOne, 2001), March 19, 1958.
6. Bruce A. Ware, *The Man Christ Jesus: Theological Reflections on the Humanity of Christ* (Wheaton, IL: Crossway, 2012), 33.
7. Hoekema, *Created in God's Image*, 75–82.
8. Ibid., 102–11.
9. Klyne R. Snodgrass, *Who God Says You Are: A Christian Understanding of Identity* (Grand Rapids: Eerdmans, 2018).
10. Ibid., 7.
11. Ibid., 9.

The Science of Practicing Presence

1. K. W. Brown and R. M. Ryan , "The Benefits of Being Present: Mindfulness and Its Role in Psychological Well-Being," *Journal of Personality and Social Psychology* 84 (2003): 822–48.
2. Michael T. Treadway and Sara W. Lazar, "The Neurobiology of Mindfulness," *Clinical Handbook of Mindfulness*, ed. Fabrizio Didonna (New York: Springer, 2009), 45–57.
3. John P. J. Pinel and Steven J. Barnes, *Biopsychology*, 10th ed. (Hoboken, NJ: Pearson Higher Education, 2017), 473–96.
4. W. C. Dement, *Some Must Watch While Some Must Sleep* (New York: Norton, 1978).

Chapter 4: Where Did All Our Time Go?

1. Yong Liu et al., "Prevalence of Healthy Sleep Duration among Adults—United States, 2014," *Morbidity and Mortality Weekly Report* 65 (2016), https://doi.org/10.15585/mmwr.mm6506a1.
2. S. G. Klauer et al., "The Impact of Driver Inattention On Near-Crash/ Crash Risk: An Analysis Using the 100-Car Naturalistic Driving Study Data," Virginia Tech Transportation Institute (Blacksburg, VA: US Department of Transportation, National Highway Traffic Safety Administration, 2006), https://www.nhtsa.gov/DOT/NHTSA/NRD/Articles/HF/Reducing%20Unsafe%20behaviors/810594/810594.htm.
3. "The Costs of Insufficient Sleep," Rand Corporation, November 29, 2016, https://www.rand.org/randeurope/research/projects/the-value -of-the-sleep-economy.html.

4. "State of American Vacation 2018," US Travel Association, May 8, 2018, https://www.ustravel.org/research/state-american-vacation-2018.

5. Amy Elisa Jackson, "We Just Can't Unplug: 2 in 3 Employees Report Working While on Vacation," Glassdoor Blog, May 24, 2017, https://www.glassdoor.com/blog/vacation-realities-2017/.

6. Isabel Thottam, "The More Money You Make, The Less Vacation You Get—Here's Why," Glassdoor Blog, August 7, 2017, https://www.glassdoor.com/blog/the-more-money-you-make-the-less-vacation-you-get-heres-why/.

7. Baron Baptiste, *Journey Into Power: How to Sculpt Your Ideal Body, Free Your True Self, and Transform Your Life with Yoga* (New York: Simon and Schuster, 2011), 33.

8. For more on mindfulness, see appendix A.

9. Leslie A. Perlow, Constance Noonan Hadley, and Eunice Eun, "Stop the Meeting Madness," *Harvard Business Review*, July 1, 2017, https://hbr.org/2017/07/stop-the-meeting-madness.

10. Ryder Carroll, *The Bullet Journal Method: Track the Past, Order the Present, Design the Future* (New York: Portfolio/Penguin, 2018).

11. Thomas Merton, *Seasons of Celebration: Meditations on the Cycle of Liturgical Feasts* (South Bend, IN: Ave Maria Press, 2009), 51.

12. Not least for the term itself, I owe much of my perspective on this to John Swinton, *Becoming Friends of Time: Disability, Timefullness, and Gentle Discipleship* (Waco, TX: Baylor University Press, 2016).

13. Thomas Merton, *Seeds of Destruction* (New York: Farrar, Straus and Giroux, 1980), xiv.

Chapter 5: The Case for Timefulness

1. As cited in Marva J. Dawn, *Morning by Morning* (Grand Rapids: Eerdmans, 2001), 242.

2. Giada Di Stefano, Francesca Gino, Gary P. Pisano, and Bradley Staats, "Making Experience Count: The Role of Reflection in Individual Learning," Harvard Business School Working Paper, No. 14-093, March 2014 (Revised June 2016).

3. Kara Chin, "Investing Legend Ray Dalio Shares the Simple Formula at the Heart of His Success," Business Insider, May 15, 2017, https://www.businessinsider.com/bridgewater-ceo-ray-dalio-learning-from-mistakes-pain-reflection-progress-2017-5.

4. Marc Wittmann, *Felt Time: The Psychology of How We Perceive Time* (Cambridge, MA: MIT Press, 2016), 101.

5. Michael Breus, *The Power of When: Discover Your Chronotype—and*

the Best Time to Eat Lunch, Ask for a Raise, Have Sex, Write a Novel, Take Your Meds, and More (Boston, MA: Little, Brown, and Company, 2016), 4.

Chapter 6: The Gift of Time

1. Developed by Philip Zimbardo and Rosemary Sword, TPT's goal is to understand a person's fundamental orientation toward the past, present, and future and, in so doing, help that person to deal with issues like depression, stress, and anxiety. See Philip G. Zimbardo and Rosemary K. M. Sword, *Living and Loving Better with Time Perspective Therapy: Healing from the Past, Embracing the Present, Creating an Ideal Future* (Jefferson, NC: McFarland, 2017).
2. Francis Turretin, *Institutes of Elenctic Theology*, ed. James T. Dennison Jr., trans. George Musgrave Giger, vol. 1 (Phillipsburg, NJ: P&R, 1992–97), 203.
3. For the following, see Leland Ryken et al., eds., *Dictionary of Biblical Imagery* (Downers Grove, IL: InterVarsity Press, 1998), 870–72.
4. For more on this reading of Ecclesiastes, see Tremper Longman III and Raymond B. Dillard, *An Introduction to the Old Testament* (Grand Rapids: Zondervan, 2006), 284–87.
5. Ibid., 285.
6. See N. T. Wright, *Simply Jesus: A New Vision of Who He Was, What He Did, and Why He Matters* (New York: HarperOne, 2011), 131–50.
7. N. T. Wright, *The Case for the Psalms: Why They Are Essential* (New York: HarperOne, 2013), 22.
8. For God, to be alive is to be in community. His life is the "fullness of unity and relation—that is, love—which God immanently is as Father, Son, and Spirit." John Webster, "On Evangelical Ecclesiology," *Ecclesiology* 1, no. 1 (2004): 13.
9. Alan Burdick, *Why Time Flies: A Mostly Scientific Investigation* (New York: Simon and Schuster, 2017), 17, 33.

Chapter 7: Leadership at the Speed of When

1. Daniel H. Pink, *When: The Scientific Secrets of Perfect Timing* (New York: Riverhead, 2018).
2. John C. Maxwell, *The 21 Irrefutable Laws of Leadership: Follow Them and People Will Follow You* (Nashville: Thomas Nelson, 2007).
3. Malcolm Gladwell, "David and Goliath: The Power of the Underdog," presented at Inbound 2014, Boston, September 18, 2014.

4. John P. Kotter, *A Sense of Urgency* (Boston, MA: Harvard Business Press, 2008), 6.

5. John H. Zenger and Joseph Folkman, *Speed: How Leaders Accelerate Successful Execution* (New York: McGraw Hill Professional, 2016).

6. *Extraordinary*, for Zenger and Folkman, means high-speed and high-quality, as quantified by their proprietary research. This and the following stats are helpfully summarized in the infographic titled "Leadership Speed" at https://zengerfolkman.com/wp-content/uploads/2019/05/Leadership-Speed%E2%80%94Infographic.pdf.

7. Tony Schwartz and Christine Porath, "The Power of Meeting Your Employees' Needs," *Harvard Business Review*, June 30, 2014, https://hbr.org/2014/06/the-power-of-meeting-your-employees-needs.

8. Carl Honore, *In Praise of Slowness: Challenging the Cult of Speed* (New York, NY: Harper Collins, 2009), 14–15.

9. Ibid., 15.

10. In *Present Shock*, Douglas Rushkoff talks about the concept of overwinding. Our world is comprised of different time scales—think of the time it takes for a volcano to form versus the time it takes to get young kids ready for school. The latter only *feels* like a million years. Overwinding describes when we transfer the expectations of one timescale to another. Markets, for example, tend to shift much more quickly than institutions. We go wrong when we try to fit one scale into another and choose the pace we'd prefer rather than what the moment demands. See Douglas Rushkoff, *Present Shock: When Everything Happens Now* (New York: Penguin, 2013), 131–97.

11. Michael Breus, *The Power of When: Discover Your Chronotype—and the Best Time to Eat Lunch, Ask for a Raise, Have Sex, Write a Novel, Take Your Meds, and More* (Boston, MA: Little, Brown, and Company, 2016).

12. Pink, *When*, 32.

13. Ibid., 61.

Chapter 8: You're Going to Die

1. Jeff Bercovici, "Silicon Valley's Latest Lifehack: Death—Future Human," Medium, July 18, 2018, https://medium.com/s/futurehuman/game-over-bf20324ba420.

2. Lucius Annaeus Seneca, *Dialogues and Essays* (Oxford: Oxford University Press, 2008), 130.

3. Cited by Bercovici, "Silicon Valley's Latest Lifehack."

4. Rob Moll, *The Art of Dying: Living Fully into the Life to Come* (Downers Grove, IL: InterVarsity Press, 2013).

5. Ibid., 32.

6. Jürgen Moltmann, *The Coming of God: Christian Eschatology* (Minneapolis: Fortress, 2004), 50–51.

7. Anthony C. Thiselton, *Life After Death: A New Approach to the Last Things* (Grand Rapids: Eerdmans, 2011), 3.

8. Sheldon Solomon, Jeff Greenberg, and Thomas A. Pyszczynski, *The Worm at the Core: On the Role of Death in Life* (New York: Random House, 2015), 7.

9. Fred Kofman, *The Meaning Revolution: The Power of Transcendent Leadership* (New York: Crown, 2018), 254ff.

10. Moltmann, *The Coming of God*, 51.

11. Peter Kreeft, *Love Is Stronger than Death* (San Francisco, CA: Ignatius Press, 1992), 22.

12. Ibid.

13. Ibid.

14. "'You've Got to Find What You Love,' Jobs Says," Stanford News, June 14, 2005, http://news.stanford.edu/news/2005/june15/jobs-061505.html.

15. Jonathan Edwards, "Resolutions," in *Works of Jonathan Edwards*, vol. 16, *Letters and Personal Writings*, ed. George S. Claghorn (New Haven, CT: Yale University Press, 1957–2008), http://edwards.yale.edu/archive?path=aHRocDovL2Vkd2FyZHMueWFsZS5lZHUvY2dpLWJpbi9uZXdwaGlsby9nZXRvYmplY3QucGw/Yy44xNTo3NDoxLndqZW8=.

Chapter 9: The Blessing of Timefulness

1. From the ancient Greek translation (Septuagint) of Isaiah 50:4.

2. Douglas Rushkoff, *Present Shock: When Everything Happens Now* (New York: Penguin, 2013).

3. "The fulness [sic] of time is the time of His emptiness in us. The fulness of time is the time of our emptiness, which draws Christ down into our lives, so that in us and through us He may bring the fullness of His truth to the world." Thomas Merton and William Shannon, *Seasons of Celebration: Meditations on the Cycle of Liturgical Feasts* (South Bend, IN: Ave Maria Press, 2009), 94–95.

4. Thomas Merton, *Raids on the Unspeakable* (New York: New Directions, 1964), 70.

5. Thomas Merton, *Seeds of Destruction* (New York, NY: Farrar, Straus and Giroux, 1980), xiv.

6. Merton, *Seasons of Celebration*, 51.
7. Ibid.

Time and the Brain

1. Albert Tsao et al., "Integrating Time from Experience in the Lateral Entorhinal Cortex," *Nature: International Journal of Science* 561 (2018): 57–62.
2. Ibid.
3. Laura Vanderkam, *Off the Clock: Feel Less Busy While Getting More Done* (New York: Portfolio/Penguin, 2018).

Chapter 10: Where Are You?

1. Jon Kabat-Zinn, *Wherever You Go, There You Are: Mindfulness Meditation in Everyday Life* (New York: Hachette, 1994).
2. "Time Flies: U.S. Adults Now Spend Nearly Half a Day Interacting with Media," Nielsen, July 31, 2018, https://www.nielsen.com/us/en/insights/article/2018/time-flies-us-adults-now-spend-nearly-half-a-day-interacting-with-media/.
3. Richard J. Foster, *Celebration of Discipline: The Path to Spiritual Growth* (San Francisco: HarperSanFrancisco, 1998), 96–109.

Chapter 11: The Case for Placefulness

1. Lindsay Lowe, "The 'Marie Kondo Effect'? Thrift Stores Nationwide See an Uptick in Donations," Today.com, January 15, 2019, https://www.today.com/home/marie-kondo-effect-thrift-stores-nationwide-see-uptick-donations-t146810.
2. Marie Kondo, *The Life-Changing Magic of Tidying Up: The Japanese Art of Decluttering and Organizing* (Berkeley, CA: Ten Speed, 2014), 114.
3. Ibid., 118.
4. Workfront, "Workfront Delivers Results of Survey Showing Employees Think Technology Is Killing Family Dinnertime," Cision PR Newswire, April 21, 2015, https://www.prnewswire.com/news-releases/workfront-delivers-results-of-survey-showing-employees-think-technology-is-killing-family-dinnertime-300066723.html.
5. Ryan J. Dwyer, Kostadin Kushlev, and Elizabeth W. Dunn, "Smartphone Use Undermines Enjoyment of Face-to-Face Social Interactions," *Journal of Experimental Social Psychology* 78 (September 1, 2018): 233–39, https://doi.org/10.1016/j.jesp.2017.10.007.
6. As it just so happens, Kondo has a new book titled *Joy at Work:*

The Career-Changing Magic of Tidying Up set to release at the same time as this book. Where there's a book, there's a market. The nerve Kondo has tapped extends out the front door and straight into the marketplace. Why? Because we need placefulness at work every bit as much as we need it at home.

7. Scott Doorley and Scott Witthoft, *Make Space: How to Set the Stage for Creative Collaboration* (Hoboken, NJ: Wiley, 2012), 4.

8. Ibid., 5.

9. Rex Miller, Mabel Casey, and Mark Konchar, *Change Your Space, Change Your Culture: How Engaging Workspaces Lead to Transformation and Growth* (Hoboken, NJ: Wiley, 2014), xiv.

10. Ibid., 16.

11. "Simon Sinek, Why Leaders Eat Last," YouTube video, by 99U, published December 4, 2013, https://www.youtube.com/watch?v=ReRcHdeUG9Y.

12. Jun Yan, "Percentage of Americans Taking Antidepressants Climbs," Psychiatric News, September 15, 2017, https://psychnews.psychiatryonline.org/doi/abs/10.1176/appi.pn.2017.pp9b2.

13. Aditi Nerurkar et al., "When Physicians Counsel About Stress: Results of a National Study," *JAMA Internal Medicine* 173, no. 1 (January 14, 2013): 76–77, https://doi.org/10.1001/2013.jamainternmed.480.

14. Health Advocate, "Stress in the Workplace: Meeting the Challenge" (Health Advocate, Inc., 2009), http://healthadvocate.com/downloads/webinars/stress-workplace.pdf.

15. Leslie Kwoh, "When the CEO Burns Out," *Wall Street Journal*, May 7, 2013, https://www.wsj.com/articles/SB10001424127887323687604578469124008524696.

16. Marily Oppezzo and Daniel L. Schwartz, "Give Your Ideas Some Legs: The Positive Effect of Walking on Creative Thinking," *Journal of Experimental Psychology: Learning, Memory, and Cognition* 40, no. 4 (2014): 1142–52, https://doi.org/10.1037/a0036577.

17. Florence Williams, *The Nature Fix: Why Nature Makes Us Happier, Healthier, and More Creative* (New York: Norton, 2017), 163.

18. Ibid, 254.

19. George Michelsen Foy, *Finding North: How Navigation Makes Us Human* (New York: Flatiron, 2016), 1.

Chapter 12: There's a Place for Us

1. A. J. Katz, "October 2018 Ratings: Fox News Channel Averaged More Total Viewers Than CNN and MSNBC Combined," TVNewser, October 30, 2018, https://adweek.it/2CP7MrC.

2. Much more needs to be said here about the place of Bethlehem in the history of redemption and the relationship between God's presence, his people, and the everyday spaces we inhabit today. However, the basic point is this: in the incarnation of Jesus Christ in a specific time, place, and body, we have the most profound affirmation of history, geography, and human embodiedness.

3. Mona Chalabi, "How Many Times Does The Average Person Move?," *FiveThirtyEight* (blog), January 29, 2015, https://fivethirtyeight.com/features/how-many-times-the-average-person-moves/.

4. Neli Esipova, Anita Pugliese, and Julie Ray, "381 Million Adults Worldwide Migrate Within Countries," Gallup, May 15, 2013, https://news.gallup.com/poll/162488/381-million-adults-worldwide-migrate-within-countries.aspx.

5. Melody Warnick, *This Is Where You Belong: Finding Home Wherever You Are* (New York: Penguin, 2017).

6. Stefan Münzer et al., "Computer-Assisted Navigation and the Acquisition of Route and Survey Knowledge," *Journal of Environmental Psychology* 26, no. 4 (December 1, 2006): 300–8, https://doi.org/10.1016/j.jenvp.2006.08.001.

7. "Taxi Drivers' Brains 'Grow' on the Job," BBC News World Edition, March 14, 2000, http://news.bbc.co.uk/2/hi/677048.stm.

8. National Research Council, *Learning to Think Spatially* (Washington, DC: National Academies Press, 2006), https://doi.org/10.17226/11019.

9. Belden C. Lane, *Landscapes of the Sacred: Geography and Narrative in American Spirituality* (Baltimore: Johns Hopkins University Press, 2001), 39.

10. Ibid.

11. Nicoletta Isar, "Chôra: Tracing the Presence," *Review of European Studies* 1, no. 1 (June 2009): 39–55.

12. Warnick, *This Is Where You Belong*, 57ff.

Chapter 13: Out of the Shadows

1. Colin Ellard, *Places of the Heart: The Psychogeography of Everyday Life* (New York: Bellevue Literary Press, 2015), 13.

2. Marc Auge, *Non-Places: An Introduction to Supermodernity*, trans. John Howe (New York: Verso, 2009).

3. Winston Churchill, speech in the House of Commons, October 28, 1943.

4. Rex Miller, Mabel Casey, and Mark Konchar, *Change Your Space, Change Your Culture: How Engaging Workspaces Lead to Transformation and Growth* (Hoboken, NJ: Wiley, 2014), 16.

5. Ibid., 16–18.

6. Ibid., 17–18.

7. Juriaan van Meel, Yuri Martens, and Hermen Jan van Ree, *Planning Office Spaces: A Practical Guide for Managers and Designers* (London, UK: Laurence King, 2010).

8. Porter Novelli/Cone, "2018 Porter Novelli/Cone Purpose Premium Index," Cone, 2018, http://www.conecomm.com/research-blog/purpose-premium.

9. Porter Novelli/Cone, "2018 Cone/Porter Novelli Purpose Study," Cone, 2018, http://www.conecomm.com/research-blog/2018-purpose-study.

10. Tonia E. Ries et al., "2018 Edelman Trust Barometer Global Report," Edelman, 2018, https://www.edelman.com/sites/g/files/aatuss191/files/2018-10/2018_Edelman_Trust_Barometer_Global_Report_FEB.pdf.

11. "Sustainable Selections: How Socially Responsible Companies Are Turning a Profit," Nielsen, October 12, 2015, http://www.nielsen.com/us/en/insights/news/2015/sustainable-selections-how-socially-responsible-companies-are-turning-a-profit.

12. "Benevity Study Links Employee-Centric Corporate Goodness Programs to Big Gains in Retention," Benevity, May 31, 2018, https://www.benevity.com/press-releases/study-links-corporate-goodness-to-retention.

13. "The Business Case for Purpose," A Harvard Business Review Analytic Services Report (Harvard Business School Publishing, 2015), https://hbr.org/resources/pdfs/comm/ey/19392HBRReportEY.pdf.

14. Adapted from Miller, Casey, and Konchar, *Change Your Space, Change Your Culture*, 4ff.

Chapter 14: Rediscovering Your Place in Nature

1. Jonathan Franzen, *Farther Away: Essays* (New York: Picador, 2013), 37–38.

2. Franzen, *Farther Away*, 38.

3. Ibid.

4. Richard Louv, *Last Child in the Woods: Saving Our Children From Nature-Deficit Disorder* (Chapel Hill, NC: Algonquin, 2008).

5. Neil E. Klepeis et al., "The National Human Activity Pattern Survey (NHAPS): A Resource for Assessing Exposure to Environmental Pollutants," *Journal of Exposure Science and Environmental Epidemiology* 11, no. 3 (July 1, 2001): 231–52, https://doi.org/10.1038/sj.jea.7500165.

6. Ihab Elzeyadi, "Daylighting-Bias and Biophilia: Quantifying the

Impact of Daylighting on Occupants Health," US Green Building Council, October 3, 2011, https://www.usgbc.org/resources/daylighting-bias-and-biophilia-quantifying-impact-daylighting -occupants-health.

7. Cary Cooper, "Human Spaces: The Global Impact of Biophilic Design in the Workplace" (Manchester, UK: Robertson Cooper, 2015), https://greenplantsforgreenbuildings.org/wp-content/uploads/2015/08/Human-Spaces-Report-Biophilic-Global_Impact_Biophilic_Design.pdf.

8. Bill Browning et al., "The Economics of Biophilia," Terrapin Bright Green, 2012, http://www.terrapinbrightgreen.com/wp-content/uploads/2012/06/The-Economics-of-Biophilia_Terrapin-Bright-Green-2012e.pdf.

9. Marc G. Berman et al., "Interacting with Nature Improves Cognition and Affect for Individuals with Depression," *Journal of Affective Disorders* 140, no. 3 (November 2012): 300–5, https://doi.org/10.1016/j.jad.2012.03.012.

10. Rita Berto, "Exposure to Restorative Environments Helps Restore Attentional Capacity," *Journal of Environmental Psychology* 25, no. 3 (September 1, 2005): 249–59, https://doi.org/10.1016/j.jenvp.2005.07.001.

11. Gen Xiang Mao et al., "Effects of Short-Term Forest Bathing on Human Health in a Broad-Leaved Evergreen Forest in Zhejiang Province, China," *Biomedical and Environmental Sciences: BES* 25, no. 3 (June 2012): 317–24, https://doi.org/10.3967/0895–3988.2012.03.010.

12. Andrea Faber Taylor and Frances E. Kuo, "Children With Attention Deficits Concentrate Better After Walk in the Park," *Journal of Attention Disorders* 12, no. 5 (March 1, 2009): 402–9, https://doi.org/10.1177/1087054708323000.

13. Marc G. Berman, John Jonides, and Stephen Kaplan, "The Cognitive Benefits of Interacting With Nature," *Psychological Science* 19, no. 12 (December 1, 2008): 1207–12, https://doi.org/10.1111/j.1467–9280.2008.02225.x.

14. David Whitemyer, "The Future of Evidence-Based Design," *Perspective*, Spring 2010, 9–14.

15. Martin Luther, *Luther's Works*, vol. 37, *Word and Sacrament III*, ed. Robert H. Fischer (Saint Louis: Fortress, 1961).

16. Bum-Jin Park et al., "Physiological Effects of Shinrin-Yoku (Taking in the Atmosphere of the Forest)—Using Salivary Cortisol and Cerebral Activity as Indicators," *Journal of Physiological Anthropology* 26, no. 2 (March 2007): 123–28.

17. Qing Li et al., "Acute Effects of Walking in Forest Environments

on Cardiovascular and Metabolic Parameters," *European Journal of Applied Physiology* 111, no. 11 (November 2011): 2845–53, https://doi.org/10.1007/s00421-011-1918-z.

18. J. Helliwell, R. Layard, and J. Sachs, *World Happiness Report 2019* (New York: Sustainable Development Solutions Network, 2019).

19. Florence Williams, *The Nature Fix: Why Nature Makes Us Happier, Healthier, and More Creative* (New York: Norton, 2017), 169–86.

20. Marily Oppezzo and Daniel L Schwartz, "Give Your Ideas Some Legs: The Positive Effect of Walking on Creative Thinking," *Journal of Experimental Psychology: Learning, Memory, and Cognition* 40 (July 2014): 1142–52, https://doi.org/10.1037/a0036577.

21. Russell Clayton, Christopher Thomas, and Jack Smothers, "How to Do Walking Meetings Right," *Harvard Business Review*, August 5, 2015, https://hbr.org/2015/08/how-to-do-walking-meetings-right.

22. Williams, *The Nature Fix*, 254.

Chapter 15: The Blessing of Placefulness

1. John Piper, "Christian Hedonism: Forgive the Label, But Don't Miss the Truth," Desiring God (blog), January 1, 1995, https://www.desiringgod.org/articles/christian-hedonism.

2. John Piper, *The Pleasures of God: Meditations on God's Delight in Being God* (Colorado Springs: Multnomah, 2000).

3. John Piper, *A Peculiar Glory: How the Christian Scriptures Reveal Their Complete Truthfulness* (Wheaton, IL: Crossway, 2016).

Chapter 16: Leadership, an Out-of-Body Experience?

1. For the sake of brevity, I collapse the ideas of mind, soul, and spirit into a single category. A fuller treatment would deal with more complicated issues of dichotomy, trichotomy, philosophy of mind, and so on.

2. S. N. Williams, "Descartes, René (1596–1650)," *New Dictionary of Theology: Historical and Systematic*, ed. Martin Davie et al. (Downers Grove, IL: InterVarsity Press, 2016), 250.

3. Christian philosopher Esther Meek laments the effects of dualism on our understanding of knowledge in general: "Descartes took the already extant penchant in western philosophy, inherited from Plato, to divide reality into 'the intelligible' and 'the sensible,' that is, that which is known by the intellect or reason, and that which is apprehended via the senses. Descartes then drew the lines even more starkly: mind and body. Mind is unextended thought; body is unminded physical extension. . . . Descartes, a mathematician, was trying to make all

knowledge as certain as he perceived mathematical knowledge to be. But in the process, all that was outside the individual mind was/is mindless, only worth measuring. Measurement gets old. My point is that as a result of this outlook, we tend to think of the world, the real, as mindless—like nobody is home." Esther Lightcap Meek, *Loving to Know: Covenant Epistemology* (Eugene, OR: Cascade, 2011), 18–19.

Chapter 17: The Case for Beingfulness

1. Amy Cuddy, "Your Body Language May Shape Who You Are," TEDGlobal, June 2012, https://www.ted.com/talks/amy_cuddy_your _body_language_shapes_who_you_are.
2. For a helpful review of the literature, see Brenda L. Connors and Richard Rende, "Embodied Decision-Making Style: Below and Beyond Cognition," *Frontiers in Psychology* 9 (July 4, 2018), https:// doi.org/10.3389/fpsyg.2018.01123.
3. Ibid.
4. Chris Weller, "In Japan, Woman's 'death from Overwork' Causes Government Stir," Business Insider, October 5, 2017, https://. www.businessinsider.com/japan-womans-death-from-overwork -government-rethinks-work-2017-10.
5. Danielle Demetriou, "'Death from Overworking' Claims Hit Record High in Japan," *The Telegraph*, April 4, 2016, https://www.telegraph .co.uk/news/2016/04/04/death-from-overworking-claims-hit-record -high-in-japan/.
6. Ibid.

Chapter 18: Embodied Stress

1. Kelly McGonigal, "How to Make Stress Your Friend," TEDGlobal, June 2013, https://www.ted.com/talks/kelly_mcgonigal_how_to _make_stress_your_friend.
2. Kelly McGonigal, *The Upside of Stress: Why Stress Is Good for You, and How to Get Good at It* (New York: Avery, 2016), 83.
3. Ibid., 38.
4. Ibid., 104.

Chapter 19: Learning to Think with Your Heart

1. Esther Lightcap Meek, *Longing to Know* (Grand Rapids: Brazos, 2003), 90–96.
2. Ibid., 94.
3. Ibid., 94.

4. Daniel Goleman, *Emotional Intelligence: Why It Can Matter More Than IQ* (New York: Bantam, 2005).

5. Daniel Goleman, "On Primal Leadership," http://www.danielgoleman.info/topics/leadership/.

6. Ibid.

Chapter 20: Practice Makes Permanent

1. This introduction is based on a Business Insider video: Alex Kuzoian, "Hitting a Major League Fastball Should Be Physically Impossible," *Business Insider*, April 15, 2016, https://www.businessinsider.com/science-major-league-fastball-brain-reaction-time-2016-4.

2. James K. A. Smith, *You Are What You Love: The Spiritual Power of Habit* (Grand Rapids: Brazos, 2016), 33.

Chapter 21: The Blessing of Beingfulness

1. Bessel van der Kolk, *The Body Keeps the Score: Brain, Mind, and Body in the Healing of Trauma* (New York: Penguin, 2014).

The Brain and the Body

1. Oswald Chambers, *Biblical Psychology: Christ-Centered Solutions for Daily Problems* (Grand Rapids: Discovery House, 1995).

2. "Understand the Facts: Symptoms," Anxiety and Depression Association of America, https://adaa.org/understanding-anxiety/panic-disorder-agoraphobia/symptoms.

3. Richard Rohr, *Everything Belongs: The Gift of Contemplative Prayer* (New York: Crossroads, 2003).

Chapter 22: The Loneliest Job in the World

1. Ironically, the photo had nothing to do with loneliness. Kennedy had a bad back and the most comfortable way for him to read the paper was to stand up and rest all his weight on his arms.

2. Thomas J. Saporito, "It's Time to Acknowledge CEO Loneliness," *Harvard Business Review*, February 15, 2012, https://hbr.org/2012/02/its-time-to-acknowledge-ceo-lo.

3. "How Much Time Do We Spend On Social Media?," Mediakix, infographic, December 15, 2016, http://mediakix.com/how-much-time-is-spent-on-social-media-lifetime/.

4. Vivek Murthy, "Work and the Loneliness Epidemic," *Harvard Business Review*, September 26, 2017, https://hbr.org/2017/09/work-and-the-loneliness-epidemic.

5. Brian A. Primack et al., "Social Media Use and Perceived Social Isolation Among Young Adults in the U.S.," *American Journal of Preventive Medicine* 53, no. 1 (July 1, 2017): 1–8, https://doi.org/10.1016/j.amepre.2017.01.010.
6. Scott Sauls, "Anxiety and Depression, My Strange Friends," March 16, 2019, http://scottsauls.com/blog/2019/03/16/mental-illness/.
7. Richard J. Krejcir, "Statistics On Pastors: 2016 Update," Francis A. Schaeffer Institute of Church Leadership Development, 2016, http://files.stablerack.com/webfiles/71795/pastorsstatWP2016.pdf.
8. Augustine, *Confessions*, trans. Henry Chadwick (New York: Oxford University Press, 1992), 1.1.1.

Chapter 23: The Case for Otherfulness

1. "New Cigna Study Reveals Loneliness at Epidemic Levels in America," Multivu, May 1, 2018, https://www.multivu.com/players/English/8294451-cigna-us-loneliness-survey/.
2. For the quote, Scott Eblin, *Overworked and Overwhelmed: The Mindfulness Alternative* (Hoboken, NJ: Wiley, 2014), 154. For the analysis, see Julianne Holt-Lunstad et al., "Loneliness and Social Isolation as Risk Factors for Mortality: A Meta-Analytic Review," *Perspectives on Psychological Science: A Journal of the Association for Psychological Science* 10, no. 2 (March 2015): 227–37, https://doi.org/10.1177/1745691614568352.
3. "Loneliness Is Bad for the Heart," European Society of Cardiology (ESC), June 9, 2018, https://www.escardio.org/The-ESC/Press-Office/Press-releases/loneliness-is-bad-for-the-heart.
4. Lynda Flowers et al., "Medicare Spends More on Socially Isolated Older Adults," Insight on the Issues, Washington, DC: AARP Public Policy Institute, November 2017, https://www.aarp.org/content/dam/aarp/ppi/2017/10/medicare-spends-more-on-socially-isolated-older-adults.pdf.
5. Emma Mamo, "How to Combat the Rise of Workplace Loneliness," Totaljobs, July 30, 2018, https://www.totaljobs.com/insidejob/how-to-combat-the-rise-of-workplace-loneliness/.
6. Holt-Lunstad et al., "Loneliness and Social Isolation as Risk Factors for Mortality."
7. Hakan Ozcelik and Sigal Barsade, "Work Loneliness and Employee Performance," *Academy of Management Annual Meeting Proceedings* 8, no. 1 (2011): 1–6, 2011, https://faculty.wharton.upenn.edu/wp-content/uploads/2012/05/Work_Loneliness_Performance_Study.pdf.
8. Gallup, "State of the American Workplace, 2017," Gallup.com,

118, https://www.gallup.com/workplace/238085/state-american -workplace-report-2017.aspx.

9. Ibid. In an earlier iteration of the study, Gallup found that individuals who had a best friend at work were 50 percent more likely to be satisfied with their job and seven times more likely to be engaged.

10. Ibid.

11. Ibid.

12. Leon Shapiro and Leo Bottary, *Power of Peers: How the Company You Keep Drives Leadership, Growth, and Success* (Brookline, MA: Routledge, 2016), 3.

13. Ibid., 3–8.

14. Cass R. Sunstein and Reid Hastie, *Wiser: Getting Beyond Groupthink to Make Groups Smarter* (Boston, MA: Harvard Business Review Press, 2014).

15. Jessica Bruder, "The Psychological Price of Entrepreneurship," Inc. com, August 20, 2013, https://www.inc.com/magazine/201309/ jessica-bruder/psychological-price-of-entrepreneurship.html.

Chapter 24: You Are Never Alone

1. Joshua Wolf Shenk, *Powers of Two: Finding the Essence of Innovation in Creative Pairs* (Boston, MA: Eamon Dolan/Houghton Mifflin Harcourt, 2014).

2. Henry Cloud, *The Power of the Other: The Startling Effect Other People Have on You, from the Boardroom to the Bedroom and Beyond—and What to Do About It* (New York: HarperBusiness, 2016), xv.

3. Ibid.

4. John T. Cacioppo, *Loneliness: Human Nature and the Need for Social Connection* (New York: Norton, 2009).

5. Kevin Hooks, "White Rabbit," *Lost*, October 20, 2004.

Chapter 25: The Journey from Dependence to Interdependence

1. Daniel Siegel, "Dopamine and Teenage Logic," The Atlantic, January 24, 2014, https://www.theatlantic.com/health/archive/2014/01/ dopamine-and-teenage-logic/282895/.

2. "State of Leadership Development 2015: Time to Act Is Now," Brandon Hall Group, 2015, http://www.brandonhall.com/mm5/ merchant.mvc?Screen=PROD&Product_Code=IP15+-+State+of+Leade rship+Development+2015.

Chapter 26: Tribes Without Tribalism

1. S. Miyagi et al., "Longevity and Diet in Okinawa, Japan: The Past, Present and Future," *Asia-Pacific Journal of Public Health* 15 Suppl. (2003): S3–9, https://doi.org/10.1177/101053950301500S03.

2. D. Craig Willcox et al., "Aging Gracefully: A Retrospective Analysis of Functional Status in Okinawan Centenarians," *The American Journal of Geriatric Psychiatry: Official Journal of the American Association for Geriatric Psychiatry* 15, no. 3 (March 2007): 252–56, https://doi.org/10.1097/JGP.0b013e3180319occ.

3. D. Craig Willcox et al., "Life at the Extreme Limit: Phenotypic Characteristics of Supercentenarians in Okinawa," *The Journals of Gerontology. Series A, Biological Sciences and Medical Sciences* 63, no. 11 (November 2008): 1201–8, https://doi.org/10.1093/gerona/63.11.1201.

4. Tara Parker-Pope, "The Power of Positive People," *New York Times*, July 10, 2018, https://www.nytimes.com/2018/07/10/well/the-power-of-positive-people.html.

5. Aislinn Leonard, "Moai—This Tradition Is Why Okinawan People Live Longer, Better," Blue Zones, August 16, 2018, https://www.bluezones.com/2018/08/moai-this-tradition-is-why-okinawan-people-live-longer-better/.

6. Seth Godin, *Tribes: We Need You to Lead Us* (New York, NY: Portfolio, 2008), 3.

7. Ibid.

8. Ibid.

9. Leon Shapiro and Leo Bottary, *Power of Peers: How the Company You Keep Drives Leadership, Growth, and Success* (Brookline, MA: Routledge, 2016), 51.

Chapter 28: What's Your Story?

1. Ron Thomas, "$24 Billion Worth of Leadership Training and What Do We Get?," TLNT, December 12, 2017, https://www.tlnt.com/24-billion-worth-of-leadership-training-and-what-do-we-get/.

2. Brené Brown, *The Gifts of Imperfection: Let Go of Who You Think You're Supposed to Be and Embrace Who You Are* (Center City, MN: Hazelden, 2010), 6.

3. Dan B. Allender, *To Be Told: God Invites You to Coauthor Your Future* (Colorado Springs: WaterBrook, 2006), 3.

4. Ibid.

5. Ibid., 6.

Chapter 29: The Case for Storyfulness

1. Becca R. Levy et al., "Longevity Increased by Positive Self-Perceptions of Aging," *Journal of Personality and Social Psychology* 83, no. 2 (August 2002): 261–70.
2. Ibid., 267.
3. Sally Lloyd-Jones, *The Jesus Storybook Bible* (Grand Rapids: ZonderKidz, 2007), 17.
4. Seth Godin, *All Marketers Are Liars: The Underground Classic That Explains How Marketing Really Works—and Why Authenticity Is the Best Marketing of All* (New York: Portfolio, 2012).
5. Daniel Montgomery, *Leadership Mosaic: 5 Leadership Principles for Ministry and Everyday Life* (Wheaton, IL: Crossway, 2016), 95–97. Brené Brown tells this story in *Daring Greatly: How the Courage to Be Vulnerable Transforms the Way We Live, Love, Parent, and Lead* (New York: Avery, 2012), 12–16.
6. Brown, *Daring Greatly*, 13–14.
7. Brené Brown, "The Power of Vulnerability," TEDxHouston, 2010, Houston, TX, https://www.ted.com/talks/brene_brown_on_vulnerability.

Chapter 30: The Stories We Tell Ourselves

1. Jim Loehr, *The Power of Story: Change Your Story, Change Your Destiny in Business and in Life* (New York, NY: Free Press, 2008), 69.
2. "Daily Affirmation," *Saturday Night Live*, NBC, New York, October 3, 1992, https://www.nbc.com/saturday-night-live/video/daily-affirmation/n10295.

Chapter 31: The Stories We Tell Each Other

1. Lori Silverman, *Wake Me Up When the Data Is Over* (San Francisco: Jossey-Bass, 2006), 149–50.
2. Matthew D. Lieberman, *Social: Why Our Brains Are Wired to Connect* (New York: Crown, 2013), 9.
3. Northwestern Mutual, "Who We Are," Northwestern Mutual, accessed August 8, 2019, https://www.northwesternmutual.com/who-we-are/.
4. Ron Hall, Denver Moore, and Lynn Vincent, *Same Kind of Different As Me: A Modern-Day Slave, an International Art Dealer, and the Unlikely Woman Who Bound Them Together* (Nashville: Thomas Nelson, 2008), 235.
5. For this story and quotes, see Arthur C. Brooks, "Empathize With Your

Political Foe," *New York Times*, January 22, 2018, https://www.nytimes
.com/2018/01/21/opinion/empathize-with-your-political-foe.html.

Chapter 32: The Stories We Tell Together

1. Annette Simmons, *The Story Factor: Inspiration, Influence, and Persuasion through the Art of Storytelling* (New York: Basic, 2006), 1–26.
2. Paul Smith, *Lead with a Story: A Guide to Crafting Business Narratives That Captivate, Convince, and Inspire* (New York: AMACOM, 2012), 79.
3. Alasdair MacIntyre, *After Virtue: A Study in Moral Theory*, 3rd ed. (South Bend, IN: University of Notre Dame Press, 2007), 216.
4. Smith, *Lead with a Story*, 68.
5. Lauren McMenemy, "What Is a Chief Storyteller? Five Business Leaders Share Their Stories," Content Standard by Skyword, March 22, 2018, https://www.skyword.com/contentstandard/marketing/ what-is-a-chief-storyteller-five-business-leaders-share-their-stories/.
6. Ibid.

Chapter 33: The Blessing of Storyfulness

1. Jennifer Brown, *Inclusion: Diversity, The New Workplace and The Will To Change* (Hartford, CT: Publish Your Purpose, 2016).

Chapter 34: Providence, Identity, and Performance

1. Emmie Martin, "Here's Why Warren Buffett Says That He and Charlie Munger Are Successful," CNBC online, May 5, 2018, https:// www.cnbc.com/2018/05/04/warren-buffett-says-the-key-to-his -success-is-luck.html.
2. Warren E. Buffett, "2014 Annual Report" (Berkshire Hathaway, Inc., 2014), 6.
3. Ibid.
4. "For a time I got lucky: Berkshire immediately enjoyed two years of good operating conditions. Better yet, its earnings in those years were free of income tax because it possessed a large loss carry-forward that had arisen from the disastrous results in earlier years." Ibid., 25.
5. Anthony K. Tjan, Richard J. Harrington, and Tsun-yan Hsieh, *Heart, Smarts, Guts, and Luck: What It Takes to Be an Entrepreneur and Build a Great Business* (Brighton, MA: Harvard Business Review Press, 2012).
6. Westminster Shorter Catechism, Question and Answer 11.

Chapter 35: The Fight for Identity on God's Playground

1. Fiona Gardner, *The Only Mind Worth Having: Thomas Merton and the Child Mind* (Eugene, OR: Cascade, 2015), 23.
2. For the quote, see John Rampton, "60 of the Most Inspirational Quotes in 'Shark Tank' History," Inc.com, September 30, 2016, https://www.inc.com/john-rampton/inspirational-quotes-from-shark-tank.html.
3. Alex Soojung-Kim Pang, *Rest: Why You Get More Done When You Work Less* (New York: Basic, 2016), 159–61.
4. For a good introduction, see Gary W. Moon, ed., *Eternal Living: Reflections on Dallas Willard's Teaching on Faith and Formation* (Downers Grove, IL: IVP Books, 2015).
5. Robert J. Anderson and William A. Adams, *Mastering Leadership, An Integrated Framework for Breakthrough Performance and Extraordinary Business Results* (Hoboken, NJ: Wiley, 2016).
6. Ibid., 29.

Appendix A: A Case for Mindfulness

1. Kevin D. Williamson, "'Mindfulness': Corporate America's Strange New Gospel," *National Review*, National Review, January 1, 2018, https://www.nationalreview.com/2018/01/mindfulness-fad-corporate-america-buddhism-without-buddha/.
2. David Gelles, "At Aetna, a C.E.O.'s Management by Mantra," *New York Times*, February 27, 2015, https://www.nytimes.com/2015/03/01/business/at-aetna-a-ceos-management-by-mantra.html.
3. Bartie Scott, "Meditation and Mindfulness Training," Inc.com, March 1, 2017, https://www.inc.com/bartie-scott/best-industries-2017-meditation-and-mindfulness-training.html.
4. Virginia Heffernan, "The Muddied Meaning of 'Mindfulness,'" *New York Times*, January 19, 2018, https://www.nytimes.com/2015/04/19/magazine/the-muddied-meaning-of-mindfulness.html.
5. Tim Lomas, "Where Does The Word 'Mindfulness' Come From?," *Psychology Today*, March 16, 2016, https://www.psychologytoday.com/blog/mindfulness-wellbeing/201603/where-does-the-word-mindfulness-come.
6. Bhante Henepola Gunaratana, *Mindfulness in Plain English* (Boston, MA: Wisdom Publications, 2011), 134.

Need More Presence?

Is your team navigating the terrain of presence-based leadership within an organization?

We believe that, with the right tools and the space to hone their craft, leaders and organizations can accelerate and create exponential impact.

NAVIGATOR
Executive Coaching &
Leadership Presence

INDIVIDUAL

ATLAS
Customized Internal
Training & Development
Programs

TRAINING   TEAM

CREW
Team Health
& Cohesion

STRATEGY

COMPASS
Business Strategy &
Strategic Development

For more information and to set up a free consultation, visit our website at leadershipreality.org today.

LEADERSHIP
— REALITY —